THE COMMENTARY OF RABBI ABRAHAM IBN EZRA ON HOSEA

THE COMMENTARY OF RABBI ABRAHAM IBN EZRA ON HOSEA

Edited from Six Manuscripts and Translated
with an Introduction and Notes

by

Abe Lipshitz

SEPHER-HERMON PRESS, Inc.

New York

THE COMMENTARY OF
RABBI ABRAHAM IBN EZRA
ON HOSEA

Published by
Sepher-Hermon Press, Inc., New York

ISBN 0-87203-127-6

Library of Congress Cataloging-in-Publication Data

Ibn Ezra, Abraham ben Meïr, 1092-1167
The commentary of Rabbi Abraham Ibn Ezra on Hosea

English and Hebrew
Hebrew text and English translation: Perush ha-R.A.b.E. al Hoshea.
Bibliography; p.
Includes index.
1. Bible. O.T. Hosea—Commentaries—Early works to 1800. I. Lipshitz, Abe. II. Title.
BS1565.I2613 1988 224'.607 88-26497
ISBN 0-87203-127-6

In Tribute

It was in Chicago on the Sabbath before Passover of 1965 when we first invited the editor and translator of this work, Rabbi Dr. Abe Lipshitz, to lead our newly-formed group, dedicated to the study of the Bible.

As a result of that invitation Rabbi Lipshitz began meeting with us regularly on Sabbath afternoons, in what was to become a long-standing association of men studying in depth the כתבי הקודש (= Sacred Writings) with their classical commentaries.

The founding members of our group were all graduates of various *yeshīḇōt* (= talmudic academies) and universities. Our motivation at the outset was based upon a common desire to improve our understanding of the original text of the Bible, a subject not sufficiently emphasized in the formative years of our respective educations. We wanted to gain a profound knowledge of our scriptural heritage by returning, as it were, to the remarkable days of our illustrious forebears, and by witnessing the events that were recorded in the Bible for posterity.

In the course of our studies we became inspired by the spirited message of the prophets, particularly as interpreted by the medieval commentators, as well as by the talmudic sages in their various expositions of biblical passages and personalities.

However, it was not only the subject matter that motivated our desire to learn. It was also our inspiring leader Rabbi Lipshitz. While still a youth his schooling had been interrupted by World War II and by the indescribable struggle of European Jewry to survive the Nazi death camps. After miraculously overcoming those immense obstacles he resumed his education in the United States, where, in a comparatively short period, he has attained the status of a world renowned scholar-writer in the fields of medieval and modern biblical exegesis.

From the very beginning of our sessions we realized that Rabbi

Lipshitz was not only a man who thoroughly mastered his subject. He also knew how to transmit it to others, a rare combination in many schools of higher learning.

To this very day Dr. Lipshitz recognizes the contribution of every participant. Every source is valuable, no matter how ancient, medieval, or modern – as long as it illuminates the text. The characters and events of Scripture come to life before our eyes, conveying to each of us a message relevant to our own times. Consequently, the ספר הספרים (= Book of Books) has become our personal guide and handbook through the travails of life.

After more than two decades we still look forward each Sabbath and festival to the opportunity, figuratively, to "cling to the dust at the feet" of our esteemed teacher, and to "drink with great thirst" his wise words (*'Ab̲ōt* 1:4).

It is indeed a privilege and honor for our group to help "bring to light" this new edition of Ibn Ezra's commentary on Hosea. We, thus, extend our heartfelt thanks to Rabbi Lipshitz for all the knowledge he has transmitted to us throughout the years at our stimulating learning sessions.

We also wish to express our appreciation to his gracious wife Hela, and their fine children for allowing us to share our mentor with them on all those memorable Sabbaths and festivals.

May Rabbi Lipshitz continue to be a source of inspiration to all of us for many years to come.

Norbert N. Rosenthal
Irving H. Skolnick

A Prefatory Note

This edition of Rabbi Abraham Ibn Ezra's commentary on Hosea is the outgrowth of a work I submitted to the University of Chicago as a doctoral dissertation in 1974.

During the intervening years my eminent teacher, Professor Norman Golb of the University, encouraged me to publish the dissertation in an expanded form for the general student of medieval biblical exegesis.

Professor Golb was constantly interested in the enhancement of this work, and he, with his great wealth of knowledge, has helped me immeasurably in presenting this complex commentary to the interested student. For his valuable contribution and unfailing kindness, I shall always be grateful.

I am also appreciative to the following libraries for providing me with copies of the manuscripts herein consulted:

The British Museum
Provinciale Biblioteek van Friesland, Holland
Bodleian Library, Oxford
Montefiore Library Collection, London
Vatican Library
The Jewish National and University Library, Jerusalem

I am equally obliged to the librarians of the Hebrew Theological College, Skokie, Illinois, Mrs. Leah Mishkin and Mr. Joseph Bachrach for their kind efforts in placing at my disposal their library's book collection and research materials.

I am, furthermore, greatly indebted to my esteemed friends of Chicago, whose company I have enjoyed for the past two decades, when on each Sabbath and festival, we studied together the words of the Prophets, related portions of the Talmud, and other classical writings of our Torah giants. This prominent group of colleagues, led by Rabbi Norbert Rosenthal and Dr. Irving Skolnick, has graciously taken upon itself the task of making the publication of this volume possible. For their encouragement and assistance I am profoundly honored.

Finally, I owe a great debt of gratitude to my dear wife Hela, a woman of valor, and our two precious daughters, Annie and Rosie, who continuously created in our home an environment of inspiration and serenity during all the years of my study and research.

Abe Lipshitz

In Gratitude

I am deeply indebted to all my dear friends in the greater Chicago area, who have provided the funding for the publication of this work. Through their generosity they have demonstrated their dedication to the furtherance of Torah scholarship.

The following merit special recognition for their substantial gifts:

Joan and Shael Bellows
Hoda and Isadore Goldberg
Sally and Maury Kaufman
Sema and Moshe Menora
Rosane and Norbert Rosenthal*

I am equally thankful to the following trusted friends, who through their benevolent financial support, have facilitated the appearance of this new study:

Rosalyn and George Bornstein
Suzette and Max Klein
Naomi and Hyman Naiman
Israel Pollack
Esther and Martin Samber
Vivian and Irving Skolnick

May all who have participated in this endeavor be rewarded for their kind and noble gestures.

A.L.

*I also would like to commend Norbert Rosenthal for his inexhaustible patience and endurance in coordinating all the necessary arrangements for the publication of this volume.

Contents

THE COMMENTARY OF RABBI ABRAHAM IBN EZRA ON HOSEA

Abbreviations and Symbols

A.V.	Authorized (King James) Version
I.E.	Ibn Ezra
J.P. S.	Jewish Publication Society
J.Q.R.	Jewish Quarterly Review
R.E.J.	Revue des études juives
R.S.V.	Revised Standard Version
LXX	The Septuagint
[ ]	Interpolation
’	א
‘	ע

Introduction

I

Modern scholarship of the last century and a half has unequivocally demonstrated the sterling qualities of Rabbi Abraham ben Meir Ibn Ezra (1092-1167) in his role as a prolific biblical exegete. Born, very likely, in Toledo, Ibn Ezra began his literary career with poetic compositions; he abruptly fled his native land (c. 1140)[1] and settled in Rome,[2] where he began his exegetical career with commentaries on Ecclesiastes and Job. Subsequently, he went to northern Italy (Lucca and other towns), where he wrote commentaries on the Pentateuch (the so-called short recensions) and Isaiah. After having established a reputation in Italy as a versatile and innovative scholar, Ibn Ezra left that country (c. 1148) for Provence and was received enthusiastically by the Jewish communities of Beziers[3] and Narbonne. In Provence, Normandy and England he continued his literary activity, which resulted not only in works of grammar and astrology but also in additional commentaries on various books of the Bible, including that on the Minor Prophets. These exegetical works were a means by which the Jews of Christian Europe came to be acquainted with many of the linguistic studies of Andalusian Jewish scholars[4] and with their newly developed methods of interpreting Scripture.[5]

Ibn Ezra won the acclaim of many of his contemporaries, who admired his learning and versatility. The questions regarding the Jewish calendar put to him by one of the representatives of the Jews of Narbonne, David b. Joseph,[6] the epigram written in honor of Ibn Ezra by Rashi's grandson Jacob Tam,[7] and the fact that the name Abraham Ibn Ezra was listed among "the great and sacred scholars" during his own lifetime[8] all attest to his high repute.

Similarly, successors of Ibn Ezra often reckoned with his scholarship by following in his footsteps and adopting his views, particularly in the field of exegesis. At the end of the twelfth century,Maimonides (1135-1204) argued that the actions of the prophet as described in the book of Ezekiel were all carried out in a vision of prophecy; similarly, the statement in the book of Isaiah "like my servant Isaiah hath walked naked and barefoot" (Is. 20:3) was interpreted by Maimonides as having happened in a divine vision. Maimonides further asserted that "the position is similar with regard to the words addressed to Hosea: 'Take unto thee a wife of harlotry and children of harlotry' (1:2). All this story...happened in its entirety in a vision of prophecy."[9] These expositions and conclusions by Maimonides strikingly resemble the interpretation given earlier by Ibn Ezra in his commentary on Hosea.[10]

Ibn Ezra's exegetical method is even more conspicuous in the commentaries of David Qimhi, who, according to Abravanel, went so far as to borrow the best and most select comments of Ibn Ezra on the Minor Prophets without mentioning his name.[11]

The influence of Ibn Ezra is furthermore perceived in the commentary on the Pentateuch of Moses b. Nachman (Nachmanides), where "R. Abraham, the Wise" is quoted with abundance, either in high esteem or "with an open rebuke directed by inner love."[12] Nachmanides also borrowed numerous interpretations from Ibn Ezra without ascribing them to their author.[13]

The sphere of Ibn Ezra's scholarly influence has, however, by no means been restricted to his coreligionists; his learning has attracted the attention and curiosity of many non-Jewish scholars from the Middle Ages down to modern times.

Less than a century after the death of Ibn Ezra, his astrological works enjoyed such popularity as to merit translation into French under the patronage of Henry Bate (c. 1264) and subsequently (1293) into Latin by Peter d'Abano.[14] At the same time that Ibn Ezra was winning acclaim as an astrologer-astronomer among the Christian scholars of France, his commentaries were being quoted abundantly by the Dominican polemicist Raymund Martin of Spain.[15] The "Abraham" who represents mathematics in a fresco of the seven arts in an Italian church has been identified as none other than Abraham Ibn Ezra.[16]

Ibn Ezra's exegetical writings were largely translated into Latin in the sixteenth and seventeenth centuries.[17] The highest degree of recognition ever extended to Ibn Ezra as a commentator by a non-Jewish scholar was that of the French biblical critic Richard Simon (1638-1712), who not only hailed him as the single Jewish authority who literally and judiciously explained the Bible, but even recommended his method of interpretation to non-Jews as well: "There are rules which Aben Ezra gives for the well-expounding of the Scripture and the Criticism of the Jewish Authors who have writ upon the Bible. There is nothing more reasonable than the rules he gives, and I doubt not but the Christians will receive his methods."[18]

II

During his lifetime, Ibn Ezra wrote commentaries not only on the Pentateuch, Isaiah, and the twelve Minor Prophets but also on a large portion of the Hagiographa, namely Psalms, Job, Canticles, Ruth, Lamentations, Ecclesiastes, Esther, Daniel, and perhaps also Proverbs. Unlike his scriptural writings on the Pentateuch and the book of Isaiah, his commentaries on the Minor Prophets and the Hagiographa have remained neglected, barely attracting the attention of even those scholars especially dedicated to the study of the history of biblical exegesis. One must, of course, neither ignore nor minimize earlier attempts to elucidate some of the difficulties found in those commentaries. However, with the exception of one or two treatises,[19] no significant supercommentary has ever appeared in which Ibn Ezra's exegesis of the Minor Prophets and the Hagiographa has been adequately treated.[20] This neglect may be attributed in large measure to the corrupt Ibn Ezra texts as they appear in the standard editions of the Rabbinic Bible (*Miqraot Gedolot*).[21] In these published texts Ibn Ezra's comments are frequently rendered with ambiguity or obscurity, which may have been one of the major obstacles that prevented readers from pursuing a comprehensive study to determine the accurate meaning of our commentator's remarks on these writings. It becomes clear that critical editions and translations of these commentaries are essential as the fundamental basis for their proper elucidation and understanding. Insofar as the commentary on Hosea represents the first of Ibn Ezra's commentaries in order of appearance of the biblical books for which a critical edition is a desideratum, we have felt it appropriate to concentrate on this task here. We also include our English translation of the work, with notes and explanatory remarks, in the hope that students as well as laymen who endeavor to widen the scope of their knowledge in the field of biblical exegesis will avail themselves of research done by preceding scholars which we incorporate into this work.

III

In his introduction to the commentary on the Pentateuch, Ibn Ezra enumerates four different classes of commentaries of whose methods of interpreting Scripture he disapproves: (1) Those who introduce an excess of extraneous matter and resort in their interpretations to the study of the profane sciences (i.e., Saadya Gaon, Samuel ben Ḥofni, and perhaps the tenth-century philosopher Isaac ben Solomon Israeli); (2) those who entirely reject tradition and rely only on their own reasoning (i.e. the Qaraites); (3) those who delight in mysticism and reject the literal sense of the text (i.e., Christian allegorists); (4) those who erroneously give preference to Midrashic explanations, which were only intended to convey figurative notions. Ibn Ezra considers himself to be the champion of a new method of interpretation designed to establish a middle course by applying common sense in analyzing the literal meaning of the word, but following traditional explanations in interpreting the legislative portions of the Torah. This method he calls "the straightway" (הדרך הישרה), his personal expression for the technical and more usual term *peshat.*

As an adherent of the *peshat* form of exegesis, Ibn Ezra remains faithful to the principle he claims to represent, not only in his writings on the Pentateuch but also throughout his commentary on the Minor Prophets.

Although this commentary, of which the one on Hosea forms an integral part, was evidently not preserved in the original form in which it was written by Ibn Ezra,[22] its salient features and characteristics are the same as those found in his other commentaries; it retains that uniqueness in style and exposition which can fit only into the framework of his exegesis. A case in point is the special treatment of syntactical repetitions in Scripture, which are, according to Ibn Ezra, common and usual in most prophecies[23] and which he simply explains by the remark that "the idea is doubled" (הטעם כפול).[24] There is also the frequent recourse to the concept of ellipsis as a means of explaining difficult biblical passages either by extending the force of a preceding word[25] or by supplying a noun that is completely missing from the text.[26] There is in addition the characteristic claim that a required object that is missing in a biblical phrase is implicitly contained in the preceding verb and may be inferred by the reader (particularly after a verb in the Hiphil form); thus the term *hōḇîshāh (lit., "she put to shame" [Hosea 2:7]) means "she put herself* to shame," *hiznētā* (lit., "you caused to commit adultery" [ibid. 5:3]) means "you caused *yourself* to commit adultery," and *hik̲'is* (lit., "he provoked" [ibid. 12:15]) means "he (Ephraim) had provoked *God*."

These instances of omissions and ellipses are employed in many variations by Ibn Ezra in his writings. Their frequent occurrence as a means of explaining striking biblical difficulties gives evidence of Ibn Ezra's unequivocal determination to establish a reasonable and more rational method for the expounding of Scripture.

There is finally the characteristic versatility in Hebrew and in Arabic making possible the explanation of difficult terms in the Bible by way of analogy between the two languages, a tendency which is rare in biblical exegesis of this period.[27]

One of the major characteristics of Ibn Ezra's exegetical writings is his attempt to establish a link between the chapters or verses of the Bible, with a view to showing the text's coherence and continuity of thought. In scope and thoroughness, this effort has no parallel in preceding medieval biblical interpretation. As a rational and intellectually gifted commentator, Ibn Ezra was certainly aware of the complexities involved in such a task. He therefore cautions the reader by saying:

> I shall provide you with a rule before I begin to explain: Every statement or precept stands independently of the other. If we are able to find a motive explaining why one statement or precept is interrelated to another we attempt to join them together with all our prowess; and if we are unable to do so, we presume that the lack is due to the inadequacy of our knowledge.[28]

This method of conjunction is quite conspicuous in Ibn Ezra's commentary on Hosea[29] and the following instances reflect his adherence to it.

Most of the medieval Jewish commentators maintain that the prophecy "and the children of Judah and the children of Israel shall be gathered together and they shall appoint themselves one head and shall go up out of the land" (2:2) is a reference to the time and circumstances of the Messianic era, when the people of Judah and Israel will "appoint one head" from the Davidic family and go up from the lands of exile to their own land of Israel.[30] However, the abrupt transition from the preceding admonition ("you are not My people and I will not be yours" [1:9]) to the promise of restoration (2:1-3) makes such an interpretation questionable.[31] Therefore, Ibn Ezra insists that the phrase "they shall be gathered" should be taken as a prediction that Judah and Israel will be gathered or subdued by Sennaherib, king of Assyria, who will subsequently become their master (viz., "one head") and remove them from their own land into exile.[32] Accordingly, the first three verses in the second chapter continue the preceding prophecy of doom (1:8-9) which includes the exile of Israel.

Similarly, when Ibn Ezra was later faced with the difficulty of coordinating the term "therefore" (2:16), he evidently refused to accept any interpretation which might have been designed to divide the verse into two opposing themes,[33] but rather preferred to link the balance of this chapter (16-25) with the prophecy previously interrupted at verse nine, and to interpret all of verse sixteen as a promise of redemption.[34] No less significant is Ibn Ezra's observation that the prophet concluded his prophecy ("and transgressors do stumble therein" [14:10]) with the same idea that had been previously expressed in the phrase "for thou hast stumbled in thine iniquity" (14:2).[35] This remark is also designed to underscore the consistency as well as continuity of thought in the book of Hosea.

IV

Ibn Ezra's view on prophecy as expressed in his commentary on Hosea may be treated in two parts:

A. *The marriage of Hosea.* In his introduction to the commentary, Ibn Ezra cites disapprovingly two different views regarding the marriage of Hosea: (1) That the prophet had unequivocally obeyed the commandment of God to marry a harlot and that such a marriage is to be regarded as one that was actually consummated;[36] (2) that this prophecy is to be taken as a parable, a purely figurative command from God, who merely ordered the prophet to proclaim to the people that he was charged with marrying a harlot, to indicate that "the land doth commit great harlotry, departing from the Lord" (1:2)[37]

According to Ibn Ezra, neither of these opinions is correct. The first one he repudiates on the ground that it is inconsistent with reason that God should command a prophet to marry a harlot and conceive children of harlotry. To say that the prophet was ordered into this extraordinary union in order to reflect the people's departure from God would be, according to Ibn Ezra, equally unthinkable, for such a marriage involves an act of indignation which, if carried out, would have rendered the prophet contemptible.[38]

It is interesting to observe that in his second introduction to the commentary on the Pentateuch, Ibn Ezra was highly critical of the digressive explanations of Scripture effected by way of allegorical exposition: "This is a method of Christian (lit., "uncircumcised") scholars who claim that the whole Pentateuch consists of parables and allegories. . . .These are useless words driven by vapor, with no parallel elsewhere."[39] In view of this statement it becomes apparent that even the second opinion cited here by Ibn Ezra, in which Hosea's marriage is treated on a purely allegorical basis, is also unacceptable to him. For such an interpretation would constitute a threat to other biblical accounts, including those of laws and precepts, which may be interpreted in a similarly symbolic sense and then be coupled with a total rejection of the literal meaning of the text.

Hence, our author proceeds with the presentation of his own theory regarding the first prophecy of Hosea by saying:

> It is therefore my view that this prophet, in a vision of prophecy or in a dream of the night,[40] perceived that God said to him: "Go take unto thee a wife of harlotry etc.", and went and took a well-known woman who conceived and gave birth – all this in a prophetic vision.

In short, the account as presented in the book of Hosea should be regarded as a psychological occurrence, which the prophet had indeed experienced inwardly but never carried out in his real life.[41]

This approach to the marriage of Hosea marks the first attempt in the field of medieval Jewish exegesis to interpret a particular biblical event in terms of a prophetic vision, a method which attracted the attention of many of Ibn Ezra's successors during the Middle Ages (see above, note 10).

B. *Unspecified historical prophecies.* The interpretation of unspecified historical prophecies in the Bible had been a major topic of discussion among medieval Jewish interpreters, (as among their Christian counterparts) with two schools diametrically opposed to each other. Some medieval scholars, like Moses Chiquitilla and Hayyim Galipapa, generally explain such prophecies in the perspective of historical events or by relating them to the contemporary period of the prophet.[42] In contrast with their view, Isaac Abravanel favors the designation of non-stipulated biblical prophecies as being "for the time to come" (*le'ātid*), meaning for the Messianic era. Abravanel further accuses Ibn Ezra of submitting to Ibn Chiquitilla by interpreting all biblical prophecies in contemporaneous terms or by reconciling them with the history of the Second Commonwealth.[43]

An analysis of most of Ibn Ezra's remarks on the prophetic books, however, makes apparent that his method of interpreting prophecy remains persistently original throughout his commentaries. This method may be perceived in his comments on the prophecies of Jacob (Gen. 49:1), Isaiah (2:1-4) and Micah (4:1), all of which are expressly ascribed in Scripture to "the end of the days."[44] Accordingly, the prophecy of Hosea 3:5 ("afterward shall the children of Israel return, and seek the Lord their God and David their king, etc.") must also be related to the Messianic era. As Ibn Ezra himself states: "The most reliable proof for the correctness of this interpretation is the phrase 'in the end of days' [ibid], meaning a distant period to which the prophets directed their prophecies" (comm. ibid.)

Ibn Ezra further maintains that the time of a prophetic event may also be determined either by way of implication from the text[45] or else when the words of the prophet are coupled with an oath of God. For according to Ibn Ezra, God's oath represents His unchangeable decree, one that can never be undone. Therefore, a prophecy coupled with an oath of God, which has not yet been fulfilled must obviously be *le'ātid* (= for a distant future).[46] When neither contextual evidence nor an oath is present, the prophecy remains vague. As he remarks: "Some of them we may be able to ascribe to the future, while with regard to others we grope 'like blind men groping for a wall' – one says this and the others says that."[47] These criteria for distinguishing prophecy designated for the future from other types of prophecy are introduced by Ibn Ezra for the first time and are unprecedented in the history of biblical exegesis. Furthermore, Abravanel's criticism leveled against Ibn Ezra for submitting to Moses Chiquitilla and interpreting all biblical prophecies in contemporaneous terms is quite clearly unwarranted.

V

As a champion and exponent of the *peshat* form, Ibn Ezra preferred to rely on the conclusions of early philologists of the Near East, Maghreb and Spain, rather than on commentators who frequently embodied in their writing Midrashic expositions in the belief that a scriptural verse may have more than one meaning. Thus Ibn Ezra quotes abundantly from the works of the Qaraites and other scholars, most of which were virtually unknown both to his predecessors such as Menahem b. Helbo and Rashi and to his contemporaries such as Joseph Qara and Eliezer of Beaugency.

Following is a list of authors cited by Ibn Ezra in his commentary on Hosea:

Ibn Chiquitilla (see Moses Hakkohen)
Ibn Janah (see Marinus)
Jeshua[48]
Joseph[49]
Marinus (= Jonah Ibn Janah)[50]
The Mishnah[51]
Moses Hakkohen (= Ibn Chiquitilla)[52]
Saadya Gaon[53]
Yefet[54]
Yiṣḥaqi[55]

In addition to the above, Ibn Ezra alludes in passing to the Midrash (1:1) and cites numerous expositions in the name of "the grammarian" (2:9), "the interpreter" (1:1, 2:2, 12:3-4), "the commentators" (10-11), "a scholar" (2:10), and "some who say" (or "the one who says"; 1:6, 2:7, 2:17, 2:21, 3:2-4, 4:17, 6:3, 11:2, 13:7-8, 13:10, 13:14, 14:5), most of which passages are discussed in our notes and traced to their respective sources.

VI

As stated above, the commentary of Ibn Ezra on Hosea represents the first of his scriptural writings in order of their occurrence in the biblical books to require a critical edition. We here present a new edition of this commentary based on the following six manuscripts:

1. **B** = British Museum 24, 896 (London)
2. **L** = Leeuwarden 4,2 (Provinciale Bibliotheek van Friesland, Holland)
3. **M** = Michael 33 (Bodleian Library, Oxford)
4. **N** = Montefiore 34,2 (Montefiore Library Collection, London)
5. **R** = Roma Angelica 80,2 (Biblioteca Angelica, Rome)
6. **V** = Vatican 75 (Vatican Library)

With the exception of a short lacuna in ms. L (2:4-3:3), all manuscripts are complete, and their variant readings have contributed immeasurably to the reconstruction of the Hebrew text.[56] However, in the course of adopting what appeared to be the correct reading, we did not ignore other versions but rather have given them in the notes as they appear in the respective manuscripts.

In addition to the Hebrew version, we present here for the first time an English translation[57] of the complete commentary on Hosea, with notes and explanatory remarks.

In our English translation we generally attempt to follow the original text faithfully. However, because of the terse style of Ibn Ezra, we have been at times compelled to modify some of his remarks, either by altering the wording or through amplification. Such modifications are either placed in brackets or remarked upon in a short note.

Our translation of biblical passages is generally based on the version published by the Jewish Publication Society (J.P.S.) of America (1963). However, the Revised Standard Version (R.S.V.), the Authorized Version (A.V.), and the Septuagint Version(LXX) were also consulted, as indicated in the text or in the notes on the respective passages.[58]

As a contribution to the history of exegesis, this work is designed to make the complex language and thought of Ibn Ezra accessible to interested readers. It is also aimed at eliciting the rules and principles that guided this classical commentator in interpreting the difficult words uttered by Hosea more than 2700 years ago.

As this work reaches its conclusion, we wish to offer a prayer of thanksgiving to the Almighty, for giving us the strength to delve into the writings of our classical commentators, whose expositions of Scripture form an almost integral part of the Bible and constitute one of the major themes of Jewish literature.

A.L.

Lincolnwood - Chicago
Tebeth, 5748
January, 1988

Notes

1 Fleischer contends that Ibn Ezra left Spain mainly because of Moslem intolerance and religious persecution which resulted in the destruction of many Spanish Jewish communities. Cf. Yehuda Leib Fleischer, "Madu'a yāṣa R. Abraham Ibn Ezra misfārad," *Mizraḥ Uma'arāb*, III (1929), 330.

It should be noted that this and the following remarks are not intended to represent a full-fledged literary biography of Ibn Ezra, which I hope to present in a separate study.

2 In the introductory poem to his commentary on Ecclesiastes, Ibn Ezra says that "he departed from his native land, which is Spain, and came to Rome in a turbulent spirit."

3 Yedayah Hapenini of Beziers describes "the joy of the scholars of the country (France), its pious men and rabbis," when Ibn Ezra passed through their communities. Cf. *Responsa of Solomon b. Adret* (Beney Beraq, 1958), No. 418.

4 At the conclusion of the second introduction to his commentary on the Pentateuch, written very likely in Normandy, Ibn Ezra complains about his contemporaries who were ignorant of the principles of Hebrew grammar: "And because the wise men of our time have not studied grammar, I will first describe its principles and rules, as a key to the perception of my grammatical remarks." Cf Michael Friedlaender, *Essays on the Writings of Abraham Ibn Ezra* (London, 1877), Hebrew Appendix p. 5.

5 In the introduction to his commentary (printed in the traditional Bible [*Miqraot Gedolot*] Ibn Ezra enumerates five schools of interpreters, rejecting the methods of four of them while accepting those of the fifth, which maintain a balance between free research and tradition.

6 One of the questions deals with the interval of nearly four weeks between the Jewish and the Christian Passover, which occurred in the year 1139. The questions and Ibn Ezra's answers were published by Moritz Steinschneider under the name *Shenēy Hame'ōrōt* (Berlin, 1847), pp. 1-3.

7 For the exchange of epigrams between Ibn Ezra and Jacob Tam, cf. Jacob Moshe Toledano, *Oṣar Genāzim* (Jerusalem, 1960), pp. 20-22.

8 Ibn Ezra is so cited by his contemporary Rabad (Abraham b. David Halevi of Toledo). Cf. *Mediaeval Jewish Chronicles,* I, ed. by Ad[olph] Neubauer (Oxford, 1887), p. 81.

9 Cf. Moses Maimonides. *The Guide of the Perplexed*, trans. by Shlomo Pines (Chicago, 1969), part II, chap. 46, pp. 405-406. (The actions of Ezekiel included placing a tile before him, lying on the left side, placing wheat and barley into a single vessel and letting a barber's razor pass over the prophet's beard [Ez. 4:19, 5:1].)

10 The similarity between Ibn Ezra's and Maimonides' interpretations of Hosea's prophecy was already noticed by Yom Tob b. Abraham of Seville (thirteenth century).

Cf. *Kitbēy Haritbā*, ed. by Moshe Yehudah Blau (New York, 1956), pp. 27-28. Cf. also Wilhelm Bacher, *Die Bibelexegese Moses Maimunis* (Budapest, 1896), p. 83, note 1. Significantly El'azar b. Matitya (fifteenth century) states in his supercommentary on Ibn Ezra that he would be inclined to believe that the philosophical principles of Ibn Ezra are borrowed from Maimonides were he not aware that Ibn Ezra's commentaries were composed before Maimonides wrote his *Guide*; cf. Naphtali Ben-Menachem, *Miginzēy Yisrael Bevatiqan* (Jerusalem, 1954), p. 135.

11 Cf. Isaac Abravanel, *Commentary on the Minor Prophets and Hagiographa* (Jerusalem, 1960), p. 13. It should be noted that of all his predecessors of the Spanish school, Qimhi cites in his commentary on Hosea only Ibn Ezra by name (1:8, 2:17, 4:13, 5:10, 6:2, 6:3, 7:9, 10:12, 11:7, 11:9, 11:10). However, the frequency with which Ibn Ezra's expositions are utilized by Qimhi without being named (cf., e.g., commentaries of Ibn Ezra and Qimhi on Hosea 12:4-7, 14-15) supports Abravanel's contention.

12 The reading in Nachmanides' introductory remark to his commentary on the Pentateuch (Moses b. Nachman, *Commentary on the Torah*, ed. by Charles B. Chavel, I [Jerusalem, 1959]) is "with an open rebuke and inner love" (instead of "directed by inner love"). However, cf. Friedlaender, *Essays*, p. 247 where the other reading ("directed by," based on Prov. 27:5) is cited.

13 Cf. Joseph Perles, "Notizen," *Monatsschrift für Geschichte und Wissenschaft des Judenthums*, VII (1885), 157: "Beidem Allem ist nich zu verkennen, dass Ibn Esra's Ansichten einen bedeutenden Einfluss auf Nachmani ausgeübt haben und dass dieser theils unbewusst, theils mit Absicht zahlreiche Behauptungen Ibn Esra's zu den seinigen machte." For additional details regarding Ibn Ezra's influence on Qimhi and Nachmanides, cf. Abe Lipshitz, *'Iyyūnim Bīleshōnōt Har'ab'a* (Chicago, 1969), pp. 9, 37-42.

14 Henry Bate occupies a high rank in the history of astronomy, philosophy and theology; his younger contemporary Peter d'Abano was received as a Doctor of Medicine and Philosophy at Paris. Cf. Raphael Levy, *The Astrological Works of Abraham Ibn Ezra* (Baltimore – Paris, 1927), pp. 19-27. For the influence of Ibn Ezra on such scholars as Roger Bacon, Pico della Mirandola, and others, cf. J.M. Millas Vallicrosa, "'Abōdātō shel R. Abraham Ibn Ezra beḥokmat hatekūnā," *Tarbiz*, IX (1928), 322.

15 Martin (*Pugio Fidei*, ed. by J.B. Carpazov [Leipzig, 1678]) quotes Ibn Ezra twenty-seven times. However, two of these quotations (viz., on Prov. 2:7 14:34; ibid., pp. 855, 925) belong to Joseph Qimhi (*Sepher Ḥūqāh* [Breslau, 1866], p. 5, 21) and are erroneously ascribed by Martin to Ibn Ezra. For a complete list of Ibn Ezra's comments cited by Martin, cf. Saul Lieberman, *Sheqī'in* (Jerusalem, 1939), p. 91.

16 Cf. Moritz Steinschneider, *Jewish Literature* (Hermon Press [New York, 1965]), p. 191.

17 Among the Scriptural commentaries of Ibn Ezra that were translated into Latin

are those on the Decalogue (by S. Munster [Basel, 1527]); on Obadiah, Jonah, and Zephaniah (by A. Pontacus [Paris, 1566]); on Canticles (by G. Genebrard [Paris, 1570]): on Lamentations (by F. Taylor [London, 1615]); on Hosea (by W. Coddaus [Leyden, 1621]); on the first five books of the twelve Minor Prophets (by J. Mercier [Giessen, 1695]). For additional information with regard to various translations of Ibn Ezra's exegetical writings, cf. Hartman, "Aben Esra," *Allgemeine Encyclopedie* (Ersch and Gruber, eds. [1818]), I, 81.

18 Cf. [Richard] Simon, *A Critical History of the Old Testament*, trans. by H.D. (London, 1682), book III, ch. IV, p. 28.

19 Cf. Isaac Sharim, *Hadar 'Ezer* [Smyrna, 1865] (on Isaiah, the Minor Prophets, and the Hagiographa) and Jonah Filwarg, *Benēy Reshef* [Piotrkow, 1900] (second sec., on the Minor Prophets and the Hagiographa). Other works on this subject, but less significant, were written by Hayyim Wolf Kaputa (*'Or Linetībah* [Lemberg, 1897]) and Meshullam Roth (*Mebassēr 'Ezrā* [Jerusalem, 1968]). The commentaries of Ibn Ezra on Isaiah, the Minor Prophets, and the Hagiographa were also explained in *Hō'il Moshe Bē'ēr*, by Moses Cremieux (b. 1776) and in *Beth Ha'ēzer* by Benjamin Spinoza (d. 1776), but these two works remain in manuscript and have never been published; cf. Friedlaender, *Essays*, p. 248. In addition to the above, fragmentary remarks on these commentaries have been published by Yehudah Leib Eisler in *Beth Talmud*, II (1882), 183-187; 213-216 and Jacob Reifman in *'Iyyūnim Bemishnat Har'ab'a*, ed. by Naphtali Ben-Menachem (Jerusalem, 1962), pp. 41-88.

20 Cf. Friedlaender, *Essays*, p. 218ff, where a long list of supercommentaries on the commentaries of Ibn Ezra on the Pentateuch is given, but hardly any significant one on the commentaries of Ibn Ezra on the Minor Prophets.

21 The absence of thought-provoking ideas in the commentary on the Minor Prophets in comparison with other scriptural writings of Ibn Ezra apparently may also have contributed to the lack of interest in it.

The Rabbinic Bible (*Miqraot Gedolot*) first published by the Bombergian Press (Venice, 1525-1526) included the commentary of Ibn Ezra on the Minor Prophets.

22 According to Ibn Ezra's statement found in some of the manuscripts at our disposal, his commentary on the Minor Prophets was composed in the year 4917 (=1156) in the city of Rodom. This commentary has not come down to us in the original form in which it was written by its author. Two such manuscripts (British Museum 24896 and Montefiore 34, 2) conclude with the following colophon:

> I, Joseph the son of Jacob of Maudeville (or 'Morville') copied this from the author's handwritten text. I have also added to his words a few remarks which he made to me when he was engaged in writing his book. However, since they are given in my own words, I marked the additional lines by two points at the beginning and at the end of my interpolations.

Rodom has recently been identified by Professor Norman Golb as the city of Rouen in Normandy. Cf. his conclusive study *Les Juifs de Rouen au moyen age* (Rouen, 1985), pp. 185-190. As for Morville, the town of Jacob's origin, cf. ibid., p. 217; note 10; idem., *Tōledōt Hayehūdim Be'ir Ru'an Biymĕy Habēynayim* (Tel Aviv, 1976), pp. 31, 55.

23 In his commentary on Ex. 14:19, Ibn Ezra points out that such repetitions occur only in prophetic, not in historical, style.

24 Cf., comm. on Hosea 4:17, 6:18, 8:3, 10:15, 13:10. Cf. also, e.g. comm. on Gen. 49:6 and Ex. 15:7.

25 Cf. comm. on Hosea 3:3, 10:7. This figure is generally described in Ibn Ezra by the phrase מושך עצמו ואחר עמו (lit., "it pulls itself and another one with it," i.e., the force of one word is extended to another). In his commentary on Is. 5:13, Ibn Ezra uses this figure "according to the rules of ellipsis." Significantly, the same rule was applied long before Ibn Ezra by the Qaraite Yefet b. 'Ali in his commentary on Hosea 12:1. Cf. *The Arabic Commentary of Yefet Ben 'Ali the Karaite on the book of Hosea*, ed. by Philip Birnbaum (Philadelphia, 1942), p. 180.

26 Cf. comm. on Hosea 2:20, 14:3, and on Is. 1:13.

27 In his commentary on the Minor Prophets, Ibn Ezra refers to Arabic terms and usages ten times (on Hosea 4:14, 13:5; Joel 2:7; Am. 5:26 [two times], 7:7, 7:15; Micah 3:11; Zeph. 1:18, 2:14). Cf. comm. on Cant. 8:11 (first part): "...for Arabic is very closely related to Hebrew....Therefore we explain biblical hapaxlegomena by similar words in Arabic, although the matter of analogy may be in doubt." It should be noted that Jewish scholars preceding Ibn Ezra already attempted to explain some biblical terms by way of analogy between these two languages. But most of these scholars focused their attention mainly on grammatical and etymological similarities (cf. S. Eppenstein's review in *'Iyyun Weḥēqer*, trans. by Ṣeb̲i Ben-Meir and Hayyim Leshem [Jerusalem, 1976], pp. 292-303), whereas Ibn Ezra wrote originally in Hebrew and used the references to the Arabic as a tool of biblical exegesis.

28 Cf. comm. on Ex. 21:2. Cf. also comm. on Lev. 19:3 and Deut. 16:18 for essentially the same statement. This rule is implemented by Ibn Ezra in comm. on Ex. 10:1; Num. 3:10, 15:2; and Deut. 2:16. In comm. on Ex. 6:28 and Lev 26:10, Ibn Ezra concedes that he does not know why the two unrelated sections are there juxtaposed.

29 Cf. comm. on Hosea 2:17, 2:22, 14:5 (twice), 14:6. In all these places Ibn Ezra uses the term הפוך (lit., "opposite") to indicate that each biblical phrase in question stands in adverse relation to a previous one. For similar attempts to conjoin the text in Hosea, cf. comm. on 2:1, 3:3, 5:6-7, 5:14, 7:1, 9:11, 10:13, 11:11-12.

30 Cf. Targum, Rashi and Qimhi, ad loc.

31 Modern scholars tend to transfer this section (2:1-2) to the end of chapter 2. Cf. William Rainey Harper, *A Critical and Exegetical Commentary on Amos and Hosea* (New York, 1905), p. 245.

32 Cf. Ibn Ezra's remark on 2:1: "This chapter is connected with the preceding one."

One of Qimhi's objections, ad loc., to Ibn Ezra's interpretation is based on the ground that the term *we'ālū* (= and they shall go up) cannot be applied to those leaving Israel for exile, because Israel is geographically located on a higher ground and those who leave it go down rather than up. However, in his commentary on 8:9, Qimhi agrees that the term *'ālū* connotes "they were removed."

33 The first clause of verse 16 is generally taken as a continuing statement of the preceding prophecy, i.e., because she (Israel) played the harlot and went after her lovers (7-15), "therefore I will allure her and bring her into the wilderness" (for retribution); and the second ("and I will speak tenderly to her," lit., "upon her heart") as a promise of redemption. Cf. Rashi, Eliezer of Beaugency (*Kommentar zu Ezechiel und den XII kleinen Propheten*, von Eliezer aus Beaugency, ed. by Samuel Poznanski [Warsaw, 1913]), and Qimhi, ad loc. Hence, verse 16 is divided into two opposing themes, viz., punishment and reward.

34 That is, because the harlot (Israel) will realize her failure by saying: "I will go and return to my first husband" (v. 9), *therefore* I (viz., God) will persuade her and bring her back into her own land (viz., the land of Israel) that had turned into a wilderness. Note Ibn Ezra's peculiar definition of the term *hamidbār* ("that turned into a wilderness"). which is designed to conjoin the first and second clauses of the verse.

35 The corrupt reading of Ibn Ezra's remark on Hosea 14:10 in the printed editions (viz., והשלם = and the complete one) led scholars to many erroneous conjectures. Cf. Filwarg, p. 5a, and Eisler, p.187. However, the correct reading in all of the manuscripts at our disposal is והשלים (= and he concluded), i.e. the prophet began and concluded his prophecy with the idea that sinners stumble in their iniquity and suffer ultimate ruin.

36 For a similar view, cf. Bab. Talmud. *Pesahim*, 87a.

37 So also Targum and Yefet, p. 15. Cf. John Calvin, *Commentaries on the Twelve Minor Prophets*, trans. by John Owen (Edinburgh, 1846), p. 45: "But it may be, and it is probable, that no vision was presented to the prophet, but that God only ordered him to proclaim what had been given him in charge."

38 Cf. comm. on 1:1: "For harlotry in departing from God is a figurative expression, whereas harlotry among men denotes an action." Cf. also E[rnst] W[ilhelm] Hengstenberg, *Christology of the Old Testament*, I, trans. by Theodor Mayer (Edinburgh, 1954), p. 180, against the view "that the law of God has been, in this special case, repealed by His command....To ascribe arbitrariness to God in this respect would be to annihilate the idea of God and the idea of Good at the same time."

39 Cf. Friedlaender, *Essays*, Hebrew Appendix, p. 1. Ibn Ezra generally speaks of Christianity in a critical tone. In his commentary on Gen. 18:1 he is critical of the doctrine of the trinity; on Ex. 16:25 he speaks of customs in Christian countries which do not compare to those among the Israelites; ibid., 29:37 (short recension, cf. *Abraham Ibn Ezra's Commentary on Exodus*, ed. by Leopold Fleischer [Vienna, 1926], p.

278), against Christian interpretation on Dan, 9:24; on Is. 7:14, against those who interpret figuratively the phrase "the children which the Lord has given me" (ibid. 8:18); ibid. 52:13, against the referral of the passage to Jesus; ibid., 52:14 against the Moslems and Christians who imagine the Jew as altogether different from his fellow creatures.

40 Cf. comm. on Jonah (introd.): "All prophets except Moses, after the divine glory had passed before him, received their prophecy in a vision or a dream."

41 Cf. C.F. Keil and F. Delitzsch, *Biblical Commentary on The Old Testament*, trans. by James Martin (Edinburgh, 1880), p.35: "Consequently no other course is left to us, than to picture to ourselves Hosea's marriages as internal events." For a more detailed discussion of the marriage of Hosea, cf. B. Uffenheimer, "Nesū'ēy Hōshē'a kesēmel neḇū'ī". *Sepher Dim* (Pirsūmēy haḥeḇrāh leḥēqer hamiqrā' beyisrā'ēl), ed. by H. Bar-Daroma, H. Gebaryahu and B.Z. Luria, (Jerusalem, 1958), pp. 269-279.

42 Moses Chiquitilla was an eleventh-century commentator and grammarian whose views on prophetic passages in the Bible are frequently quoted by Ibn Ezra; cf. below, note 51. For a discussion of the view of Galipapa (fourteenth century) on prophecy, cf. *Sepher Ha'iqqārim*, ed. and trans. by Isaac Husik, IV, part 2 (Philadelphia, 1946), pp. 418-423.

43 Cf. Abravanel, introd. to comm. on Joel 3, and on Zech. 9:8, 13.

44 In his commentary on Gen. 49:1, Ibn Ezra remarks: "The prophecy is designated *le'ātid* "(= for the future), because of the phrase *be'aḥrit hayāmim* ("in the end of the days"); so also in comm. on Micah 4:1: "No doubt that this prophecy is meant *le'ātid*, therefore [the prophet] said 'in the end of the days.'" "The end of days" is taken by Ibn Ezra to mean the furthermost period of time with the highest degree of perfection. Those days, in his view, have not yet come; cf. *The Commentary of Ibn Ezra on Isaiah*, ed. and trans. by Michael Friedlaender (London, 1873), p. 14.

45 Cf. comm. on Is. 34:8: "This verse shows that the prophecy refers to the Messianic period," a remark which is obviously designed to disprove Chiquitilla's contention (quoted by Ibn Ezra, ibid., v. 2) that the prophecy in Isaiah should be referred to the Assyrian conquest. Cf. also comm. on Micah 4:11-12; Ob. 1:21: Zeph. 3:8; Zech. 13:1, 14:8, 14:21. All of these prophecies are designated by Ibn Ezra *le'ātid* on the basis of textual evidence.

46 For similar remarks with regard to the oath of God, cf. comm. on Gen. 22:16; Num. 23:21; Is. 45:23, 52:1, 62:8.

47 Cf. *Yesōd Mōrā*, pub. by Naphtali Ben-Menachem (Jerusalem, 1970), p. 24. Cf. also comm. on Hosea 2:25, where Ibn Ezra reluctantly remarks: "This prophecy may either refer to the time to come or else it is syntactically connected with what precedes."

48 Jeshua is an unidentified, eleventh-century Qaraite quoted by Ibn Ezra, on Hosea 5:7. He is also named among other Qaraites and criticized by Ibn Ezra, in his introduction to the commentary on the Pentateuch.

49 The unidentified Joseph is quoted by Ibn Ezra, on Hosea 14:3. Significantly, there are certain similarities between the remarks of Ibn Ezra and those of his older French contemporary Joseph Qara in their respective commentaries on Hosea 1:6, 1:9, 2:7, 2:22 (and 13:5, as quoted by Qara in the name of Menahem b. Helbo). However, such similarities are not sufficient to prove a direct relationship between the two commentators.

50 His full name is Abulwalid Merwan Jonah Ibn Janah (c. 990-1050), who is also quoted by Ibn Ezra as R. Jonah or R. Marinus; the latter designation is used in the comm. on Hosea 2:14, 2:18, 11:4, and 14:3.

51 Ibn Ezra quotes the Mishna on Hosea 8:13 in the name of "Our Masters of blessed memory."

52 His full name is Moses b. Samuel Hakkohen Ibn Chiquitilla (eleventh century) and he is quoted by Ibn Ezra, under "R. Moshe" or "R. Moshe Hakkohen" on Hosea 8:13, 10:8, and 13:1. For a fragmentary list of Ibn Chiquitilla's biblical expositions, cf. Samuel Poznanski, *Mose b. Samuel Hakkohen Ibn Chiquitilla* (Leipzig, 1895), pp. 95-117.

53 Saadya (882-942) is quoted by Ibn Ezra on Hosea 11:9 under the term "the Gaon," but the source for this quotation is no longer extant.

54 Yefet b. 'Ali (Abu Hasan, second half of tenth century) is quoted by Ibn Ezra on Hosea 3:4, 4:3, 5:3, 5:5, 5:7, 5:11, 8:1, 8:4, 8:13, 10:8, and 14:8 (2). All, with the exception of three quotations (on 4:3, 8:4, and 14:8) are found in Yefet's commentary on Hosea. Poznanski says: "Mais Yefet a du rédiger une deuxième version aussi sur d'autres ecrits bibliques" (cf. Samuel Poznanski, "Bibliographie," *Revue des études juives*, XLI [1900], 306), which may explain why one does not find in Yefet all of the statements Ibn Ezra assigns to him.

55 The anonymous Yiṣḥaqi is quoted by Ibn Ezra on Hosea 1:1 and is also cited and ridiculed in his commentary on Gen. 36:32 and Job 42:16. This author has been identified by some with the tenth-century physician-philosopher Isaac b. Solomon Israeli and by others with Ibn Janah. For the latest suggestion regarding the identity of Yiṣḥaqi, cf. Ezra Fleischer, "Leṣibyōn hash'ēlot ha'atiqōt ulbe'āyat zehut meḥabbrān," *Hebrew Union College Annual*, XXXVIII (1976 [Hebrew section]), 17-23.

56 For a more detailed description of mss. B, L, and V, cf. Friedlaender, *Essays*, pp. 204, 206, and 208-09; for ms. M, cf. Ad[olf] Neubauer, *Catalogue of the Hebrew Manuscripts in the Bodleian Library* (Oxford, 1886), No. 301; for ms. N, cf. Hartwig Hirschfeld, *Descriptive Catalogue of the Hebrew Mss. of the Montefiore Library* (London, 1904), No. 34; for ms. R, cf. Angelo d. Capua, "Cataloghi dei Codici ebraici della Bibl Angelica" in: *Cataloghi dei codici orientali di alcune biblioteche d'Italia* (Firenze, 1878), no. 18.

57 Ibn Ezra's commentary on Isaiah (ed. and trans. by Michael Friedlaender [London, 1873]) and the one on Canticles (ed. and trans. by H.J. Mathews [London, 1847]) are the only ones of his scriptural writings ever to have been translated into English.

58 The Authorized (King James) Version and the Revised Standard Version both are cited in the present work as they appear in *The Interpreter's Bible*, IV (New York-Nashville, 1955), pp. 566-725; while citations from the LXX are as given in *The Septuagint Version of The Old Testament*, trans. by Lancelot Charles Brenton (London, 1844), pp. 833-875. In addition, we here refer to the commentaries of Ibn Ezra and David Qimhi on the Minor Prophets (as well as those of Rashi and Joseph Qara) as printed in the traditional Bible (*Miqraot Gedolot*), VIII (Jerusalem, 5724 = 1964). The Commentary of David Qimhi on Hosea, ed. by Harry Cohen (New York, 1966), was also consulted.

Chapter I

(1-2) This Hosea was one of the honored prophets of God. Yiṣḥaqi uttered falsehood against him in his book in saying that he was the son of Elah [II Kings 15:30] because Beeri is Elah; for he had found a passage stating, "and the howling thereof unto Beer-elim"[1] [Is. 15:8]. Elah, however, is not Elim; for on account of the presence of an additional letter, the name becomes different, e.g., "Ziph and Zipha" [I Chron. 4:16].[2] Furthermore, it is not in accordance with the rules of biblical Hebrew[3] to refer to an individual by saying he is the son of a city except in reference to a group, e.g., "daughter of Zion" [II Kings 19:21]; rather, one would only show a relation to the city by [using a form] similar to *Shōmrōnī* [= a Samaritan].[4] There were two things that impelled [Yiṣḥaqi] to make his assertion: The first is that he found in Chronicles [the statement] "Beerah, his son, whom Tiglath-pileser,[5] king of Assyria, exiled, was prince of the Reubenites" [I Chron. 5:6] – hence he was the father of this prophet; while the second is that [the prophet] said: "And to punish Jacob according to his ways" [12:3]. He interpreted this latter passage in reference to our forefather Jacob who took the birthright away from Reuben [I Chron. 5:1].[6] Its correct interpretation, however, is not as he thought, for he forgot what was written concerning Hosea, the son of Elah, "and he did evil in the eyes of the Lord" [II Kings 17:21].[7] Yiṣḥaqi argues that [Hosea actually] took a harlot for a wife, but did not this blinded man see written *when the Lord spoke at first with Hosea, the Lord said* [1:2]. Far was it from him to violate the commandment of God.[8] The fact [moreover] remains that Hosea, the son of Beeri, is not Hosea, the son of Elah. Compare "Enoch," which is a general name for four different people in the Pentateuch [Gen. 4:17, 5:18, 25:4; Num. 2:5]. [Compare also] "Shaul of Rehoboth by the River" [Gen. 36:37], "Shaul the son of the Canaanitish woman" [ibid. 46:10] and "Shaul the son of Kish" [I Sam. 10:21]; there are many such instances.

This prophet began his prophecy concerning the reign of Jeroboam, the son of Joash, king of Israel, forty years before the exile of Samaria, assuming his prophecy took place at the end of Jeroboam's days – for after him Zechariah, his son, did not reign for more than six months and then the reign of the dynasty of Jehu, of the kings of Israel, ceased [II Kings 15:8, 9-12].[9]

Another exegete maintained that [the words] *lēḵ qaḥ* [= go take] mean "to instruct," in the sense of "good instruction" [*leqaḥ ṭōḇ* (Prov. 4:2)].[10] He further maintained that the meaning of "and she conceived" [1:3] is like "ye conceive chaff, ye shall bring forth stubble" [Is. 33:11]. He further said that the name *Gomer* implies being consummated [*gemūrāh*] by harlotry[11] and the "daughter of Diblayim" is symbolic of Judah and Israel.[12] Still another [commentator] said that [by the phrase] *take unto thee a wife of harlotry*, the prophet was told: "If you come to take a moral woman you will not find one, *for the land had committed harlotry*, i.e., all the people of the land committed harlotry in departing from God. Yet another exegete said [that the prophet was asked to] take unto himself *a wife of harlotry and children of harlotry* because the people of the land had equally committed harlotry in departing from the Lord and "it is enough for the servant to be like his master."[13]

Thus says Abraham [Ibn Ezra] the author: It is inconceivable that God should command one to take a harlot and to conceive children of harlotry. Furthermore, the concept that "it is enough for a servant to be like his master" cannot be applied to this case, for harlotry in departing from God is a figurative expression, whereas harlotry among man denotes an action. It is therefore my view that this prophet, in a vision of prophecy [or] in a dream of the night, perceived that God said to him, *go take unto thee a wife of harlotry*, after which he went and took a well-known woman who conceived and gave birth – all this in a prophetic vision, as God [Himself] explained: "If there be a prophet among you" – [that is to say,] except Moses our teacher alone – "I, the Lord, do make myself known unto him in a vision, I do speak with him in a dream" [Num. 12:6]. Be not surprised how he [Hosea] could see in a dream such acts as "he went and took [a woman of harlotry, etc." (v. 3)], since even in a layman's dream, without prophecy, "the cows consumed..." [Gen. 41:4].[14] Compare "like as My servant Isaiah hath walked naked and barefoot" [Is. 20:3], which was also [said] by way of prophecy; for why should the prophet walk naked because of Ethiopia and Egypt?[15] Similarly, "take thee a tile" [Ez. 4:1], also "lie thou upon thy left side" [ibid. 4:4], and "take thou unto thee wheat" [ibid. 4:9], as well as the story of the beard [ibid. 5:1][16] – all of which is confirmed by what Ezekiel said at the beginning of his book: "I saw a vision of God" [ibid. 1:1]. [Ezekiel moreover said]: "In the visions of God, He brought me unto the land of Israel[17] [ibid. 40:2]. Be not surprised, [however], that no visions are mentioned at the beginning of our prophecy, for the same is the case with regard to the words of God that came to Zechariah [Zech. 1:1].[18] Only afterward is it there stated: "I saw in the night" [ibid. 1:8], "I lifted my eyes and saw" [ibid. 2:1]. It is written [also] of Abraham [that the Lord came to him] "in a vision" [Gen. 15:1]; such was his every prophecy. Thus [the Lord] explained to him [viz., to Hosea] by way of prophecy why he should take a harlot, viz., *for the land hath committed great harlotry.*

(3) **So and he went and took** the woman mentioned above. All this he perceived in a vision.[19] [The phrase] *and she bore a son* is to be understood [metaphorically] as the generation following Jeroboam, the son of Joash.[20]

(4) **[I will visit] the blood of Jezreel:** Meaning, I will visit the blood of the house of Ahab[21] *upon the House of Jehu* because he did not follow God [II Kings 10:1-11; 31]. Also his son Jehoahaz, his grandson Jehoash, as well as our Jeroboam and his son Zechariah, all did what was evil in the eyes of God, for so is it written [ibid. 14:6, 14:24, 15:9].

(5) **[I will break] the bow of Israel:** [Meaning,] the kingdom of Zechariah; for it was then that the dynasty of Jehu ceased.[22]

(6) **And she conceived...and bore a daughter:** This means the following generation. He called it *daughter* for it is written of Jeroboam that "he restored the border of Israel" [ibid. 14:25]. After the death of his son Zechariah, Menahem reigned, and in his days the king of Assyria entered the land [ibid. 15:17-19]; there is no need to mention the kingdom of Shallum because he only reigned one month [ibid. 15:13].[23] Then, in the days of Pekah, the son of Remaliah, Tiglath-pileser exiled many [people] of the cities of Israel; and in the days of Hosea, the son of Elah, Samaria was seized. For this reason he called this generation *daughter.*[24] He then explains [the calling of his daughter] *Lōrūhāmāh*[25] [by saying] *for I shall no more have compassion.* The conjunction *shin* [= that] is missing; the passage means that I shall no more proceed to have [lit., "that I have"] compassion. Compare "we shall know, that we may follow" [6:3], "do not exceed [that] you

talk" [I Sam. 2:3].[26] There is an opinion that [the phrase] *that I will utterly carry them [kī nāsō' 'essā' lāhem]* relates to their sins for which I have pardoned them until now.[27] However, there is no mention of sin [here]. It is my view that this [latter] word is used in a manner similar to its use in [the phrase] "they slew Abner" [II Sam. 3:30].[28] The meaning is similar to [that in the phrase] "will my maker take me away" [*yīssa'ēnī* (Job. 32:22)].[29] Thus he was here foretelling the exile of the tribes.

(7) **[But I will have compassion upon] the house of Judah:** For the people of Jerusalem escaped from Sennaherib. **And I will save them by the Lord their God** refers to the angel of God proceeding to smite the whole Assyrian camp [II Kings 19:30-35].

(8-9) **When she had weaned [she conceived and bore a son . . . Loammi:** Meaning,] the exiled tribes begot children in exile. There they stayed and did not return to their land.[30] Therefore, He named them *Loammi*[31] and [told them] *I will not be* their God; however, he did not mention the word *God* because of great anger.[32]

Notes

1 The question raised here by I. E. is that of identification of the father of Hosea, viz., Beeri (1:1). Yiṣḥaqi maintains that Beer-elim is the name of one place – with "Elim" understood as being synonymous with Beer. Therefore, Beeri and Elah are, in his view, one and the same person. Consequently, Hosea b. Beeri, the prophet, is, according to Yiṣḥaqi, identical with Hosea b. Elah, the last king of Israel. For various suggestions regarding the identity of Yiṣḥaqi, see Introduction, sec. 4, note 55.

2 I.e., Ziph and Zipha are two individuals whose names are made distinct by the addition of a letter in the second case.

3 Lit., "the holy tongue," a term used frequently in I. E.'s writings. Cf. Wilhelm Bacher, *Abraham Ibn Esra als Grammatiker* (Strassburg, 1882), p. 6, note 2, and p. 33, note 1; Leo Prijs, *Die Grammatikalische Terminologie des Abraham Ibn Esra* (Basel, 1950), p. 68.

4 As opposed to *ben Shōmrōn* (= a son of Samaria). Therefore, Hosea cannot be referred to as the son of Beeri, i.e., the son of a place called Beer.

5 I. E. and Qimhi (comm., Introd.) both spell this name "Tiglath-pileser," as in II Kings 15:29, 16:7, 16:10. Cf. *Pesiqta Derab̲ Kahana*, ed. by Solomon Buber (Lyck, 1868), p. 159b: "Pileser King of Assyria." However, Yefet, in his commentary, transcribes "Tillegath-pilneser," which corresponds with the Masoretic text in I Chron. 5:6. Cf. *The Arabic Commentary of Yefet b. 'Ali the Karaite on the Book of Hosea*, ed. by Philip Birnbaum (Philadelphia, 1942), p. 6.

6 Yiṣḥaqi had evidently claimed that Beerah, the prince of the Reubenites, was exiled by Tiglath-pileser during the reign of Pekah, the son of Remaliah, king of Israel (I Chron. 5:6). According to him, this Beerah and Beeri, the father of the prophet, are the same person, for the Hebrew letters *hē* (last consonant in Beerah) and *yod* (last consonant in Beeri) are interchangeable. Soon after Hosea conspired against Pekah and ascended the throne of Israel, Shalmaneser, king of Assyria, besieged Samaria and imprisoned the king (II Kings 15:30, 17:30-6). Thus, Beerah, the father of this prophet, was a contemporary of Tiglath-pileser and Pekah, while his son, Hosea, who later became king of Israel, was subjugated by Shalmaneser. Yiṣḥaqi further adduces from the passage "and to punish Jacob according to his ways" (12:3) that Hosea was a Reubenite and therefore he complained about the birthright Jacob removed from his forefather and gave to Joseph (Gen. 49:3-4). It should be noted that others also identify Beer with Beerah the Reubenite, cf. *Pesiqta Deraḇ Kahana*, op. cit., p. 159b; Qimhi, comm., Introd., but it is Yiṣḥaqi alone who maintains that Beeri was Elah and that Hosea the prophet was King Hosea, the son of Elah.

7 I.e., it is unlikely that such a pejorative statement would be made about the prophet Hosea.

8 According to I. E., Yiṣḥaqi holds that by taking a harlot, Hosea also did evil in the eyes of God.

9 According to I. E., Hosea evidently began his prophetic activity during the last years of Jeroboam II and continued throughout the reigns of the remaining kings of Israel (the period from c. 765 to c. 725). This remark is probably designed to synchronize the two periods of Judah and Israel given at the beginning of Hosea. For a discussion of the matter, cf. W. R. Harper, *A Critical and Exegetical Commentary on Amos and Hosea* (New York, 1905), p. 203, and J. D. Wynkoop's commentary in *Biblia Hebraica* (Kiew, 1906), p. 7. Cf. also *Pesiqta Rabbati*, ed. by Meir Friedmann (Vienna, 1880), p. 153b, where Hosea is assigned a prophetic span of 90 years.

10 The entire passage in Hosea reads: "Go take (*lēḵ- qaḥ*) unto thee a wife of harlotry." According to this exegete, the word *qaḥ* [lit., take] means "instruct" in consonance with the meaning of the word *leqaḥ* in the phrase *leqaḥ tōḇ* (= "good instruction" or "good doctrine"). I.e., Hosea was asked to give instruction to the harlot "Gomer daughter of Diblayim," a name (viz., Diblayim) which is taken allegorically for Judah and Israel. Cf. below, note 12. According to Abravanel in his *Commentary on the Twelve Minor Prophets* (Tel-Aviv, 1960, p. 19), there is no doubt that this exegete and the Targum are of the same opinion. Cf. also Rashi, ad loc. (after quoting the Targum): "The word *qaḥ* that is used here connotes instruction: Instruct them to repent."

11 A similar view on the name Gomer is expressed in Bab. Talmud, *Pesahim*, 87a, and by Jerome. Cf. M. Rahmer, "Die Hebräischen Traditionen in den Werken Hieronymus," *Monatsschrift für Geschichte und Wissenschaft des Judenthums*, XIV (1865), 221; Rashi, and Qara, ad loc.

12 The name *Diblayim* (figcakes) in its dual form is taken allegorically for Judah and Israel. Cf. Jacob b. Reuben, *Sepher Ha'ōsher* (appeared in print with *Mibḥar Yeshārim* by Aaron b. Joseph the elder [Eupatoria, 1836]), ad loc.

13 That is to say, if the people have committed adultery by going astray after other gods, the servant (i.e., the prophet) may also marry an adulteress; for "it is enough for the servant to be like his master." Cf. *Midrash Shōḥēr-tōb* (on Psalms), ed. by Solomon Buber (Vilna, 1891), 27:5.

14 The layman I. E. refers to is Pharaoh, who saw in his dream seven fat cows consuming seven lean ones. In his commentary on Hosea (p. 20), Abravanel is of the opinion that whenever Scripture confirms the action of a prophet by saying "and he did so walking naked and barefoot" (Is. 20:2) or "so he went and took" (1:3), it cannot be dismissed as a mere prophetic vision. This comment by I. E. may have been designed to combat such an opinion, which was perhaps already circulating in his own time.

15 In his commentary on Is. 20:3, I. E. remarks: "It would be a strange thing that the prophet should have gone naked as a sign for Egypt. I shall explain this circumstance with the help of God at the beginning of the Minor Prophets." The translation is that of M. Friedlaender in *The Commentary of Ibn Ezra on Isaiah*, p. 92.

16 Sharim (*Hadar 'Ezer*, [Smyrna, 1865], p. 26b) erroneously read in I. E. *hazāqēn* (= the old man), referring this remark to the elderly prophet from Bethel (I Kings 13:11). It goes without saying that I. E. had in mind the beard (*hazāqan*) Ezekiel was told to shave. Cf. below, note 17; N. Krochmal, *Mōreh Nebūkēy Hazemān*, ed. by Shimon Rawidowicz (Berlin, 1924), p. 316; David Qimhi, *Dictionary*, ed. by Biesenthal and Lebrecht (Berlin, 1847), p. 118.

17 A remarkably similar exposition is given by Maimonides in *The Guide of the Perplexed*, trans. by Shlomo Pines (Chicago-London, 1969), part II, chapt. 46, pp. 405-406:

> So was his saying to him: "Thou also . . . take thee a tile," and so on. "Moreover lie thou upon thy left side," and so on. "Take thou also unto thee wheat and barley," and so on; as well as his saying to him: "And cause it to pass upon thy head and upon thy beard," – seen, all of it, in a vision of prophecy in which he saw that he carried out the actions he was ordered to carry out. God is too exalted than that He should turn His prophets into a laughing stock and a mockery for fools by ordering them to carry out crazy actions. And this in addition to ordering them to commit acts of disobedience; for [Ezekiel] was a Priest, and every side of beard or of hair he cut made him guilty of transgressing two prohibitions. But all this happened merely in a vision of prophecy. In the same way, when He says: "Like as My servant Isaiah hath walked naked and barefoot," this only happened in the visions of God . . . . The position is similar with regard to the words addressed to Hosea: "Take unto thee a wife of harlotry and children of har-

lotry." All this story concerning the birth of the children and their having been named so and so happened in its entirety in a vision of prophecy.

18 This is not an exact quotation from Zechariah as suggested in mss. L, N, and in the printed editions. The reading adopted here ascribes these words to I. E. and is based on mss. M, R, V.

19 Cf. above, note 14 for our remark on I. E.'s earlier comment on this verse.

20 So also Yefet, p. 23, and Jacob b. Reuben, ad loc.

21 I.e., the massacre committed in Jezreel by Jehu against the family of Ahab (II Kings 10:11). Cf. Rashi, Qara and Qimhi, ad loc. Cf. also below, comm. on 2:24.

22 Cf. Poznanski's note to Eliezer of Beaugency's opening remark in his *Kommentar zu Ezechiel und den XII kleinen Propheten* (Warsaw, 1910-1913), p. 117. This exegete apparently meant to say that with Zechariah, the kingdom of Israel almost ceased. For the following kings were already subjugated to the Assyrian kings and their kingdom was considered insignificant.

23 Viz., the reign of Shallum was only of a month's duration in contrast to the reigns of other kings, which lasted for years.

24 The personification of the nation first as a son (v. 4) and then as a daughter represents, respectively, the better days under Jeroboam II, who restored the borders of the land, and the following years of weakness, when Israel was subdued by Assyria. Cf. Jacob b. Reuben, ad loc.: "He called them *daughter* because they were weak."

25 *Lōrūḥāmāh*, lit., "the unpitied one," i.e., she is not pitied. Cf. Harper, p. 212.

26 Our translations of the above passages of Ibn Ezra are necessarily hyperliteral. The method of supplying omitted conjunctions such as the Hebrew *shin* is frequently used by I. E. to explain textual difficulties. Cf. below, comm. on 6:3 and comm. on Is. 52:1, Ps. 118:24. In *Ṣaḥot*, ed. by Gabriel Lippman (Fürth, 1827), p. 22b, I. E. disagrees with the grammarians who said the word is missing a *waw* (= and): "They have not spoken correctly. Rather it is missing a *shin* (= that) which is like *'asher*."

27 J.P.S. translates the last phrase, thus: "That I should in any wise pardon them." Cf. Bab. Talmud, *Pesahim*, 87b, and commentaries of Eliezer of Beaugency and of Qimhi, ad loc. The Hebrew root *ns'* means both "to pardon" and "to carry."

28 Instead of the literal translation "they slew *to* Abner," so here as well (1:6), "I will utterly carry *them* away," instead of "to them" (*lāhem*).

29 The same root *ns'* is used here, but in the sense "to carry away" rather than "to pardon." Cf. Yefet, p. 21, and the anonymous Arabic translation of Hosea, ed. and trans. by R. Schroeter in *Archiv für Wissenschaftliche Erforschung* (Halle, 1869), I, 49: "Sondern sie in die Länder tragen," but closer to Ibn Janah, *Dictionary* (*Sepher Haschorāschim*), ed. by Wilhelm Bacher (Berlin, 1896), p. 322: "I will remove and uproot them."

30 In his *Commentary on the Twelve Minor Prophets*, ed. by I. D. Markon (Jerusalem, 1957), p 1, Daniel al-Qumisi interprets this prophecy as a warning to the people

of the diaspora after the exile of Israel and Judah, uttered because they accepted traditional law, i.e., Rabbinic Judaism. I. E., however, makes reference only to the ten tribes of Israel, who were exiled and never returned to their land.

31 I.e., not my people.

32 Cf. also Qara, ad loc.: "And I will not be your God; this is [one] of the elliptical verses." Note the strange reading in I. E..: "And I will not be to them" (*lāhem*), instead of that in the text: "To you" (*lāḵem*).

Chapter II

(1) This chapter is connected with the preceding one in the following way: It is in the place of their exile that they will give birth to many children, but they will not be God-fearing. The meaning of the word *bimqōm* [= in place of] is similar to that of *taḥat* [= in retribution for] in the phrase *tahat 'āsher lō' 'ābadtā* [= in retribution for your not having served (Deut. 28:47)], viz., they [the exiles] will call themselves *the children of a living God*, but in reality they are *not my people* in retribution for their evil deeds.[1]

(2) **[The children of Judah and the children of Israel] shall be gathered:** The meaning of [the phrase] *they shall be gathered* is that Sennaherib had captured numerous people of Judah, as is stated [in Scripture]; namely, he seized "all the fortified cities of Judah" [II Kings 18:30]. **They shall appoint themselves one head**, that is Sennaherib;[2] **and they shall go up out of the land for great shall be the day of Jezreel** – for the iniquity of the house of Israel was visited [upon them].[3] Thus, this entire passage is to be interpeted as a rebuke rather than as praise; or else, it means that the day of their calamity will be as great as the day of Jezreel.[4] The one who interprets the passage in the sense of "greater than the day of Jezreel"[5] [erred], for it is contrary to the grammatical rules of biblical Hebrew to drop a comparative *mem* [= than] because the concept would then become reversed.[6] Furthermore, the phrase "greater than [the day of Jezreel]" is meaningless, since there is no indication what is [greater than that day].

(3) **Say [ye unto your brethren, *'ammī*** (= that is My people)]: [For a similar sarcasm,] compare "Elijah mocked and said: 'Cry aloud'" [I Kings 18:27]; "rejoice, O lad, in your youth" [Ecc. 11:4]; "come to Bethel" [Am. 4:4] and many such cases.[7] Therefore, [the prophet] continued [to say]: "Plead with your mother, plead," [meaning] how can you claim to be the children of a living God [v. 1] when your mother [i.e., your ancestors] had played the harlot [v. 7].

(4) **Plead [with your mother . . . and let her put away her harlotries]:**
The prophet reprimands the exiles in the hope that they will repent;
then God will cause them to return from their captivity. Or else he
[here] sounds a warning to the contemporary generation before their
going into exile. The second radical of the verb in the word *zenûnehā*
[= her harlotries] is doubled; compare *hāgîgî* [= my meditation (Ps.
5:2)]. The third radical of the verb in the word *wena'afûfehā* (= and
her adulteries] is likewise doubled; compare [also] *sagrîr* [= rainy
(Prov. 27:15)].[8]

(5) **Lest [I strip her naked and set her] as in the day she was born:**
That is [the day] when she was in Egypt; as Ezekiel mentioned: "Yet
thou wast naked and bare" [Ez. 16:7].[9] [For the meaning of the word]
wehiṣṣagtîhā [= and I will set her,] compare "he [Jacob] set [*wayaṣṣēg*]
the rods" [Gen. 30:38]. **I will make her as a wilderness** uninhabited
by man; *and [slay her] with thirst* because she claims "[I will go after
my lovers] who give me my bread, my water ... and my drink." [v. 7].

(6) **And I will not have compassion upon her children**, those who
will go into exile.[10]

(7) **She put to shame:** [Supply the word] "herself."[11] The Piel participle *me'ahăbay* has a causative meaning, since they sought that I
should love them in exchange for their gifts.[12] The one who identifies
my waters with "the wine" [v. 10] and adduces as evidence the passage "and my wine in the season thereof"[13] [v. 11] is incorrect;[14] for
the phrases "the wine" [v. 10] [and] "and my wine" [v. 11] correspond
to *my drinks.* For the meaning of *my waters* compare "I fed them
with bread and water" [I Kings 18:13]; similarly the prophet [Moses]
said: "I did neither eat bread nor drink water" [Deut. 9:9] and "give
me water for money" [ibid. 2:28].[15]

(8) [For the meaning of the verb] *śāk* [= hedge up], compare
lesikkîm [= as hedges (Num. 33:55)].[16] Compare also "hast not Thou
made a hedge [*śaktā*] about him" [Job 1:10]. *Sîrim* [means] thorns,
as in "for as the crackling of thorns" [*hasîrim* (Eccl. 7:6)[17] and in "like
tangled thorns" [*sîrim* (Nah. 1:10)]. **[She will not find her] paths:**
These are conspicuous places that can be recognized by their signs.[18]
And I will make a wall against her: [That is to say,] I will set up a
fence on her ways; compare "he hath enclosed my ways with hewn
stone, [he hath made my paths crooked" (Lam. 3:9)].

(9) **And she shall run [after her lovers** (*weriddefāh 'et me'ahăbehā*)]:
The one who says that the *Dagesh* in the *dalet* [of *werriddefāh*]
denotes a persistent action in which a person is endlessly engaged [is

mistaken].[19] Will this grammarian perhaps explain to us the difference between the Qal form of the verb in *hadōḇer bī* [= that speaks with me (Zech. 1:19)] and its Piel form in *dibber bī* [= spoke by me (I Sam. 23:2)] or between the Qal form of the verb *gōresh* [= drive out (Ex. 34:11)] and its Piel form in the expression *agareshennū* (= I will (not) drive them out (ibid. 23:29) and] *vayegāresh* [= he drove out (Gen. 33:24)]? These derivative words can be found in Qal as well as in Piel, and there are many such cases. [Rather,] the correct [explanation] is that the verb *rādaf* [= to run after] in Qal is always used when pursuing someone who flees. However, the verb in *yeraddef ḥōsheḵ* [= darkness shall pursue (his enemies) (Nah. 1:8)], which is in Piel, becomes causative.[20] [The present phrase] *weriddefāh et me'ahaḇehā* means she will pursue them [viz., her lovers] when she escapes to them [from her enemies].[21] **And she shall seek them** [*ūḇiqshātam*]: There is a *Dagesh* missing in the *qaf* [of the word *ūḇiqshātam*] although it is in the Piel form. [The *Lamed* in the word] *shilḥū* [within the phrase] *shilḥū bā'ēsh miqdāsheḵā* [= they have set fire to Thy sanctuary (Ps. 74:7)] is also missing a *Dagesh*,[22] all this in order to facilitate the pronunciation.

(10) **For she [did not know]** until now [*that it was I who gave her the corn*, etc.],[23] because she used to say that the Baalim,[24] to whom she offered sacrifices, nurtured her. Compare "but since we ceased offering to the queen of heaven ... [we have wanted all things" (Jer. 44:18)].[25] **[And gold] they used for Baal:** [That is to say,] the craftsman made images from gold and silver to decorate the Baal. In Spain there was a scholar[26] who interpreted the name Baal in astrological terms, i.e., the "master" of an ascending zodiacal house";[27] for the [twelve] constellations are called "houses". They worshiped them, because they are "the host of heaven."[28]

(11) **Therefore [I will take back my corn in time thereof]:** Viz., at the time when I will bring over her enemies to take it [the corn] away.[29] **And I will rescue** [*wehiṣṣaltī*][30] means I will separate; every occurrence of the term "rescue" connotes separation, and [the verse thus means] *I will separate*[31] *My wool and My flax* that I had given her *to cover her nakedness.*[32]

(12) **Now I will uncover her shame**: The word *naḇlūtāh* [= her shame] is derived [from the same root as] *neḇālāh* [= a vile deed (Gen. 34:7)], but the vocalization [of *naḇlūtāh*] follows the [same] pattern as *hayaldut wehashaḥrut hāḇel* [= childhood and youth are vanity (Ecc. 11:10)]; to reveal nakedness is a vile deed.[33]

(13) **I will cause to cease [***(wehishbattî)*** . . . **her new moon and her
Sabbath** (*ḥodshāh weshabbattāh*)]: In order not to join two *taws*
together[34] they dropped one.[35] There is also a *taw* missing in the word
Shabbattō [= his Sabbath], for the three root letters are *shin, bet* and
taw.[36] There is similarly a *taw* missing in the word *wekāratî* [= and
I will cut (v. 20)], for the three root letters are *kaf, resh* and *taw*. All
this because it is [grammatically] improper to join two of the same
consonants [in one word] and to pronounce *wehishbatetî, wekāratetî*,
[which would otherwise have been the correct pronunciation]. By the
word *ḥodshāh* [= her new moon] the first of the month is meant, when
the moon's cycle begins.[37] [It should be noted that] the word
shabbattāh [= her Sabbath] is also missing a *taw*.[38] It is possible, however, that the missing *taw* is assimilated in the *Dagesh* of the remaining one.[39]

(14) The *aleph* in [the word] *'etnāh* [= hire] is added [as a
performative to the root]; compare *mattānāh* [= gift (Num. 18:7)].[40]
R. Marinus compares the word with *'etnān* [= hire (Deut. 23:19)].[41]

(15) **I will visit [upon her the days of the Baalim] ... wherein [she]
decked herself out** like a harlot who puts on *a nose ring and necklace*
to embellish herself, so that she might find favor in the eyes of the
adulterer.

(16) **Therefore [will I entice her]:** That is, after she realizes that all
this evil resulted from the fact that she forgot Me and did not know
at the beginning that I had done her good.[42] [Moreover,] when she
says: "I will go and return to my first husband" [v. 9], then will I
persuade her with words,[43] *and bring her* back into her land that had
turned into a desert.[44]

(17) **I will give her her vineyards:** [This promise was made] in contrast with the warning "I will lay waste her vines" [v. 14]. Similarly,
the *Valley of Akor*, i.e., the Valley of Jezreel,[45] which I have disturbed,[46] will turn into a gateway to hope.[47] The meaning of the word
we' āntāh is "and she will play and sing";[48] compare *wata'an Miriām*
[= and Miriam sang[49] (Ex. 15:21)]. Some interpret [the phrase
we'āntāh shāmāh in the sense of] "she will live there"; compare
mā'ōn [= a dwelling place (Ps. 90:1)].[50] They similarly explain the passage "jackals shall dwell [*we'ānāh*] in their castles"[51] [Is. 13:22]. This
[explanation] is in my view farfetched.[52]

(18) **Thou shalt call Me no more *ba'alî*:** For so it is written "[I will
visit upon her] the days of the Baalim" [v. 15]. However, R. Marinus
said that [the phrase means that] one will no longer mention even an

ambiguous name such as *Baal*, which [is a term used homonymously for an object] of idolatrous worship and [for taking a wife] as in the passage "for as a young man espouseth [*yib̲'al*] a virgin," [Is. 62:5].[53]

(19) [For the meaning of the phrase] *I will remove [the names of the Baalim from her mouth],* compare "the Lord thy God will circumcise thy heart." [Deut. 30:6]; for when the rebel turns away from his sinful act, God assists and makes him return wholeheartedly.[54]

(20) **I will make a covenant [for them ... with the beasts of the field]**: This prophecy was made in contrast with the threat that "the beasts of the field shall eat them" [v. 14]. **[I will break] the bow and the sword and war:** I.e., the weapons of war,[55] Compare "among those who eat" *bread* "at thine own table"[56] [II Sam. 19:29]; "an ass" *laden* "with bread" [I Sam. 16:20].[57] [All this was promised to them] because [the text] previously stated "I will break the bow of Israel" [1:5]; that is to say, from now on they would live in security.

(21) **And I will betroth thee** [(*we'ērastik̲*) **unto Me in righteousness and in justice, in loving kindness and in compassion**]: [For the meaning of the word *we'ērastik̲*,] compare *me'ōrāsāh le'ish* [= betroth unto a man (Deut. 22:23)]. Some explain[58] this passage by saying: If you [viz., the people] will do *righteousness and justice*, then I will likewise bestow upon you *kindness and mercy*; however, there is no need [for such an explanation].[59]

(22) **And I will betroth thee unto Me with faithfulness:** That is to say, you will be faithful only to Me. [The phrase] *and thou shalt know the Lord* is in contrast [with admonition] "for she did not know [that it was I that gave her the corn, the wine, and the oil" (v. 10)].[60]

(23) **I will answer** [(*'e'eneh*) **saith the Lord, I will answer the heavens:**[61] Meaning, I will provide the heavens]. Compare "money answereth [*ya'aneh*] all things" [Eccl. 10:19], which [also] means it provides [all things].[62] The repetition of the word *'e'eneh* [= I will answer] signifies permanence; compare "the floods have lifted up, O Lord [the floods have lifted up their voice" (Ps. 93:3)], as I have explained.[63] [The promise] *I will answer the heavens* is made in opposition to [the warning] "I will make your heaven as iron" [Lev. 26:19]. **And they will answer the earth:** [I.e., the heavens will answer] by providing their dew and their rain in the proper time.

(24) **They shall answer Jezreel:** This is the name of the place mentioned above [1:4-5; 2:2]. It will be restored to what it was before, with a multitude of people.[64]

(25) **I will sow her [unto Me in the land].** That is to say, they [the people of Northern Israel] will multiply and thrive like the seed of the earth. **And I will have compassion upon Loruhamah:**[65] [The name *Lōrūhāmāh*] signifies the earlier forebears, and the name *Lō'ammi*[66] represents those who were born in exile. This prophecy may refer either to the age to come[67] or else it is syntactically connected [with what precedes]. [In the latter case], it means if the exiled would have turned away from their evil way, they would have returned to their land.[68] Be not surprised how they could have returned to their land after God had already decreed upon them to stay in exile for many years. For Jeremiah also said of Jerusalem, "Thou shalt be delivered into the hand of the king of Babylon" [Jer. 37:17], and yet he instructed [the people], "Execute ye justice" [ibid. 22:3]. By this, the prophet meant to say that if you will do [justice], the temple will not be destroyed, but otherwise it will be cast into ruin.[69]

Notes

1 I. E. regards the word *bimqōm* (in the phrase *wehāyāh bimqōm*, 2:1) not as having reference to place (as indicated by the Targum), but as equivalent to "in recompense for" or "in retribution for." I. E.'s assertion, however, would appear to require the interchange of the two final clauses. On the interconnection of chaps. I and II, see below, note 3.

2 Cf. Qimhi's objection to this view, ad loc.: "Those who interpret this subject in terms of exile are incorrect. For why should one who goes into exile appoint a head? Furthermore, the prophet should have said 'and they should go down' or 'go out [from the land]' (instead of 'and they should go up'), for Israel is higher than all other lands." However, in his commentary on 8:9, Qimhi agrees that the word *'ālū* (= they are gone up, viz., to Assyria) connotes "they were removed."

3 In Bab. Talmud, *Pesahim*, 88a and in the commentaries of Rashi, Qara, Qimhi, and Eliezer of Beaugency, the "day of Jezreel" is seen as a day of salvation. I. E. maintains that this chapter is connected with the preceding one and that the first three verses (2:1-3) continue with the prophecy of doom which includes the exile of Israel. Hence, "the day of Jezreel" is regarded as the day when the massacre against the family of Ahab was avenged by the house of Jehu. Cf. comm. on 1:4-5.

4 The prophecy may thus refer to the day when the iniquity of the house of Israel was visited upon them because of the bloodshed in Jezreel (1:4); or the prophet may simply be calling the day of their calamity "the day of Jezreel" metaphorically, because they are both equal in their misfortune. I. E. could not have meant that the sentence

was to be read as if a *kaf* (= as) preceded the phrase "the day of Jezreel," for in the following sentence he rejects a similar notion.

5 Cf. Qara, ad loc.: "The day of their ingathering from exile will be greater than the day they were scattered and dispersed thither"; he thus interprets *gādōl yōm Yizr'e'el* in the sense of "greater than the day of Jezreel," instead of "great shall be the day of Jezreel."

6 I.e., the reading rendered in the text without the *mem* (= than) prefixed to the word *yōm* (= day) indicates the opposite, i.e., "for great shall be the day of Jezreel."

7 Similarly, our prophet derides the people by mocking them sarcastically: "Say to your brethren *'ammī* (= that is My people) and to your sisters *rūhāmāh*" (= they have obtained compassion); but in reality you are the children of a harlot. Cf. comm. on Eccl. 11:9 where the passages from Ps. 60:10 and Lam. 4:21 are also cited.

8 The three radicals of the verb are *zayin, nun* and *hē*, but in the word *zenūnehā* the second radical (*nun*) is doubled. Similarly in the word *hagīgī*, the second radical (*gimel*) is doubled, while in the words *wena'afūfehā* and *sagrir*, the third radicals (*fe* and *resh* respectively) are doubled. Cf. *Sāphā Berūrāh*, ed. Gabriel Hirsh Lippmann (Fürth, 1839), p. 30b.

9 Cf. Rashi, ad loc. Cf. also Targum on Ez. 16:4-9 where Ezekiel's prophecy is referred to Israel's redemption from Egypt.

10 Cf. Abravanel, ad loc.: "It is possible to interpret [v. 6] as Ibn Ezra explains it, i.e., I will have no compassion even on those children who are going into exile and are no longer attached to the worship of the Baal for they are children of harlotry."

11 The entire passage reads as follows: "She that conceived hath put shame (*hōḇīshāh*), for she said: 'I will go after my lovers (*me'ahaḇay*) who give me my bread, my water . . . and my drink'" (*weshīqūyāy*). The causative verb *hōḇish* (= to put to shame) in its Hiphil form requires a direct object. Hence, the term *nafshāh* (= herself) is to be supplied, i.e., she that conceived them put herself to shame. I. E. is of the opinion that the required object is implicitly contained in the verb even when it is not directly mentioned. Cf. comm. on 4:10; 5:3; Is. 10:31; Ps. 38:6. In all these places where the direct object is missing, I. E. supplies either "herself," "themselves," or "myself."

12 The Hebrew *'āhaḇ* (=loved) in its Qal form is a transitive verb. Thus, *me'ahaḇay* (= my lovers), in the Piel form, becomes doubly transitive, i,e., those who make me love them. According to I.E., the prophet had here in mind the neighboring people who demanded loyalty from the Israelites in exchange for the favors extended to them. For a similar comment, cf. comm. on Lam. 1:19. Cf., however, below, note 25 for a different view.

13 Cf. Qara, ad loc.: "When the prophet says here '[my lovers] that gave me my bread and my water,' I do not know the meaning of 'my water,' but from the answer given below, 'therefore I will take back. . . my vine in the season thereof' (v. 11), it may be learned that 'my water' is nothing else but wine."

14 The consideration of Qara appears to be that it is unlikely that the Israelites should expect from their lovers water which is available almost everywhere. Cf., however, the following note.

15 I.E. points out that water, when needed, is just as valuable as bread. This becomes obvious from the fact that Obadiah supplied bread and water to the prophets in hiding (I Kings 18:13). Similarly, Moses marked his stay on Mount Sinai for forty days and forty nights by saying: "I did neither eat bread nor drink water" (Deut. 9:9). He also asked to buy water for money (ibid. 2:28). Therefore, the word *ūmēymay* (v.7) is to be taken literally (viz., "and my waters"), and the wine mentioned in vv. 10-11 is included in the word *weshiqūyay* (= and my drinks, ibid.).

16 The entire clause reads thus: "Therefore I will hedge up *(sāk̲)* thy way with thorns" *(besirim).* Cf. comm. on Num. 33:55 where the passages from Hosea 2:8 and Is. 5:5 are communicated.

17 Cf. comm. on Eccl. 7:6: "That is to say, he will place on their way thistles and thorns."

18 According to I.E., the prophet implies that by hedging up the ways the "sinning mother" will be unable to find even her well-known places (*netīb̲ōtehā*). Note that I.E.'s last two remarks on v. 8 invert the order of the text.

19 Qara, ad loc., quotes the tenth-century grammarian Dunash b. Labrat, who maintains that the Piel form of the verb *rādaf* (= to run after, with a *Dagesh* in the second radical) represents a continuous and perpetual pursuit. For a discussion of I.E. 's objection to this view, cf. J. Zlotnik, "Binyan pi'ēl," *Leshōnēnū*, II (1939), 31.

20 In the phrase "and the angel that spoke to me" (Zech. 1:9) the participle *hadōb̲er* (lit., "that speaks") is in Qal, with no *Dagesh* in the *bet.* Yet in I Sam. 23:2, the same verb (*dibber* = spoke) appears in Piel with a *Dagesh.* Similarly, when God promised the people: "Behold I am driving out before thee the Amorites" etc. (Ex. 34:11), the verb *gōresh* (= driving out) is used in Qal without a *Dagesh.* However, the verbs *agareshennū* (= I will drive them out, ibid., 23:29) and *wayegāresh* (= so he drove out, Gen. 3:24) are both in Piel with a *Dagesh* in the *gimel.* I.E. is of the opinion that none of these actions indicated a durative process. Therefore he concludes that the only difference between the two forms of the verb is that *rādaf* in Qal is transitive, i.e., to run after one who escapes, whereas *riddēf* in Piel becomes causative. Cf. Qimhi, *Dictionary,* s.v. רדף: "God causes darkness to pursue and the enemies are the pursued."

21 Friedlaender suggests that the last explanation of the difference between the Qal and the Piel of the verb *rādaf* is an interpolation by one of I.E.'s students. Cf. M. Friedlaender, *Essays on the Writings of Abraham I. E.*, (London, 1977), p. 167, note 1.

22 The *Dagesh* forte is designed to double the sound of the consonant in which it occurs and it usually represents an assimilated letter. For a similar remark on the missing *Dagesh* in the *qof,* cf. comm. on Ex. 2:23 and on Esther, ed. by Joseph Zedner (London, 1850), 2:15.

23 Viz., until she realized her error by saying, "I will return to my first husband" (v. 9, cf. comm. on v. 16), she did not know that it was God who gave her sustenance.

24 Here, as in the preceding occurrences, "she" evidently refers to the ancestors mentioned by I.E. in verse 3 of this chapter.

25 Al-Qumisi (in his comm. on 1:3) and Joseph Qimhi (quoted by his son David in his comm. on v. 7) both rely on the passage from Jeremiah and interpret "my lovers" (v. 7) to mean the moon and the stars, as objects of worship.

26 In his commentary on Deut. 7:13, I.E. calls this anonymous scholar "a great interpreter." For a conjecture identifying this scholar with the poet R. Yehudah Halevi, cf. N. Ben-Menachem. *'Inyānēy Ibn Ezra* (Jerusalem, 1987), p. 230, note 29.

27 The Hebrew *Ba'al* denotes husband, owner, and master, as well as a Canaanite deity.

28 Medieval astrology and astronomy describe the twelve zodiacal constellations as being subordinate to the then-known seven planets (Sun, Moon, Mercury, Venus, Mars, Jupiter, and Saturn), all of which were supposed to revolve around the Earth. Each planet is called "the master of the house," i.e., the master of the particular ascending constellation it dominates. For a more detailed discussion on this matter, cf. David Rosin, "Die Religionsphilosophie Abraham Ibn Esras," *Monatsschrift*, XLII (1898), 312-313, and J. Bonfils, *Ṣophnath Pa'anēaḥ*, vol. II, ed. by David Herzog (Heidelberg, 1930), p. 71.

29 According to Rashi, the word *be'ittō* (= in time thereof) means that time when the fruits become ripe.

30 J.P.S. renders the phrase thus: "And [I] will snatch away my wool and my flax."

31 I.e., I will take away.

32 Cf. also Rashi and Qara, ad loc.

33 The noun *neḇālāh* (= a vile or obscene deed) with third person feminine singular suffix is *niḇlātāh* (= her vile deed), with a *hiriq* and *qamaṣ* under the *nun* and *lamed* respectively, rather than *naḇlūtāh* with a *patah* and *qubuṣ*. I.E., however, is of the opinion that the vocalization *naḇlūtāh* here indicates the abstract noun form, as in *yaldut*, etc. With the last statement, "for to reveal nakedness is a vile deed," I.E. intends to explain that the word *naḇlūtāh* equals *erwātāh* (= her nakedness, v. 11). That is to say, the meaning of vv. 11 and 12 taken together is that God will take away the garments covering sinful Israel, thus revealing its shame to all the idolatrous nations.

34 One of which is supposed to serve as the third radical of the verb and one as the verbal afformative.

35 I.e. והשבתי with one *taw* instead of והשבתתי with two *taws*; cf. below, note 38.

36 The translation is based on the readings found in some mss. as well as in our printed edition. The term *shabbattō*, per se, however, is not in the Bible. Accordingly,

I.E. probably had in mind the word *beshabbattō* (lit., "on his Sabbath," Num. 28:10; Is. 66:23). This reference seems to be quite superfluous, particularly in view of I.E.'s immediately following remark that the word *shabbatāh* (= her Sabbath) in v. 13 is also missing a *taw*. It would seem, therefore, that the two words *wek̲āk̲ah shabbatō* (= there is also a *taw* missing in the word *shabbatō*) is a scribal interpolation and should be disregarded. Hence, the following alternative translation: "In order not to join two *taws* together, they dropped one, for the three root letters are *shin*, *bet*, and *taw*, etc." This reading is also supported by mss. B and L, in which the two aforementioned words are missing.

37 The Heb. *ḥōdesh* means month; however, in his commentaries, I.E. points out that this word also bears the meaning "new moon," or the first of the month, called *Rosh-ḥōdesh*. Cf. comm. on Is. 1:13 and Zech. 8:18. Cf. also the short dialogue between R. Moses Hakkohen and his opponents in comm. on Ex. 12:1. It should be noted that with the remark on חדשה (= her month), I.E. interrupts here his grammatical discussion on the word שבתו.

38 Lit., "or else the missing *taw* is assimilated in the *Dagesh* of the remaining one." In his commentary on Ex. 16:23; 31:15 (short recension) and *Ṣaḥot*, p. 37[b], I.E. holds that the original form of the noun *shabbat* (= Sabbath) was *shabbetet*, like *daleket* (= inflammation, Deut. 28:22). Accordingly, "her Sabbath" should be *shabbatettāh* with an additional possessive *taw*, instead of *shabbatāh*. However, due to the difficulty in pronouncing two of the same consonants, one was dropped. Cf. above, v. 13, notes 34-35. Filwarg suggests emending the text of I.E. as follows: "The word *shabbattāh* (= her Sabbath) is also missing a *taw* and it (the missing *taw*) is assimilated in the *Dagesh*, etc.," instead of "or else [the missing *taw*] is assimilated in the *Dagesh*, etc." Cf. Yonah Filwarg, *Benēy Reshef*, (Piotrkow, 1900), part 2, page 4[b]. This reading, although it seems preferable, could not be found in any of our mss.

39 For a similar remark, cf. *Ṣaḥot*, 37b. Cf. also above, note 22, for a short explanation of the *Dagesh* forte and its function.

40 The opening clause of our verse reads, "And I will lay waste her vine . . .whereof she said: These are my hire." According to I.E., the words *'etnāh* (= hire) and *mattānāh* (= gift) are derived from the verb *nātan* (= gave) with the radicals *nun*, *taw* and *nun*. Hence, the *aleph* in the word *'etnāh* is a preformative.

41 Lit., "with *'etnan zōnāh*." Abulwalid Merwan Ibn Janah, an eleventh-century grammarian (also referred to by I.E. as R. Marinus and R. Jonah). Cf. his *Dictionary*, p. 545. Cf. also Qimhi, ad. loc., and on 8:9-10.

42 Cf. above, comm. on v. 10: "And she [did not know until now], etc."

43 I.E. holds the promise of Israel's restoration, expressed in the rest of this chapter, not to be a direct transition from the punishment prescribed in vv. 11-15. He rather maintains that the conjunction "therefore" in v. 16 is related to the prophecy interrupted at v. 9. That is to say, because the people will realize their failure and admit

their error (v. 9), God will attempt to persuade them and bring them back to their land (vv. 16-25).

44 Note I.E.'s explanation: "I will bring her back into her land (viz., the land of Israel) that had turned into a desert." This interpretation stands in sharp contrast with that of most commentators, who interpret the phrase as meaning that God will bring her either into exile for retribution or into the desert for a reunion with Him. Cf. Rashi, Qara, Eliezer of Beaugency, and Qimhi, ad loc.

45 The Valley of Jezreel mentioned in 1:5.

46 *'Ēmek 'ak̲ōr*, lit., "Valley of Troubling." Comp. Josh. 7:25-26. I. E. is of the view that the valley was called "Akor" because God "troubled" or "disturbed" it (Heb. *'ak̲ōr*).

47 In his commentary on Is. 65:10 (written while he was still in Italy) I.E. communicates our passage, but rejects this explanation: "Others render it ('Ēmek 'ak̲ōr) 'Valley of Trouble' . . .but there is no need for such an explanation." Moreover, I.E. describes there the Valley of Akor to be located near Jerusalem, which is in Judah. It can hardly be seen how this valley can be identified with the valley of Jezreel, which was known to be located in the kingdom of Israel.

48 Unlike the translation given in R.S.V.: "And she shall answer."

49 Cf. also, Targum, Saadia (quoted by Qimhi, ad loc.), Yefet and Qara (ad loc.), all of whom interpret *we'āntāh* as "And she will sing." According to this explanation, the three root letters of the verb are *ayin*, *nun* and *hē*. For a similar view, cf. *Iggeret R. Yehudah b. Quraish*, ed. by M. Katz (Tel-Aviv, 1950), p. 199.

50 Hence, the three radicals would be *ayin*, *waw* and *nun*.

51 Cf. also Menahem b. Saruq, *Mahberet*, ed. by Hirsch Fillipowski (Edinburgh, 1854), p. 135 and Eliezer of Beaugency, ad loc.

52 This latter view is also rejected by Joseph Qimhi in his *Sepher Hagālūy*, ed. by H.J. Matthews (Berlin, 1887), p. 131. However, in his commentary on Is. 13:22, I.E. had agreed that the meaning of the phrase *we'ānāh 'īyim* can be either "the jackals will sing" or "dwell."

53 Comp. v. 19: "And they [the Baalim] shall no more be mentioned by their name." The source of the comment of R. Marinus (= Ibn Janah) could not be located. For another reference by I.E. to the same comment, cf. comm. on Eccl. 5:1 where Ibn Janah, however, is not quoted.

54 This comment is consistent with I.E.'s explanation in his commentary on v. 16 that the restoration of Israel will take place only after the people will declare their readiness to return to their "first husband" (v. 9). Cf. below, comm. on 10:12, note 44, and Qimhi, ad loc., who quotes from Bab. Talmud, *Yoma*, 38b: "Heaven helps him who would be improved." Cf. also Abravanel, ad loc., who quotes I.E. almost verbatim without mentioning his name.

55 Supply the word "weapons," which is missing in the text. For a similar remark, cf. comm. on Ps. 76:4 and Yefet on 1:7. A.V. and J.P.S. translate ומלחמה as "and the battle."

56 Supply the word "bread," which is missing in the text.

57 Supply the missing word "laden." In these two examples, I.E. discusses the ellipsis of a crucial word, which he contends appears implicitly in this passage in Hosea as well.

58 Cf. Rashi and Qara, ad loc.

59 According to I.E.'s explanation, the prophet foretells Israel's betrothal to God "in righteousnes, in justice, in loving kindness and in compassion," with all of these qualities ascribed either to God or the people.

60 Cf. Qara, ad loc., for a similar remark.

61 So R.S.V.; J.P.S. renders: "I will respond to the heavens."

62 In his commentary on Ex. 20:13 (short recension) I.E. is of the opinion that the word *'e'eneh* (lit., "I will answer" or "respond") is transitive. This opinion is consistent with our explanation that the meaning of the phrase in Hosea is indeed "I will provide the heavens" with rain, etc. For a similar view, cf. comm. on Gen. 41:16 and Eccl. 5:19; ibid. 10:19. Cf. also below, comm. on 14:9.

63 According to I.E., the repetition of a biblical phrase is not only given for the sake of rhetorical fancy but rather to indicate a process of duration and continuity. Cf. also comm. on Ps. 29:1; ibid. 93:3.

64 The three root letters in the name *Yizreel* (= Jezreel) are *zayin*, *resh* and *ayin*, and they denote "to sow" or "to scatter." Rashi interprets the name *Yizreel* allegorically: "And they shall respond to 'Jezreel,' viz., to the children of the exile who were scattered and then gathered;" cf. also Rashi on 10:14. Menahem (*Mahberet*, p. 84) and Qara (ad loc.) both ascribe the name Yizreel to the people who sow the land. However, Dunash (*Teshūḇōt Dunash ben Labrat*, ed. by Hirsch Filipowski [London-Edinburgh, 1855]), p. 49, Jacob Tam (ibid.), and I.E. maintain that Jezreel is the name of a location.

65 R.S.V. translates *Lōrūḥāmāh* as "not pitied." Comp. 1:6.

66 I.e., "not-my-people." Cf. above, comm. on 1:8-9.

67 Viz., to the days of the Messiah. Since the prophecies described in vv. 16-25 had not been fulfilled at the time when the exiles returned from Babylonia (c. 538 B.C.), they probably refer, in I.E.'s view, to the Messianic period.

68 I.e., if the prophet does not have in mind the Messianic era, he may be here referring to the immediate future, by promising the exiles the return to their land if they would only repent of their sins.

69 Similarly, if the exiles would have improved themselves through good deeds, they could have been restored to their own land.

Chapter III

(1) **And [the Lord] said** by way of prophecy:[1] **Go yet love a woman:** [That is,] take her for a wife, for this is the meaning of the word *'îshāh* = woman].[2] Moreover, he [the prophet] did not [here] mention a harlot.[3] The passage "so I bought her unto me [for fifteen pieces of silver]" [v. 2] proves the correctness of this interpretation.[4] Thereupon she would become *beloved of her friend,*[5] meaning another man with whom she would commit adultery. This figure signifies *God's love toward the children of Israel,* viz., that He loved them, but *they turned unto other gods*; hence [the comparison with] one *beloved of her friend.* However, they [the people] did not love God, but rather loved wine that caused them to err.[6] [For the meaning of the] word *"ashîshēy* [in the phrase *'ashîshēy 'anābim* (= flagons of grapes),] compare "stay ye me with flagons" [Cant. 2:5], meaning with flagons of wine.[7] So also [the people of the Northern Kingdom *turn unto other gods and love] flagons of grape wine.* Similarly, [(David) "dealt among the people]... one flagon" [II Sam. 6:19].[8] There was [thus] no need to mention "wine" [here explicitly].

(2) According to some, [the meaning of the first word], *wā'ekrehā*, is "and purchased her" [the woman];[9] compare *tikrū mē'îtām* [= ye shall purchase (food) of them, viz., of the children of Esau (Deut. 2:6)]. This explanation, however, agrees neither with the context[10] nor with Hebrew grammar.[11] Rather, for the meaning of *wā'ekrehā* compare *haker nā'*;[12] it would only have been more appropriate [for the prophet] to say *wā'akîrāh.*[13] Or else *wā'ekrehā* may yet be the Qal form, for although it is not found elsewhere, (that is to say] even if the Qal form of *haker* [= know; discern] is not found elsewhere);[14] it [viz., *wā'ekrehā*] may still be formed on the pattern of *wā'ettnehā* [=and I gave it, i.e., I, the Lord, gave the kingdom to Jeroboam (I Kings 14:8)]. Or else [it is indeed the Hiphil form and] the *segol* [under the *aleph*] replaces a *patah.* Compare *wā'e'dēk* [= I decked thee (Ez. 16:11)], which is derived from *'dh* [a verb meaning "to deck;[15]

or] *'akelkā* [= I consume thee (Ex. 33:3)], which is derived from *klh* [a verb meaning "to consume"].[16] This word [viz., *wā'ekrehā*] is similar [in form] to *wayadbeqū* [= and they followed (I Sam. 31:2)];[17] there are many such cases. The plain explanation of the *fifteen pieces of silver* is [that they were given to the woman] as a dowry.[18] [On the other hand,] **a ḥomer** [of barley] **and a half ḥomer** [of barley][19] refers to her sustenance.[20] This [i.e., all these amounts] in my opinion [may also be taken] as a metaphor referring to [the kingdom of] Judah. These *fifteen [pieces of silver]* represent the kings of Judah beginning with King Rehoboam;[21] for you should not regard the reign of the sons of Josiah as more than one, since they were brothers.[22] Similarly, the *ḥomer* and the *letek* signify the High Priests[23] who were [serving] during the kingdom of Judah in Jerusalem[24]

(3) **And I said [to her] thou shalt sit solitary [for me many days]:** That is to say, if you want to remain mine, you must stay faithful *many days* so that *thou shalt not play the harlot and thou shalt not be any man's wife*,[25] meaning you shall not worship other gods in secrecy. The force of the word *lō'* [=not (in the phrase *thou shalt not be any man's wife*)] is carried over to the last clause, meaning *and also I will* not come in *to thee*,[26] whereas some interpret [this passage in the sense of] "if you will return to Me, I will also return to you." The prophet [further] explains this vision by saying:

(4) **For [the children of Israel shall sit solitary] many days without a King:** [The reign of] the Hasmoneans cannot serve as a basis for contradicting [the truth of this prophecy] for they were not the descendants of Judah.[27] **Without a sacrifice [and without a pillar]:** Yefet b. Ali said that this is what [the phrase] "thou shalt sit solitary for me" [(v.3) refers to], viz., that you will provide for me neither a *sacrifice* nor *a pillar.*[28] According to his opinion, there would be no prohibition to erect a pillar except [if erected] in the manner described in Scripture – but what would he do with the word *teraphim*?[29] Others say that all of these objects [viz., sacrifice, etc.] are meant to be used for the rites of idolatry,[30] but we do not elsewhere find *ephod* in a negative sense.[31] It is my view that [the meaning of the passage is as follows: [*The children of Israel will sit. . .] without a sacrifice* to God *and without a pillar* to Baal, *without an ephod* for God and without *teraphim* for idols – those that Laban called his gods [Gen. 31:30].[32]

(5) **Afterward shall the children of Israel return:** Meaning, that the people of Judah and [also the people of] Israel who were exiled earlier

[shall return], it was for this reason that the prophet included them [viz., the people of Israel].[33] By the phrase *David their King*, the Messiah is meant; compare "David my servant shall be their prince forever" [Ez. 37:25].[34] **They shall come trembling unto the Lord:** That is to say, when the Messianic era will arrive, they will return speedily to their land in a sudden haste. Compare "they shall come trembling as a bird out of Egypt" [11:11], and the passage following thereafter, "I will make them dwell in their house, saith the Lord." The most reliable proof for [the correctness of] this interpretation is our closing phrase *in the end of days*; i.e., a distant period to which the prophets directed their prophecies.[35] Compare "it shall come to pass in the end of days that the mountain of the Lord's house shall be established" [Is. 2:2]. There it is written: "And they shall beat their swords into plowshares"; all this refers to the distant future.[36]

Notes

1 Cf. above, I.E.'s introduction to chap. I.

2 I.e., without the definite article, instead of *ha'īshāh* (= *the* woman).

3 This distinction refers to 1:2, "go take unto thee a wife of harlotry."

4 I.E. later explains this passage (3:2) in the sense of "to know her," or "to recognize her," rather than "to buy her" and insists that the fifteen pieces of silver were given to her as a dowry. This explanation would imply that, according to I.E., God instructed the prophet in a second dream to take another woman, in addition to Gomer (1:3), and to marry her legally.

5 R.S.V. renders this as "Beloved of a paramour."

6 Comp. below 4:11-12: "Harlotry, wine and new wine take away the heart. . . for the spirit of harlotry had caused to err." Comp. also Is. 5:12: "The harp . . . and wine are in their feasts but they regard not the work of the Lord."

7 In his commentary of Cant. 2:5, I.E. calls *'ashīshōt* a vessel or glass full of wine.

8 I.e., one flagon of wine.

9 In Ibn Jana's *Dictionary*, p. 230 *wā'ekrehā* is listed under *kaf, resh, hē*, and the passage "Ruth the Moabitess have I acquired [i.e., purchased] to be my wife" (Ruth 4:10) is quoted in support of this view, Cf. also Bab. Talmud, *Hullin*, 92a, and Rashi, ad loc.

10 Since the prophet in his second dream married the woman legally (comm. 3:1), it would be appropriate to say *wā'eqqāḥehā* (lit., "and I took her," i.e., and I married her) instead of "and I purchased her."

11 For the *Dagesh* in the *kaf* of *wā'ekrehā* is superfluous.

12 *Haker nā'*: "know now," "discern I pray" (Gen. 37:31; 38:25). Hence, the three radicals of *wā'ekrehā* are *nun*, *kaf* and *resh* (i.e., "to know" or "to recognize," instead of *kaf*, *resh* and *hē*, i.e., "to purchase") with a *Dagesh* forte in the *kaf* to compensate for the missing *nun*. Accordingly, the entire phrase *wā'ekrehā lī* means "and I made her [the woman] known to me." For a similar view, cf. *Pesiqta Derab̲ Kahana*, p. 102b; Jacob b. Reuben, ad loc.; and Schroeter, *Archiv*, II (1869), 153, note 2.

13 I.e., "and I knew her." *Wa'akīrāh* is the Hiphil form of *nkr*, a verb meaning "to know." For an alternate vocalization of the verb *wa'akīrāh*, cf. Symha Pinsker, *Einleitung in das Babylonisch-Hebräische Punktationssystem* (Vienna, 1863), p. XLIV, foot.

14 This explanation, which I put here in parentheses, seems redundant and is marked in ms. N with the term *hagāhāh* (= marginal note). Cf. Friedlaender, *Essays*, p. 167, note 1 and Y.L. Eisler, "Mîk̲tab bîqōret," *Beth Talmud*, II, 168, where this explanation is regarded as a later addition.

15 Since the word *wā'e'dēk̲* is transitive, meaning "[and] I decked thee," its proper vocalization would be *wa'a'dēk̲* in Hiphil with a *patah* and a *hataph* under the *aleph* and *ayin* respectively, instead of a *segol* and a *shewa*.

16 In his commentary on Ex. 33:3 (short recension) I.E. points out the irregular utilization of the *segol* in the word *'ak̲elk̲ā* (= I consumed thee); for in the Piel form it should be vocalized *'ak̲allk̲ā* with a *patah* under the *kaf* and the *Dagesh* forte in the *lamed* instead of *'akelk̲ā* with a *segol* and no *Dagesh*.

17 I.e., the Philistines followed upon Saul. This last example is designed to characterize the Hiphil form of the verb *dbq* in which the additional *yod*, usually placed between the second and the third radical, is sometimes dropped, e.g., *wayadbeqū* (=and they followed, I Sam. 31:2) without a *yod*, instead of *wayadbīqū* (Jud. 18:22) with a *yod*. I.E. maintains that *wā'ekrehā* may also be considered a Hiphil form, where the *yod* is missing and the *patah* under the *aleph* is replaced by the *segol*.

18 This explanation is consistent with I.E.'s view that this woman (3:1) was not the harlot mentioned in 1:2, but one whom the prophet was told to marry legally. Thus the fifteen pieces of silver represent the dowry which always goes with marriage.

19 R.S.V. renders it thus: "And a homer and a letheh of barley."

20 Lit. "her food." According to I.E., part was given to the woman in cash as a dowry and part in kind for her sustenance.

21 The total number of Judean kings from Rehoboam until Sedeqiah, not including Athaliah the daughter of Ahab, is nineteen, but in Midrashic sources the number is reduced to fifteen. Cf. *Bemidbar Rabbah*, 13:13, and M. M. Kasher, *Torāh Shelēmāh*, vol. X-XI (New York, 1946), p. 53. See following note.

22 I.e., Jehoiaqim and Zedeqiah, both sons of Josiah, may be considered one for they were brothers. With the exception of Jehoahaz and Jehoiakin, who reigned for three months each, and perhaps also with the exclusion of Ahaziah, the son of Athaliah, whose reign lasted only one year, we arrive at fifteen kings.

23 The measures of *ḥomer* and *letek̲* come up to fifteen *ephas* (viz., *ḥomer* = 10 *ephas*; *letek̲* = a half *ḥomer*). Furthermore, an *epha* (3 *seahs*) is traditionally rated as being worth one shekel. Hence, the price of the barley would be fifteen shekels. According to I.E., this price is significant for the High Priests who served in Jerusalem during the reign of the fifteen kings. It should be noted that the number of High Priests who served during the first commonwealth is traditionally given as eighteen. Cf. L. Greenwald, *The History of the High Priests* (New York, 1932), pp. 18-20. However, by excluding Zadoq, who served during the times of Solomon (the latter having reigned during the period of the united monarchy) on the one hand, and Seraiah and Jehozadaq, who served during the times of Jehoiakin and Zedeqiah (after the reign of Jehoiaqim) on the other hand, the number of thee High Priests would be reduced to fifteen. For other allegorical interpretations of the fifteen pieces of silver, the *ḥomer*, and the *letek̲*, cf. Targum, Rashi, and Qimhi, ad loc. Cf. also M. Rahmer, *Monatsschrift*, XIV (1865), 465.

24 It should be noted that I.E. holds the prophecy in chap. 3 to be independent of chap. 1. That is to say, the harlot mentioned above (1:2) signifies the Kingdom of Israel, while the woman the prophet was told to marry legally represents the Kingdom of Judah, cf. comm. on 3:1. Furthermore, the vision in 3:2 and the following explanation of the prophet's acted-out allegory (in v. 4) both seem to have a substantial resemblance to each other. Thus, by interpreting the fifteen pieces of silver, the *ḥomer*, and the *letek̲* as a metaphor for the fifteen kings and the High Priests of Judah, our passages would be connected by relating the prophetic vision "go yet love a woman, etc." (v. 1-2) to the following explanation: "For the children of Israel shall sit . . . without a king . . . and without a sacrifice . . . and without an *ephod* " (v. 4, i.e., without a king or a priest). For a remark of a similar nature, cf. comm. on Is. 1:22: "'Thy silver' is a metaphor for the judges and princes; this verse is therefore followed by 'thy princes are rebellious.'" It should be noted, however, that the disapproval in I.E.'s introduction to his commentary on the Pentateuch of those who delight in allegorism and reject the literal sense of the text (cf. above, Introduction, sec. III), leads us to conjecture that this allegorical interpretation of the fifteen pieces of silver, etc., is an alternative one which has not been penned by I.E.

25 Cf. Qara, ad loc.: "Why do I say to you, 'Thou shalt sit solitary for me many days and not play the harlot'? Because the children of Israel will stay in exile many days, etc."

26 I.e., you shall have no marital relations nor will I be a husband to you; with the force of the word *lō'* (= not) being carried over from the preceding. For I.E.'s method of adducing ellipses as a means of explaining difficult passages in the Bible, cf. Bacher, *Abraham Ibn Esra als Grammatiker*, p. 146, notes 15-16.

27 The Hasmonean dynasty was established in the latter half of the second century B.C., long after the prophet proclaimed that the people would be without a king or a

prince. The Hasmoneans were a family of priests, however, and not the descendants of the royal family of King David. Therefore, they were not considered the rightful heirs to the Kingdom of Judah. In his commentary on Gen. 31:19, I.E. remarks: "For God chose a king only from the family of David. The verse [Hosea 3:4] is therefore followed by 'and the children of Israel shall seek the Lord their God and David their King.'"

28 Cf. Yefet, p. 53, lines 4-7, from which I.E. appears to draw this conclusion.

29 According to I.E., Yefet is of the opinion that the prohibition to set up a pillar (Deut. 16:22) does not apply to those that are erected for the purpose of worshiping God. This opinion is contrary to the traditional view, which prohibits the erection of any pillar no matter what its purpose. Cf. Maimonides, *Mishneh Torah*, Madda, vi, 6. Yefet further interprets the "sacrifice," the "pillar," and the *ephod* in v. 4 to have been objects of the worship of God that the people would miss in exile. Hence, the question remains how Yefet would explain *teraphim*, which always denotes images or household gods. Cf. comm. on Gen. 31:19: "It seems to me that the *teraphim* are figures designed to receive the influences of the supernal beings, but I cannot [fully] explain." It should be noted, however, that in his commentary on Deut. 16:22, I.E. seems to agree with the aforementioned opinion of Yefet concerning the prohibition of erecting a pillar. He only objects to Yefet's interpretation of Hos. 3:4 "because of the mention of *teraphim* in the passage.

30 The prophet will thus have said that while in exile the people will have no king and will not be able to worship idols either by offering them sacrifices and setting up altars or by utilizing the *ephod* and *teraphim*.

31 I.E.'s commentary on the Early Prophets has not come down to us; it would be of interest to know how he interpreted the *ephod* mentioned in Jud. 18:40 other than in a negative sense.

32 This last explanation preferred by I.E. probably regards the "king" and the "prince" as part of a series of contrasts mentioned in v. 4, viz., "the children of Israel shall remain for many years without a king (God's representative) and without a prince" (Baal's representative or the representative of the stars they worshiped, cf. comm. on Dan. 8:24: "Michael is the great prince and there are many princes, i.e., stars, under him"); "without a sacrifice" to God "and without a pillar" for Baal worship; "without an *ephod*" for God and without *teraphim*. Cf. Abravanel, ad loc., and Sharim, p. 27b, who anticipate W. R. W. Gardner, "Notes on Certain Passages in Hosea," *American Journal of Semitic Languages and Literature*, XIII (1901-1902), 178.

33 According to I.E., this prophecy refers to the Kingdom of Judah, cf. above, comm. on 3:2, 4; but "the children of Israel" (v. 5) who will return during the Messianic era include both the southern and the northern people of Israel, who were exiled before. See following note.

34 I.e., for the Messianic days, when Israel and Judah will become "one nation in the land . . . and My servant David shall be king over them." (Ez. 37:22-24).

35 This entire passage beginning with the words "a distant period" reads literally, "which are the end of the prophecy of the prophets."

36 I.E. may have had doubts about the period to which a given prophecy was directed (e.g., comm. on 2:25), but he accepts the fact that whenever the phrase "in the end of days" is used, the prophecy refers to "the time to come" rather than to the events of the prophet's lifetime. Cf. comm. on Gen. 49:1; Is. 2:1; and Micah 4:1

Chapter IV

(1) **Hear ... ye children of Israel, [for the Lord hath a controversy] with the inhabitants of the land:** That is, the land of Israel which God had chosen;[1] the more correct phrase would be *the inhabitants of* His *land;*[2] Compare "[the people] have gone forth out of His land" [Ex. 36:20].

(2) The term *'ālōh* [in the phrase *'ālōh wekaḥēsh* (=swearing and lying)] denotes taking an oath. [Compare] *we'at 'ālit*[3] [=and thou didst utter an oath (Jud. 17:2)] which is derived [from *'ālōh* implying] an oath. [The word] *pārāṣū* [=they broke out] is derived from [the same root as] *periṣim* [=robbers (Jer. 7:11].[4] **And blood [touched blood]:** I.e., the blood of one slain person was touching the blood of another.[5]

(3) **Therefore . . . [everyone that dwelleth therein doth languish]:** The *lamed* in the word *umlal* [=languished] is doubled.[6] The phrase *with the beasts of the field and the fowl of the heaven* indicates that they will not find anything to hunt for, and the passage *and even the fishes of the sea also are taken away* proves the correctness of this explanation. Yefet said that this calamity would be worse than the one that befell Noah's generation,[7] for then the fish of the sea did not die.[8] This is a homiletical interpretation.[9]

(4) **Yet [let no man strive, neither let any man reprove]:** I.e., there is no man to contend with or to reprove him. It was the regular practice of the priest to reprove the people of Israel, but now, conversely, it is they who reproved the priest; for he also is a malefactor, as [the prophet] explains [v. 5, etc.]. This is the meaning [of the phrase] *for thy people are as they that strive with the priest.*[10]

(5) **Therefore shalt thou stumble:** The prophet [now] addresses the High Priest of his time and prophesies concerning him: *You shall stumble by day,* meaning during the day–when there is light–as if it were night; you and the false prophet who persuades you.[11] This is the meaning of [the phrase] *the prophet also shall stumble with thee*

in the night; [the closing phrase] *wedāmītī ['īmmekā]* means "I will cut off [your mother]."[12]

(6) **My people are destroyed** *[nidmū 'ammī]* **for the lack of knowledge:** This word *[nidmū]* if derived from *demūt* [=likeness, resemblance], should be followed by *'el* [=to], with a *segol* [under the *aleph*]. Compare "whom art thou like" [Ez. 31:2].[13] Without the word *'el*, however, [*nidmū*] denotes "cutting off" [14] as in the phrase "I will cut off [*wedāmītī*] thy mother" [v. 5], meaning that she would give birth no more to another [son] who might become a priest in your place, but that you will soon stumble and your children will also die. [With the phrase] *nidmū* [*'āmmī* the prophet] addresses the priest [by telling him]: *For the lack of* your *knowledge My people* were cut off.[15] **Because thou hast rejected knowledge, I will also reject thee, that thou shalt be no priest to me; seeing thou hast forgotten the law of the God:** [By inclusion of the words *because thou hast rejected knowledge*] the idea is repeated.[16] The law was given to the priest[s][17] who, moreover, were the judges. [Compare] "for the priest's lips should keep knowledge, [and they should seek the law at his mouth" (Mal. 2:7)].[18] **I will forget the children:** [Since] it is inconceivable that God should forget [anything, the phrase is to be taken] only [in a metaphorical sense], i.e., the priest's children will stumble and will be destined for destruction.[19]

(7) **The more they were increased:** Meaning, the more I increased their children,[20] *the more they sinned against Me*[21] by committing many sins. Therefore, *I will change ['āmir] their glory into shame*; [*'āmir* means] I will change.[22]

(8-9) **They feed on the sin of My people:** Viz., the sons of the priest [*feed on the sins of My people*], and *they set the soul* of My people upon their iniquity,[23] as if to say: "You can rely on me to forgive you for your sin."[24] Compare "he setteth his soul upon it" [Deut. 24:15].[25] This is a great offence; consequently wickedness will befall the priest as well as the people, and there will be no superiority of the priest over the Israelites.

(9) **It is [like the people, like the priest** (*ka'ām kakkōhēn*)]: I have already said that when two nouns follow each other with the prefixed *kaf*, the phrase is elliptical; [thus the meaning of this passage is that] the people will be like the priest and the priest like the people,[26] [which is] similar [in construction to the phrase "I am as thou art], my people are as thy people" [I Kings 22:4]. **I will punish him:** Every one of them.[27]

(10) **And they shall eat [and not have enough]:** This is the punishment. *Hiznū* [means] they caused themselves as well as others to commit harlotry;[28] and yet they shall not increase [*welō' yifrōṣū*]. Compare "the man increased" [*wayifrōṣ* (Gen. 30:43)].[29] **Because they have forsaken God to heed:** Supply "His ways" or "His law."[30]

(11) **Harlotry, [wine and new wine take away the heart** (*yiqqaḥ lēḇ*)]: With no conjunction *waw* [= and];[31] compare "the sun the moon stand still in their habitation" [Hab. 3:11]. That is to say, that the harlotry and the wine, each one of them takes away [*yiqqaḥ*] the *heart.*[32] Taking away the heart implies that they remained without a heart for [spiritual] understanding.[33]

(12) **My people [asks counsel of their stock]:** The proof that they are heartless is that My people turned to inquire of its wooden [image], viz., the idol.[34] **For the spirit of harlotry hath caused to err:** [Supply] "him."[35] **They have all gone astray from under their God:** *My people* mentioned above is the implied subject.[36]

(13) **[They sacrifice (*yezabbēḥū]* upon the tops of the mountains:** *Upon the tops* [*of the mountains*] indicates [that it was done] conspicuously, and the phrase *upon the hills* signifies the same. *Yezabbēḥū* [means] they tell the priests of Baal to sacrifice.[37] [The prophet further continues his admonition by saying]: Because the men go to offer sacrifices outside of the cities, the daughters and the brides remain [alone] at home and therefore [tend to] commit adultery.[38]

(14) **I will not [punish your daughters, ... for they themselves consort** (*yefārēdū*) **with harlots]:** That is to say, it is not surprising if the daughters commit adultery. For when [the men] go up to the tops of the mountains to offer sacrifices they [themselves] eat and drink with harlots, and all of them commit adultery. The word *yefārēdū* connotes that people known to each other [consort] with one harlot.[39] The [last] word *yillāḇēṭ* in Arabic indicates one who is perplexed and does not know what to do.[40] Compare "but a parting fool will be perplexed" [*yillāḇēṭ* (Prov. 10:8)].[41] By the phrase *I will not punish* [*your daughters* the prophet] did not mean to say that [God] will not [at all] punish them, but rather he said this in contrast to the parents,[42] who instructed [their daughters] to commit adultery and to emulate their [evil] deeds. [Or else] perhaps the daughters were young and it was for that reason that [he said] *I will not punish* [*your daughters*]. [43]

(15) **If** Israel sinned together with Jeroboam [I]–who feared that the kingdom would revert to the Davidic family–by way of his establishing two [golden] calves in the two extremities of the land,[44] why,

then, should Judah take on guilt[45] by leaving the Temple, which was in their part [of the land],[46] and by going to a distant place to worship idols? The prophet thus admonishes them [by saying]: *Yet let not Judah become guilty, and come not to Gilgal,*[47] *neither go ye up to Beth-aven*, which is Bethel,[48] because of the [golden] calf Jeroboam erected there.

[Further to this thought] it is written in Scripture:[49] ["Thou shalt fear the Lord thy God; Him shalt thou serve, and to Him shalt thou cleave], and by His name shalt thou swear" [Deut. 10:20]. The passage "thou shalt fear the Lord thy God" means [to caution] that no one shall disobey a prohibitory law out of fear of a monarch, or slander, or physical harm, but rather [one should obey the law] because of reverence to God. "Him shalt thou serve" signifies the positive laws, some of which [are fulfilled] by mouth[50] and some by deed; [the phrase] "to him shalt thou cleave," [means to say that a man shall always] direct the thoughts of his heart [toward God]; that he should endeavor with all his prowess that no moment shall pass without him thinking in his heart both of God's work and wonders [as reflected] in the phenomena of the upper and the lower [worlds],[51] as well as of the marvels of the prophets. After achieving a close relationship with the Almighty, a man is obliged to refer to the Name [i.e., to God] in all his affairs, taking oaths by His name [alone]; in order that all other people shall understand therefrom that he is attached to God and the love of Him, whereby His name and the remembrance thereof are always on his lips. Consequently, by his love for God, all other people will pay heed and learn from him [to emulate the same] love and reverence–thus was it the habit of the prophets to swear [by the name of God], as David, Elijah and Elisha [have done];[52] compare "to Me . . . every tongue shall swear" [Is. 45:23]. Hence, [the exhortation *nor swear: As the Lord liveth*] means: Why pretend that you are children of God while you are coming into a house of vanity?[53] –it would be much better to do neither the one thing nor the other. Or else [the phrase *nor swear*, etc.] may be interpreted in reference to the accusation of "swearing and lying" mentioned at the beginning of the chapter [v.2].[54]

(16) **For [Israel is disobedient like a disobedient cow]**:[55] Disobedient in the sense that they turned toward a way [of life] prohibited by God.[56] [Thus the prophet] compares Israel to a *disobedient cow*, with whom no man is able to plow [the soil]. The meaning of the phrase *now the Lord will feed them*, etc., is that [God would have fed them]

like a lamb in a broad pasture if they would not have been rebellious.[57] Or else the meaning is: Now God will feed them like a lonely and bewildered lamb *in a broad pasture*.

(17) **[Ephraim] is joined [to idols** (*'aṣabbîm*)]:[58] Some say that *'aṣabbim* [means money];[59] compare "[and you will exact] all your money" [*'aṣṣḇēḵem* (Is. 58:3)] The correct meaning, however, is as in "the despised idol" [*'eṣeḇ* (Jer. 22:28)]; "unto the idols of [*'aṣabbēy*] Canaan" [Ps. 106:39], all of which are derived from *'iṣāḇōn* [= toil (Gen. 3:17)]; for there is no value in [the making of] their images, only toil.[60] [Thus the prophet declares] that they [the people of Northern Israel] are attached to the images and are their companions. **Let him alone**,[61] until their wine will pass by,[62] perhaps [then] they will open their eyes.

(18) **[When their drunkenness is] over [they indulge in harlotry** (*hiznū*) **they love** (to say) **give ye** (*'āhaḇū hēḇū*)]:[63] [That is to say], trouble beset them in that their drunkenness passed due to the lack of new wine, and nevertheless they did not turn away from their evil way; rather, their kings led others to adultery[64] because of what they [viz., the kings] said: 'Give us gifts.'[65] The pattern of the word *hēbū* [= give ye] is similar to that of *'ēfū* [Ex. 16:23], which means basically "bake ye." For it [viz., *'ēfū*] as well as *hēḇū* and also *hāḇū* [= get (Deut. 1:13)], are all [in the imperative] just as *redū* [= get down], *ṣe'ū* [= get out] are.[66] However, due to the guttural letter,[67] the vocalization is changed.[68] [The word] *māginnehā* [= her shields] signifies the kings;[69] compare "for the Lord is our shield" [*māginnēnū* (Ps. 89:19) in which latter case] the end of the passage proves [my interpretation],[70] for it is a repetition of the same idea. The antecedent [viz., "her"] refers to Beth-aven [v. 15].[71]

(19) **[The wind] hath bound her up [in her skirts** (*biḵnāfehā*)]:[72] This is a figure of speech, as a man who wraps up the wind in the corners of his [garment] and finds nothing in it.[73] Or else the antecedent [viz., "her"] refers to the corners of Beth-aven (v. 15).[74] **And they shall be ashamed:** Viz., the rulers, *of their sacrifices,* [which they offered] in Beth-aven.

Notes

1 I.E. was probably prompted by the definite article ("the land") to explain that the prophet refers to the inhabitants of the chosen land, i.e., the land of Israel and not to "the inhabitants of the earth" (Ps. 33:13). For a similar remark, cf. comm. on Joel 1:14.

2 With the word *shelō* (= His) missing from the text.

3 The example given by I.E. is the only other place in the Bible where the verb *'lh* is clearly conjugated in Qal. For the same paradigm, cf. *Grammatische Werke d. R. Jehudah Chajjug*, trans. from the Arabic by Ibn Ezra and ed. by Leopold Dukes (Stuttgart, 1844), p. 108 where our phrase אלה וכחש is cited. Cf. also below, comm. on 10:4, notes 13-14.

4 A.V. translates *pārāṣū* as "they break out" and J.P.S. renders it as "they break all bounds." I.E. maintains that in our case *pārāṣū* means they acted in violence (probably because of its juxtaposition to "blood"); whereas in v. 10 the same verb connotes "to increase." Cf. Eliezer of Beaugency, ad loc., where *pārāṣū* is interpreted as "they are robbers, ... hence the following phrase, 'and blood touched blood.'"

5 Cf. Rashi, ad loc.: "Bloodshed increased to the stage that the blood of one slain person was touching (= intermingling with) the blood of another."

6 The three radicals of the verb meaning "to languish" are *aleph, mem* and *lamed.* Hence in the word *umlal* the *lamed* is doubled. cf. Ibn Janah, *Hariqmah*, I, ed. by Michael Wilensky (Jerusalem, 1964), p. 166; *Dictionary*, p. 37.

7 Lit., "the generation of the flood."

8 This interpretation is not found in the Arabic commentary of Yefet b. 'Ali on Hosea, but we are inclined to share the view of Poznanski (*REJ*, XII [1900], 306) that I.E. quoted here from another recension of Yefet's commentary which is no longer extant.

9 Cf. Bab. Talmud, *Kiddushin*, 13a. Homiletical expositions such as this one are according to I.E., not to be taken generally as the literal sense of the text. Cf. below, comm. on 13:5. In the Introduction to his comm. on Daniel, I.E. remarks: "Sometimes they (viz., the midrashic explanations of the biblical text) are of homiletical character . . . but it was generally agreed that the text never loses its literal sense." Cf. "Ibn Ezra's Short Commentary on Daniel," ed. by Henry J. Matthews in *Miscellany of Hebrew Literature*, II (1877), 1 (Heb. Sec.). Cf. also comm. on Ex. 13:18 (short rec., p. 84): "It is merely a homiletical explanation and therefore of no authority."

10 Lit., "and your people are like those who contend with the priest." According to Qimhi, ad loc., the *kaf* prefixed to *kimrīḇēy* (= like those who contend) denotes reciprocity, i.e., the people will indeed reprove and admonish the priest for he is as wicked as they are. This view, shared by most commentators, is contrary to that of I.E.

11 Cf. Targum, ad loc., for a similar interpretation.

12 *Wedāmītī* may also mean "and I will silence," i.e., I will silence thy mother. Cf.

Yefet (p. 60), Rashi, Qara, Eliezer of Beaugency, and Jacob b. Reuben, ad loc.; but I.E. and before him Menahem (*Mahberet*, p. 65) and Ibn Janah (*Dictionary*, p. 111) prefer the meaning "and I will cut off," i.e., I will destroy thy mother. Cf. also comm. on v. 6, 10:15; Is. 6:5; 15:1, and *Sephat Yether*, ed. by Gabriel Hirsh Lippman (Frankfurt a. M., 1843), No. 69, p. 21a.

13 Lit., to whom did you liken yourself [(*'el mî dāmîtā*) in your greatness].

14 I.e., [My people] were cut off, viz., destroyed.

15 Cheyne (*The Book of Hosea*, ed. by T.K. Cheyne [Cambridge, 1905], p. 64, bottom) and Harper (p. 254) render: "My people will be destroyed by reason of their lack of knowledge," ascribing the "lack of knowledge" to the people. I.E. maintains that the priest addressed by the prophet was being blamed for his lack of knowledge which resulted in the destruction of the people. See notes 16-18, below.

16 The idea of blaming the priest is repeated, i.e., "for lack of your knowledge . . . ; because you have rejected knowledge." See preceding note.

17 Comp. Deut. 31:9: "And Moses wrote this law and delivered it unto the priests, the sons of Levi."

18 The priests, however, have "rejected knowledge" and failed in their duty to judge the people, therefore God will reject their priesthood.

19 Similarly, in Bab. Talmud, *Yoma*, 39b: "The phrase 'I will forget thy children' is to be understood metaphorically as the priest being deprived of his high office." For a lengthier dıscussion on the use of metaphoric terms in Scripture, cf. Ibn Quraish, pp. 59, 61 where our passage is included. Cf. also below, comm. on 11:8.

20 By using "they were increased" in the third person, the text refers to the sons (or the children) of the priests mentioned in v. 6.

21 A.V. renders our phrase thus: "As they increased, so they sinned against Me."

22 The last remark is probably directed against the rendition given by the Targum, "*They* have exchanged their glory for infamy," which may be a modification of the type known in rabbinic literature as *Tiqqûnēy Sōferim*; cf. *Midrash Tanhuma* on Ex. 15:7. (One purpose of these "Seribal modifications" was to remove possibly opprobrious attributions from association with God in scriptural passages.)

23 J.P.S. renders the entire phrase thus: "And set their heart on their iniquity:" lit., "and unto their iniquity they lift up their soul."

24 Thus encouraging the people to sin by assuring them of forgiveness.

25 Lit., "and to it he lifts up his soul," i.e., the hired servant depends upon his hire.

26 I.e., neither shall fare any better than the other. For a similar remark, cf. comm. on Gen. 18:25; 44:18; Is. 24:2, and *Sephat Yether*, No. 32, p. 13a.

27 J.P.S. translates the entire phrase thus: "I will punish him for his ways." I.E. apparently aims to explain the discord between the singular in v. 9 and the preceding plural in vv. 7-8. Hence the remark: "Upon every one of them." Cf. below, note 32.

28 J.P.S. renders *hiznû* as "they shall commit harlotry." Cf. also Qimhi, ad loc.,

where *hiznū* is interpreted as an intransitive verb. However, according to I.E., *hiznū* in Hiphil is transitive, i.e., they caused one to commit harlotry. For references to I.E.'s remark, cf. above, comm. on 2:7, note 11.

29 Here, as in Gen. 31:43, the verb *prṣ* means "to increase," i.e., they will not increase, but will remain childless, whereas in v. 2 it connotes, according to I.E., acting in violence. Cf. Ibn Janah, *Dictionary*, p. 414; and note 4 of this chapter.

30 I.e., by not heeding His ways, they have forsaken God. Saadya reads the first word in v. 11 ("harlotry") with v. 10. So also R.S.V.: "Because they have forsaken the Lord to cherish harlotry." By supplying the missing "His ways" or "His law" in v. 10, I.E. seeks to reject such a conjunction. For a similar remark, cf. *Ṣaḥot*, pp. 56b; 74a. In *Moznayim*, ed. by Wolf Heidenheim (Offenbach, 1791), p. 4b, I.E. cautions against heeding the words of one of the Geonim (viz., Saadya) that in ten different cases, two biblical verses following each other are to be conjoined. Two such cases are cited from Hosea 4:10-11: 12:11-12. For a detailed discussion of the matter, cf. Joseph Bonfils, *Ṣophnat Pa'aneaḥ*, I, ed. by David Herzog, (Heidelberg, 1930), p. 114; Bacher, *Abraham Ibn Esra als Grammatiker*, p. 39, note 14; and Moshe Zucker, *Rav Saadya Gaon's Translation of the Torah* (New York, 1959), pp. 250-251.

31 From our mss. it is clear that in the biblical text available to I.E., either the first *waw* conjunctive was missing (i.e., "wine" instead of "and wine") or both (i.e., "wine, new wine" instead of "and wine and new wine"). Wilensky maintains that in the text used by Saadya, both *waw* conjunctives were missing; cf. Ibn Janah, *Hariqmah*, p. 140, note 7. Such a reading is not apparent, however, in *Hā'emūnōt Wehadē'ōt* (Josefow, 1885), sec. X, chap. 6, where our passage is quoted with only the first *waw* missing.

32 I.E., explains why the Heb. *yiqqaḥ* (= will take) may indeed be in singular, i.e., harlotry and wine *each* takes away the heart. For a similar remark, cf. above, note 27, and below, comm. on 8:14, 10:5.

33 Comp. v. 14: "The people that is without understanding is distraught."

34 Like the Targum and not like Qimhi who quotes in the name of his father that the wooden stock signifies the false prophet.

35 *Hiṭ'āh* (= he caused to err) in Hiphil requires a direct object. I.e., the spirit of harlotry caused *him* to err, viz., the people. Cf. above, comm. on 2:7, note 11.

36 The Hebrew *'am* (= a people) can be referred to in singular or in plural. ("My people asks counsel"; "*they* have gone astray.")

37 I.E. is of the opinion that *yezabbēḥū* in Piel is transitive, i.e., they tell the priests of Baal to sacrifice. This view is rejected by Qimhi, ad loc.

38 For the same remark, cf. Qara and Qimhi, ad loc.

39 It is not quite clear what I.E. means by this remark. He begins with "the word *yefāredū*" but fails to explain its literary meaning. Cf. Filward, p. 3a. Our translation is based on the similarity of I.E.'s comment to that of the Targum ("they group together with a harlot and with a harlot they eat and drink")

40 J.P.S. translates the last clause of this verse in a similar sense: "And the people that is without understanding is distraught" (ילבט), meaning that the lack of moral understanding will bring upon the people bewilderment and perplexity resulting in failure. I.E. here uses the word *mishtabbēsh*, which in his comm. on Dan. 5:9, he explains as follows: "[The word *mishtabbēsh* is to be understood] literally, viz., like a man who does not know what do do."

41 J.P.S. renders it thus: "But a parting fool shall fall." I.E.'s remark on the word *yillāḇēt* seems to be closer to Qimhi's second interpretation given in the name of his father in *Dictionary*, s.v. לבט. Cf. also Qimhi, ad loc.; Bacher, *Abraham Ibn Esra als Grammatiker*, p. 168; Schroeter, *Archiv*, II (1869), 156, note 6; and Samuel Poznanski, "The Arabic Commentary of Abu Zakariya Yaḥya Ibn Bal'am on the Twelve Minor Prophets," J.Q.R. (N.S.), XV (1924-1925), 16, note 23.

42 I.e., guilty as they may be, the daughters' punishment will not be as severe as that of their parents.

43 Cf. Yefet, p. 69, for a similar comment.

44 Viz., in Bethel and in Dan. Compare I Kings 12:26-29.

45 I.e., why should Judah be involved in Israel's idolatry?

46 Viz., in the southern portion of the once-united monarchy.

47 Comp. below 12:12: "In Gilgal they sacrifice unto bullocks," an admonition which, according to Qara, ad loc., includes the people of Ephraim and Judah. Cf. also comm. on 12:3.

48 "Beth-aven, 'house of vanity,' or 'of wickedness' is a keenly sarcastic substitute for the desecrated name Bethel, 'house of God'" (Cheyne). Cf. Rashi and Qimhi, ad loc. Comp. also below, 10:5, and Am. 4:4 5:5. This view is rejected, however, by Eliezer of Beaugency in his commentary on Hosea 5:8: "For Beth-aven belonged to Benjamin, not to Ephraim."

49 I.E. now engages in a moralizing discourse wherein the reader is reminded that a man who draws nearer to God should demonstrate his love and reverence for Him. For a similar discussion, cf. *Yesōd Mōrā*, ch. 7.

50 In *Yesōd Mōrā*, I.E. enumerates the commandments that are implemented by the mouth, viz., the prayer of thanksgiving (Deut. 26:5-10), taking a vow (ibid. 23:22-24), grace after meals, the chanting of Hallel, prayer, and the duty of teaching the children undivided allegiance to God (ibid. 6:7).

51 In his more technical discussion, the universe is divided by I.E., into three separate worlds: (1) the "world of glory," as the "upper world"; (2) the middle world, which he designates as that of the heavenly bodies; and (3) the world beneath, i.e., the earth and its atmosphere. Cf. comm. on Ex. 3:15; Dan. 10:21. For a closer view of the tripartition of the universe mentioned in the writings of Ibn Ezra, cf. Friedlaender, *Essays*, p. 13, note 2, and comm. on Is. 6:1, p. 34, note 5.

52 Comp. I Sam. 20:3; I Kings 17:1; II Kings 2:4, 6.

53 I.e., why swear by the name of the Lord and commit idolatry at the same time.

54 Thus the prophet would be admonishing the people for swearing falsely. Cf. Qimhi, ad loc.

55 J.P.S. renders the phrase thus: "For Israel is stubborn like a stubborn heifer."

56 Lit., "he turns away from a restrictive way [of life]" by breaking all prohibitions and throwing off the yoke of the law.

57 According to this interpretation, the prophet's statement may be taken as an exclamatory question; viz., Israel being like a disobedient cow, how then, can she expect to be treated like a lamb? Cf. Cheyne, p. 69, and Harper, p. 264. Cf. also R.S.V., where this passage is construed as a question: "Israel is stubborn; can the Lord now feed them like a lamb in a broad pasture?"

58 A.V., J.P.S. and R.S.V. all translate *'aṣabbim* as "idols."

59 In his (earlier) commentary on Isaiah, Ibn Ezra says: "*'Aṣabbim* means money . . . . It is probably derived from *'ṭṣābōn*" [= labor].

60 For a similar remark, cf. comm. on Ps. 115:4

61 I.e., the prophet should let Ephraim alone and not try to reform him as long as his bonds with the idols are indissoluble.

62 The reading in the printed editions עד שיסיר אותו (= until he will remove it, probably the idols) seems uncertain and the minute changes in our mss. make no material difference with regard to the sense. Our translation is based upon the reading in I.E. as quoted by Abravanel (p.41): עד שיסור יינם (= until their wine will pass by), which is supported by I.E.'s opening remark on v. 18. For an additional suggestion to emend the text in I.E., cf. Sharim, p. 27b.

63 The translation "they love (to say) give ye" is based on the interpretation given by I.E. and Qimhi, ad loc. R.S.V. and Harper (p. 265) view the last line of our verse as uncertain.

64 *Hiznū* being in Hiphil is transitive, i.e., they led others to adultery. Cf. comm. on 2:7 and 4:10.

65 Cf. Qimhi, ad loc.: "The princes love to say: 'Give us a bribe for the perversion of justice' and this is shameful for them."

66 Hence they should all have a *shewa* under the first letter, instead of *ṣēre* or a *qamaṣ*.

67 The guttural letters being the *hē* in *hēḇū* and the *aleph* in *'ēfū*.

68 Friedlaender (*Essays*, p. 167, note 1) claims that in our instance "it is left to the reader to find out who is the author" of the explanation following the remark that *hēḇū* is formed like *'ēfū*. Although none of the extant manuscripts omit the words in question, Abravanel, in quoting I.E., ad loc., indeed omits the whole passage, including the aforementioned remark.

69 The closing phrase of our verse is *qālōn māginnehā*, which A.V. renders: "Her

rulers with shame . . ."; thus translating *māginnehā* (a word which means literally "her shields" or "protectors") figuratively as "her rulers."

70 The end of the passage reads: "And the Holy One of Israel is our King."

71 I.e., shame upon those who shield and protect Beth-aven (= house of vanity). According to I.E., *bayit* (= house) can be used in the feminine as well as in the masculine. Cf. comm. on Cant. 1:3.

72 So J.P.S.; A.V. renders *bik̲nāfehā* as "in her wings."

73 For a similar remark, cf. Menahem bar Helbo, as quoted by Qara, ad loc. Cf. also Samuel Poznanski, "R. Menahem bar Helbo's interpretations of the Holy Scripture," *Sokolow Jubilee Volume* (Warsaw, 1904), p. 425, and Qimhi ad loc. That is to say, Israel's reliance was upon what proves to be wind, i.e., nothing. Note that I.E. does not comment on the inconsistency between the masculine verb *ṣārar* (= bound) and the feminine "her corners" (or "her wings,"), but Qimhi extends to our passage the biblical license whereby such changes are warranted.

74 I.e., through the wind (viz., idolatry) Israel became absorbed in the corner (or wings) of Beth-aven. For a similar remark, cf. above, comm. on v. 18.

Chapter V

(1) [With the phrase] *hear this, O priests*, also *give heed, O house of Israel*[1] [the prophet addresses] those who had been rebuked [earlier].[2] Or else the *house of Israel* signifies the Sanhedrin,[3] [the prophet then continuing] *hearken, O house of the king*, for they are all judges.[4] **For you have been a snare on Mizpah**, by not letting the pilgrims go up to the house of God.[5]

(2) [**The idolators** (*sēṭim*) **are gone deep** (*he'emṭqū)]* **in making slaughter:** I.e., in making slaughter on the way [to Jerusalem].[6] The word *sēṭim* denotes the Baal worshipers,[7] [and the word *he'emṭqū* (= they are gone deep)] refers to those mentioned above who deepened the trap[8] [in the hope] the passersby would not notice it. However, *I will punish all of them*[9] for this evil [deed] which they have committed, because what they have concealed *is not hidden from Me*. Hence the following verse, "I [know Ephraim and Israel is not hidden from Me]."

(3) You should know that our forefather Jacob's [desired] wife was Rachel, but Leah took her place.[10] Similarly, [when] Rachel gave him [viz., Jacob] her handmaid [Bilhah for a wife], Leah, too, gave him the other handmaid [Zilpah for a wife] out of envy. Subsequently, when Rachel had borne Joseph, [Jacob] said [to Laban]: "Send me away" [Gen. 30:25]. Furthermore, Jacob said concerning Ephraim and Manasse: "Let my name be named in them" [ibid. 28:15]; therefore all of Israel is called Ephraim.[11] However, Yefet said that perhaps the dynasty of Jehu was originally from Ephraim.[12] Consequently, when he found [the passage] "and Ramoth in Gilead for the Gadites" [Deut. 4:43], he was compelled to say that it [viz., this Ramoth] is not the same [place as the one] cited in the accounts concerning Jehu.[13] In [the commentary on] the book of Amos, I shall explain that he [Jehu] was [indeed] from Ephraim.[14] It is my view that when our ancestors came into the land of Canaan, the [tribe of] Judah abode in its borders on the south, and the house of Joseph, which is the

whole tribe of Ephraim and half of the tribe of Manasse, [was situated] to the north [of Judah].[15] Therefore, [the prophet] mentions [in v. 5] Judah and Ephraim. Similarly, [it is written] in Jeremiah [31:20]: "Is Ephraim a darling son unto me?" and [yet] there was no longer a king hailing from Ephraim in those days.[16] *Hiznētā* [means you caused to commit harlotry][17] yourself, as well as others[18]

(4) **They will not set out** [*lō yittnū*] **their deeds**[19] means they will not perform [their] deeds so as *to return [to their God].*[20] Or else [the meaning of the phrase is that their bad deeds] will not permit them [*to return to their God*].[21] Compare "therefore I permitted thee not [*(lō' nettatiḵā)* to touch her]" [Gen. 20:6].

(5) Yefet said [that the meaning of] *we'ānāh* is the same as *ya'aneh* [in the phrase "my leanness will testify] to my face" [Job. 16:8].[22] This [explanation] makes no sense; rather *we'ānāh* is derived from *'ānî* [= humble].[23]

(6) **With their flocks ... they shall go to seek the Lord:** The antecedent is Judah only [in v. 5],[24] for the Temple was in their possession; *but . . . He hath withdrawn* His glory *from them,*[25] as stated [in v. 15]: "I will go and return to my place."[26] The reason He had withdrawn [His glory] is that "they have dealt treacherously against the Lord" [v. 7].

(7) **Now shall** an evil *month [ḥōdesh] devour* these children *with their portions.*[27] Compare "for the day of their calamity is at hand" [Deut. 32:35].[28] R. Jeshuah[29] said that this was the month of *Ab.*[30] Yefet said the word *ḥōdesh* connotes a sword; compare *ḥadāshāh* [II Sam. 21:16].[31]

(8) **Blow [the horn]:** Meaning, proclaim this [announcement] so that all may know that "Ephraim [shall be desolate]" [v. 9].[32]

(9) [The phrase] *hōda'tî ne'emānāh* [means I made known] a faithful judgment; it is like a decree, etc.[33]

(10) **[The princes of Judah] were** doing harm to those in their [own] domain, *like them that trespass* secretly. Therefore, I will punish them.[34]

(11) **Ephraim is oppressed:** I.e., his [own] kings oppressed him and deceived him; *because he willingly walked [(hō'il hālaḵ) after the commandment]:*[35] These two verbs [*hō'il hālaḵ)*] in the past tense [follow each other without the conjunction *waw* (= and)] as in [the phrase] "the rain is over, it is gone" [Cant. 2:11].[36] [That is to say, Ephraim] agreed to follow man-made precepts,[37] which is [the meaning of the word] *ṣāw* [= precept]. compare *ṣaw lāṣāw* [= precept by precept (Is.

28:10]. Yefet said [the prophet cautioned the people by telling them that] *Ephraim will be oppressed* by the [other] nations.[38]

(12) **I will be [unto Ephraim as a moth]:**[39] Meaning, I will destroy them.[40]

(13) **When . . . [Judah] saw his wound:** [The word *mezōrō* (= his wound) connotes] a sore that that needs to be treated.[41] **Then he sent [to the king of Yareb]:**[42] Viz., Judah [sent to the king of Jareb] for [Judah] follows [Ephraim].[43] *Yārēḇ* is the name of a place in Assyria.[44] [For the meaning of the word] *yigheh* [= cure], compare *yēṭiḇ gēhāh* [= "(a merry heart) makes good relief," (Prov. 17:22)]. [For when a patient recovers from his illness, his face is shining and his] appearance [lights up].[45]

(14) **For [I will be unto Ephraim as a lion]:** At the beginning [(in v. 12) the prophet] said, "I will be [upon Ephraim] as a moth," [which is a figure] for internal punishment[46] and now [the punishment is compared] to a lion [who attacks] from the outside.[47] [Consequently,] who will be able to heal you? **[I will tear] and go away:** That is to say, I will get Me away and no one will [be able to] chase after Me; or else I will go away with the prey.[48] [However], the [most] correct explanation is that I will tear them [apart] and walk away, as [stated] in the following verse.[49]

(15) **I will go . . . till they acknowledge their guilt** [*ye'shmū*]: Meaning, until they will admit they sinned; or else [the word *ye'shmū*] signifies desolation. Compare "Samaria will be desolate" [*te'sham*(14:1)], "that the land be not desolate" [*tēshām* (Gen. 47:19), but there] the *aleph* is missing.[50] [The last word] *yeshaḥarūnenī*, [means] they will seek Me as the [going forth of the] dawn [*keshaḥar*][51] and will say to one another: "Come [and let us return unto the Lord," (6:1)].[52]

Notes

1 We here follow the translation given in R.S.V.

2 Lit., "those I have rebuked," viz., the priests who had been rebuked above in 4:6-10. According to this interpretation, the following phrase "for judgment pertains to you," refers neither to the aforementioned "house of Israel" nor to the "priests," but only to the preceding "house of the king."

3 I.E. here alludes to the assembly of seventy-one scholars (Sanhedrin) who, according to the Mishnah (*Sanhedrin* 1:16), formed the supreme judicial legislature in Israel.

4 I.e., on the latter interpretation, the priests, the house of Israel (viz., the Sanhedrin), and the royal family all participate in the administration of justice, For the priestly judges, comp. Deut. 17:9 and Ez. 43:24. Cf. also above, comm. on 4:6 and Ps. 132:9.

5 Comp. I Kings 12:28: "Whereupon the king took council. . . and he said unto them 'Ye have gone up long enough to Jerusalem.'" Some rabbinic sources suggest that beginning with Jeroboam I, the kings of Israel continued to set up military posts near the sites of Mizpah and Tabor to prohibit any pilgrimage from Northern Israel to Jerusalem; cf. Bab. Talmud, *Ta'anit*, 28a; Rashi, Qara, and Qimhi, ad loc.

6 The Targum interprets the first clause in v. 2: "And they slaughter numerous victims for idols." I.E. evidently held that these victims were the pilgrims who were slaughtered on their way to Jerusalem.

7 *Sĕtim* (lit., "apostates") depicts, according to I.E., the Baal worshipers who victimized those who dared to go up to Jerusalem. Cf. Rashi on Bab. Talmud, *Sanhedrin*, 102a where *sĕtim* is interpreted in a similar sense.

8 I.e., those mentioned above concealed the trap. However, it is not quite clear whether I.E. had in mind the preceding *sĕtim*, viz., the Baal worshipers; the priests, etc., mentioned in v. 1; or both. For I.E.'s method of supplying a direct object (viz., "the trap") after a transitive verb (viz., העמיקו, lit., "they have deepened"), cf. above, comm. on 2:7, note 11.

9 J.P.S. translates the last clause in v. 2 thus: "And I am rejected of them all." However, R.S.V.'s rendering, "but I will chastise all of them," is closer to I.E.'s interpretation. Cf. also Targum and Rashi, ad loc.

10 Comp. Gen. 29:20-23. Cf. also below, comm. on 12:13 where the passage "did not I serve with thee for Rachel" (Gen. 29:25) is cited.

11 Jacob also placed the younger son Ephraim above the older one Manasse, just as if Ephraim had been endowed with his birthright. Comp. Gen. 48:18-19. For a similar remark, cf. comm., ibid. 48:16

12 According to Yefet, as quoted here by I.E., the people of Northern Israel were called Ephraim after king Jehu, who came from Ephraim and founded a new dynasty after the house of Omri was annihilated. This opinion could not be located in Yefet's commentary on Hosea. Cf. above, comm. on 4:3, note 8. It should be added that according to Rashi in his commentary on Gen. 48:4, Jehu is associated with Manasse; but at the same time, Jehu may have come from the territory that was originally allotted to Ephraim. Cf. below, note 14.

13 Comp. II Kings 9:4-6: "So the young man, even the young man the prophet, went to Ramoth-Gilead . . . and he poured the oil on his [viz., Jehu's] head." According to Yefet, Ramoth-Gilead, where Jehu the Ephraimite was anointed king, could not have been the same "Ramoth in Gilead" that was located in the territory of the Gadites (Deut. 4:43).

14 In his commentary on Amos 7:13, I.E. contends that Jehu came from Bethel, which is indeed located in the territory of Ephraim; however, he was anointed king in Ramoth-Gilead because he conspired there against Joram, king of Israel, who was wounded in the war with the Arameans. Comp. II Kings 9:14-15.

15 I.E. refers here to the conquest of Canaan by Joshua whereby the portion allotted to Judah on the south was adjacent to the one allotted to Ephraim on the north. Comp. Josh. 18:5.

16 I.E. evidently maintains that the names "Judah" and "Ephraim" signify their respective geographical locations rather than the ruling kings and their dynasties. For a similar remark, cf. comm. on Ps. 60:9. However, in his commentary on Is. 7:2, I.E. had agreed with the traditional view (Bab. Talmud, *Sanhedrin*, 104b) that "the kingdom of the ten tribes is called Ephraim because their first king, Jeroboam, was of that tribe" (I Kings 11:26). Cf. also below, comm. on 13:1.

17 Unlike the translation given in J.P.S.: "Thou hast committed harlotry."

18 For the same remark, cf. above, comm. on 4:10.

19 A.V. renders the opening phrase, as "they will not frame their doings," while J.P.S. translates it as "their doings will not suffer them."

20 I.e., they will make no effort to improve their relations with God. The Targum translates the first clause in v. 4: "They will not give up their needs in order to return to the worship of their God."

21 That is to say, they have sinned so much that a return to God is now impossible. Cf. Qimhi, ad loc.

22 Hence the translation of the first clause in v. 5: "And the pride of Israel shall testify (*we'ānāh*) to (lit., "in") his face." Cf. Yefet, p. 79, lines 20-24. However, the passage from Job 16:8 quoted by I.E. is missing there.

23 I.e., Israel's pride shall be humbled to his face. It should be noted that Yefet's interpretation is shared by Dunash, Jacob Tam (*Teshūḇōt*, p. 79), and Eliezer of Beaugency, despite I.E.'s rejection. However, the LXX, the Targum, Menahem (*Mahberet*, p. 135), Rashi (ad loc.) and (according to Menahem's students in *Sepher Teshūḇōt Talmidēy Menahem Wetalmid Dunash*, ed. by Salomon Gottlieb Stern [Vienna, 1870], sec. 1, p. 74) also Saadya, interpret *we'ānāh* "and . . . shall be humbled" as preferred by I.E. Cf. also Joseph Qimhi, *Sepher Hagālūy*, p. 48, where the latter explanation is favored.

24 I.E. maintains that the prophet here speaks only of the people of Judah, who will seek God "with their flocks and with their herds," i.e., with their sacrificial offerings. This prophecy relates, according to Qimhi, ad loc., to the days of King Josiah, when the people removed the idols and kept the Passover "to the Lord in Jerusalem" (II Kings 23:23). However, Wynkoop (p. 23), Cheyne (p. 72) and Harper (p. 271) agree that the prophet had Northern Israel in mind, not Judah.

25 I.e., the people of Judah will seek the Lord but will not find Him, for "He hath withdrawn His glory from them." A.V. and J.P.S. render it "He hath withdrawn Himself from them," but in R.S.V. "Himself" is omitted. I.E. seems to maintain that *ḥālaṣ* (= He withdrew) is a transitive verb that requires a direct object: Hence "He hath withdrawn His glory." However, Qimhi, ad loc., and before him Ibn Janah (*Dictionary*, p. 156) insist that the verb is intransitive.

26 Cf. Maimonides, *Guide*, part 1, chap. 23, p. 53: "It says accordingly, 'I will go and return to my place' the signification of which is that the indwelling that had been among us is removed."

27 Thus יאכלם (= shall devour them) relates back to the "strange children" mentioned earlier in the verse. According to Ibn Janah (*Dictionary*, p. 144), "*ḥelqēhem* (lit., their portions) means 'their land,' as stated (in Am. 7:4) 'and [the fire] would have eaten up the land'" (*haḥēleq*). Cf. also Qimhi, ad loc.

28 Similary, the phrase "now shall a month devour them" implies that the time for punishment is imminent.

29 Jeshuah is a tenth-century Qaraite exegete often quoted by I.E. in his commentaries. See Introduction, above, sec. V, note 48.

30 So also Rashi and Qara, ad loc. The month of *Ab* (which corresponds roughly to the month of August) has long been traditionally designated as a month of sorrow. Cf. Mishnah, *Ta'anit* 4:6: "With the start of *Ab* we diminish rejoicing." For an account of the various trials and tribulations in Jewish history that are related to the month of *Ab*, cf. Abravanel, ad loc.

31 J.P.S. renders *ḥadāshāh* as "new armour," but according to Yefet, as quoted by I.E., *ḥadāshāh* signifies a sword. Note that in Yefet's commentary on Hosea (p. 69) *ḥōdesh* is translated "the beginning of the month." However, Ibn Bal'am in his commentary on the Minor Prophets (ed. by Poznanski in *JQR* [N.S.]., XV, 17) interprets *ḥōdesh* as "sword."

32 "This is the announcement toward which v. 8 pointed" (Harper, p. 274).

33 *Ne'emānāh* (= faithful) is according to I.E. an adjective that requires a noun (as in "faithful city," Is. 1:21). Hence, "I make known a faithful judgement," viz., "Ephraim shall be desolate." This judgment is, according to I.E., like a decree that cannot be revoked.

34 Thus v. 10 suggests no seizure of northern territory, but rather indicates the deceptive practices the princes of Judah were engaged in against their own people. Therefore, "I will pour out my wrath upon them," i.e., I will punish them.

35 So A.V.; J.P.S. renders it as "after filth" instead of "after the commandment."

36 "It is gone" instead of "and gone" as rendered in J.P.S. For I.E.'s method of supplying omitted conjunctions, cf. above, comm. on 1:16, note 25.

37 For a similar remark, cf. Yefet, ad loc. In using the phrase *miṣwōt 'anāshim* (lit., commandments of man, Is. 29:13), I.E. had in mind such precepts as were instituted

by Jeroboam I (comp. I Kings 12:32-33). He obviously did not mean to use this phrase in the same sense as employed in various places by Yefet and other Qaraites to condemn Rabbinic Judaism by asserting that rabbinical law commenced with Jeroboam I.

38 This is unlike I.E., who maintains that in the beginning of the verse the prophet depicts the oppression and deception of Ephraim by his own kings. Cf. Yefet, p. 86 where the passage "thou shalt be only oppressed and robbed" by the enemy (Deut. 28:29) is quoted in support of this interpretation. For a similar remark, cf. Rashi and Qimhi, ad loc.

39 So A.V.; R.S.V. renders: "I am . . ." instead of "I will be."

40 Comp. Is. 51:8: "The moth shall eat them." This figure depicts, according to I.E., God's retribution upon Ephraim by a gradual process of internal dissolution. Cf. below, comm. on v. 14.

41 Comp. Jer. 30:13: "None deemeth of thy wound that it may be bound up" (*lemāzōr*).

42 So A.V.; J.P.S. translates מלך ירב as "King Contentious," and R.S.V. renders it: "Great king." Cf. below, note 44.

43 In the first clause of vv. 13 and 14, Judah is mentioned after Ephraim. Subsequently, in the second clause of v. 13 parallelism suggests that the subject of the word *wayishlaḥ* (lit., "and he sent") is Judah, i.e., and Judah sent to the king of Jareb; cf. Rashi, Qara, and Qimhi, ad loc.

44 Rashi and Qara, ad loc., claim that Yareb is an epithet for Tiglat-Pileser (II Kings 16:7). Cf. also Cheyne, p. 76, quoting Nowak who prefers an identity with Tiglath-Pileser II, to whom the epithet Jareb (= fighter) would accurately apply. However, the Syriac renders: "The King of Jareb," which is closer to the interpretation given by I.E. and Qimhi, ad loc. Cf. Rahmer, *Monatsschrift*, XXIV (1865), 470.

45 The last words in I.E. of most printed editions (מראית העין= appearance) are obscure and all attempts to explain them are to no avail. Cf. Sharim, p. 28b; Filwarg, pp. 5-6; Roth, p. 117. Our translation is based on the interpretation given by Quraish, pp. 113, 173, and on the remark made by Qara, ad loc, which suggests that *yigheh* is derived from the verb *ngh* (= to brighten) with the first radical missing in the word. Cf. also Eliezer of Beaugency, p. 125, note 4. The last clause of our verse is thus interpreted in the sense that king Jareb will neither be able to cure Judah nor will he be able to brighten Judah's appearance by treating his wounds, i.e., Judah can expect no outside help.

46 Lit,. "like a moth inside the body," a figure depicting, according to I.E., a process of internal dissolution. Cf. above, note 40.

47 Hence, the metaphor of the "moth" and the "lion" signifies Israel's destruction from within and from without.

48 I.e., "I will tear and go away" by carrying the prey with Me like a lion who drags away the prey "and none shall [dare to] rescue it." Cf. Rashi and Qara, ad loc., for a similar interpretation.

49 Comp. v. 15: "I will go and return to my place," which indicates the removal of God's providence from the people of Israel. Cf. comm. on v. 6.

50 Comp. 14:1: *Te'sham* (= will be desolate), with an *aleph* as the first radical. The same word appears in Gen. 47:19 without an *aleph*. From I.E.'s commentary on Gen. (ibid.) it becomes apparent that, in his view, the three radicals of the word *tēsham* are *yod, shin*, and *mem*. However, in *Moznayim*, p. 20a, he states that the radicals from which *tēshām* is derived are *aleph, shin* and *mem*; hence the "missing" *aleph* in Gen. 47:19. For a similar remark, cf. comm. on 10:2. Cf. also G.R. Driver, "Confused Hebrew Roots," *Gaster Anniversary Volume* (London, 1936), p. 76, where seven biblical passages (including three from Hosea 5:15, 10:12, 14:1) are quoted in which the verb אשם means "to be desolate."

51 I.e., in their trouble they will seek the Lord "as the [going forth of the] dawn." For the meaning of the word כשחר (lit., as the dawn), cf. comm. on 6:3: "The wise man at first [only] knows God through His works, as the dawn when it goes forth, etc." By adding here the word *keshaḥar*, I.E. may have intended not only to explain the word *yeshaḥarūnenī* but also to interpret our last verse as a link between chaps. 5 and 6:1-3. See following note.

52 Cf. Targum, Rashi, and Qara on 6:1 where "they will say" or "and they will say" is supplied before the opening phrase. So also R.S.V.: "And in their distress they will seek Me saying, etc."

Chapter VI

(1) **[For He hath torn** (*ṭārāf*). **and He will heal us, He smites** (*yak̲*), **and He will bind us up]**: [The prophet] says *He hath torn* because of [the previous appearance of the phrase] "as a young lion."[1] [The meaning of the word] *yak̲* is "He smites";[2] [for the meaning of the phrase] *He will bind us up* compare "[wounds and bruises, and festering sores; they have not been pressed], neither bound up [neither mollified with oil" (Is. 1:6)] – for [to heal] a sore, it requires to be treated, bound up and finally softened with oil. The word *ṭārāf* [=He hath torn], a verb in the past tense, [occurs here] with *yak̲*, which is the future tense, in the sense of the present, as I have explained in [my commentary on] the book of Isaiah.[3]

(2) **He will revive us:** [That is to say], He will heal us. Compare "lay it for a plaster upon the boil and he shall revive" [Is. 38:21]; "until they were revived" [Josh. 5:8]. The phrase [*He will revive us*] *after two days* implies that [He will deliver us] in a short time. [Moreover,] *on the third* [*day He will raise us up,*] which is not the normal rule among sick people. For then [viz., on the third day] they suffer [the most].[4]

(3) **Then shall we know** that **we shall follow on to know the Lord:**[5] For this [knowledge of God] is the [most profound] idea[6] of the sciences; and it is for this [purpose] alone that man was created. However, no man is able to know God until he devotes himself to the study of many sciences, which serves as a ladder leading to this highest degree [of knowledge].[7] The phrase [*to know the Lord*] *as the dawn* means that the wise man at first [only] knows God through His works, as at the beginning of the dawn, but gradually the light increases until he sees the [complete] truth. **He shall come [unto us] as the rain** means that God will assist us and teach us the truth; compare "my teaching shall drop as the rain" [Deut. 32:2].[8] Others say, [this figure signifies] a cure which will come to us from God [alone]; as the rain "that is not looked for from man" [Micah 5:6]; that is to

say, there is no other cure except [the one that comes] from Him.[9] **As the latter rain** and **former rain** [(*yōreh*) unto] **the earth:** [The word *yōreh* (= former rain)] is missing a conjunctive *waw* [= and], as in the verse "Adam, Seth, Enosh" [I Chron. 1:1]. There is also a prepositional *beth* [= on, in] missing [before the word *āreṣ* (=earth)], as in the phrase "for [in] six days [the Lord made heaven and earth]" [Ex. 20.11].[10] Thus [the meaning of the last clause is that *He shall come unto us*] *as the latter rain*, and as *former rain* [comes] *unto the earth.*[11]

(4) **What [shall I do unto thee, O Judah? For your kindness is as a morning cloud]**: That is to say, this *loving kindness* [i.e., this resolution whereby] you say you will return to know God, [v. 3] [is] *as a morning cloud*, that does not last. The word *mashkim* is not a verb [but rather a noun][12] as in the phrase *mashkim hāyū* [Jer. 5:8];[13] as if the [word *mashkim*] were here a synonym of "dawn. " It is my opinion [that by using the phrase] *mashkim hāyū* [the prophet Jeremiah meant to say] that each one of them rose early [in the morning];[14] therefore, the meaning of our phrase [viz., *kaṭal mashkim*] will be the same.[15]

(5) **I have hewed [the prophets** (*ḥāṣab̲tī baneb̲ī'im*)]: [For the meaning of the word *ḥāṣab̲tī*], compare "hewer [*ḥōṣēb̲*] in the mountain" [I Kings 5:29; II Chr. 2:1, 17]; that is to say, I slew some of their prophets who misled them in order not to return to God.[16] **I have slain them,** because they speak falsely by uttering the words of their mouth,[17] therefore *I have slain them* likewise *by the words of My mouth.*[18] Perhaps [then] will Israel return [to God]. [For the meaning of the phrase] *thy judgment goeth forth as the light*, compare, "He will make thy righteousness to go forth as the light [and thy right as the noonday" (Ps. 37:6)]. Furthermore, [the prophet compares *judgment* to *light* that goes forth] because of what he said before: "His going forth is sure as the dawn" [v. 3].[19]

(6) **For I desire love:** I.e., true love,[20] not love [that vanishes] like a cloud [v.4].

(7) **But they:** Viz., the false prophets, [*like* [ordinary] *men have transgressed the covenant*].

(8) **Gilead ... is deceitful** [(*'aqūbāh*) **of blood**]:[21] [For the meaning of the word *'aqūbāh*] compare "the heart is deceitful" [(*'aqōb̲*) Jer. 17:9], "Jehu acted deceitfully" [(*b̲e'oqb̲āh*) II Kings 10:19.[22] Similarly, *Gilead is] deceitful*, because of the [innocent] blood that was spilled [there].[23]

(9) **And [as bands] lie in wait** [*ūkeḥakēy*) **for a man, so are the priests banded together**]: The *yod* [in *ukeḥakēy*] replaces a *hē.*[24] Compare *lekalē' hapesh'a* [= to finish the transgression (Dan. 9:24), in which case] the *aleph* similarly replaces the *hē.*[25] Both of these words [viz., *ūkeḥakēy* and *lekalē'*] are rare; for the proper form of the infinitive construct [when derived from] a *lamed-he* verb is *lekalōt, leḥakōt* [=to finish, to wait].[26] [By the phrase *as bands lie in wait for a man* the prophet] meant to say that the banded priests are likened to bands [of robbers] who *lie in wait* for an oncoming man in order to despoil him. Note that [the text] mentions the false prophets [v. 5,] as well as the priests. [For the meaning of the word] *shekmāh* [= in consent], compare "to serve Him with one consent" [*shekem 'eḥād* (Zeph. 3:9)].[27] The force of the word *gedūdim* [=bands] is carried over to the following phrase; [that is to say], they are all as bands [of robbers] who murder on the road [in consent] – meaning that the priests grab their contributions by force.

(10) **In the house [of Israel I have seen] a horrible thing** [*sha'arūrīyāh*]: I.e., a vile thing. Compare "like vile [*hashō'arim*] Figs" [Jer. 29:17]. **There harlotry is found in Ephraim**: [The prophet] alludes to the calves[28] [that were erected] in Bethel, which [latter] belonged to Ephraim [I Kings 12:28].

(11) **Also Judah [appointed a bough** (*qāṣir*) **for thee]:**[29] After having mentioned Ephraim [the prophet now speaks of Judah. For the meaning of the phrase] *he appointed a bough* compare [the tree] "will put forth a bough [*qāṣir*] like a plant" [Job 14:9]; that is to say, he [viz., Judah] put forth for you [viz., Ephraim] a bough by assisting you in the worship of Baal in Bethel at the very time that I [God] had planned *to restore the captivity of My people*,[30] that they might say: "Come, let us return to the Lord" [v. 1].[31] [However], because Judah abandoned My house and assisted you, I will not restore your captivity.[32]

Notes

1 Comp. 5:14: "For I will be . . . as a young lion to the house of Judah. I, even I, will tear" (*'eṭrōf*). Cf. Qara, ad loc., for a similar remark.

2 Qara and Qimhi, ad loc., interpret *yak* (lit., "He will smite") in the sense of "He smote". So also J.P.S.: "He hath smitten." I.E. seems to agree with Rashi that the imperfect *yak* expresses continuity or the duration of an action. Hence, "He smites, etc." See following note.

3 We follow here ms. L. In his commentary on Is. 6:4, I.E. states: "The Hebrew language has no special form for the present tense: past and future are therefore intermingled." For a discussion on this matter, cf. Bacher, *Abraham Ibn Esra als Grammatiker*, p. 126, note 3.

4 I.E. interprets v. 2 figuratively. For him, "He will revive us after two days" means that Israel would emerge from its troubles after a short while; while "on the third day He will raise us up" means that He would altogether cure them of their ills in short order. For the apogee of an illness on its third day, cf. comm. on Gen. 34:25: "On the third day [the pain] is always severe." For a similar remark, cf. Eliezer of Beaugency, ad loc.

5 A.V. renders the passage as " . . . if we follow on to know the Lord," instead of "that we shall follow to know the Lord." Our translation here is based on I.E.'s interpretation which suggests that the word נרדפה is missing a conjunction (= that). For I.E.'s method of supplying omitted conjunctions, cf. above, chap. 1, note 25.

6 The Hebrew *sōd* is generally translated "secret," or "counsel," but in I.E.'s writings *sōd* is evidently synonymous with *yesōd* i.e., a fundamental idea which requires deeper insight. Cf. Friedlaender, *Essays*, p. 128, note 1; M. Steinschneider, *Gesammelte Schriften* (Berlin, 1925), p. 444, note 96.

7 I.E. holds that the knowledge of God can be obtained only through the study of God's works (i.e., the study of practical sciences). This study is as a ladder by which a man, climbing upward, is led to attain the knowledge of God Himself. Cf. comm. on Ex. 20:1-2, at I.E.'s response to R. Yehuda Halevi: "A man who prides himself on the study of sciences, which serves as a ladder leading gradually to the place of his desire, will recognize the work of God displayed in minerals, plants, animals, and in the body of man himself . . . ; thus from the ways of God will the wise man obtain the knowledge of God [Himself]." For a similar remark, cf. *Yesōd Mōrā*, chaps. 7, 10. I.E.'s lengthy comment may have been prompted here by Hosea's repeated stress upon the knowledge of God; comp. 2:22, 4:1, 6; 5:4; 6:6; 8:2

8 I.e., my teaching will refresh and stimulate the people to begin a new spiritual life. Similarly, I.E. interprets the phrase "He shall come unto us as the rain" in the sense that God will rejuvenate the Israelites as the rain refreshes the plants, thereby assisting them in their pursuit of the truth.

9 In his commentary on Micah 5:6, I.E. explains that the Israelites who will remain in exile after the redemption of Zion "shall depend on God alone, not on the kings of the nations in whose land[s] they are; as the dew which is not at man's disposal but rather at the hands of God." This comment, surprisingly, appears to be identical with the one quoted here in the name of others.

10 In the first case the verse reads: "Adam, Seth, Enoch," instead of "and Enoch"; in the second case the phrase reads literally: "for six days," without the prepositional *beth* (= in), instead of "for *in* six days." See following note.

11 J.P.S. translates *yōreh* as "that watereth"; *yōreh* thus being construed as a verb. Cf. also R.S.V.: "As the spring rains that water the earth." I.E. is of the opinion that *yōreh* is a noun, as in Deut. 11:14, *yōreh ūmalqōsh* (= former rain and latter rain); except that in our case the conjunction *waw* (= and) between *malqōsh* and *yōreh* is missing. Similarly, there is a prepositional *beth* missing in the word *āreṣ* (= earth), as in the phrase *shēshet yāmin* (= six days) instead of *beshēshet yāmim* (= in six days). Hence the meaning, "as the latter rain *and* former rain [comes] unto the earth." For a similar remark, cf. comm. on 10:12.

12 Unlike Qara, ad loc., where the closing phrase is interpreted: "As the dew that rises early and vanishes quickly," with *mashkim* (= rises early) taken as a verb. Cf. below, note 15. The translation "but rather" is based on Roth's suggestion (p. 115) that the Hebrew word *raq* (= but rather) is missing from the text of I.E.'s commentary. This reading makes I.E.'s comment more intelligible.

13 J.P.S. translates *mashkim hāyū* as "they became . . . lusty stallions". By quoting the phrase from Jer. 5:8, I.E. evidently had in mind to establish that *mashkim* can also be taken as a noun instead of a verb. For as a verb ("to rise early") in singular, *mashkim* would be difficult to conjoin with the following plural *hāyū* (= they were). Similarly, the word *mashkim* in Hosea is also a noun, which is equivalent to *shaḥar* (dawn, i.e., "and as the dew of the dawn that passes away"). For the Hebrew term *mashkim* as a noun in the sense of "morning," "dawn," cf. Mishnah, *Bikkurim* 3:2. It should be noted that I.E.'s commentary on Jeremiah has not come down to us, and therefore we can hardly ascertain how he explains the aforementioned phrase. However, according to Qimhi (*Dictionary*, p. 404), I.E. interprets *mashkim hāyū* as horses attributed to *Meshek̲* (a people of Asia Minor, Gen. 10:2). This strange statement could not be traced in any of I.E.'s writings.

14 In an attempt to explain the juxtaposition of the singular *mashkim* and the plural *hāyū* (see preceding note), I.E. apparently concludes that Jeremiah scorned the adulterers by saying, "that each one of them rose early, in the morning," boasting about his indulgence in harlotry "with his neighbors wife" (Jer. 5:8). For a similar remark, cf. above, comm. on 4:1.

15 In this closing comment I.E. seems to contradict himself by suggesting that in both cases *mashkim* remains a verb; hence the interpretation of our phrase, "and as the dew that rises early [and] goes away," which is similar to the one given by Qara, ad loc. (see above, note 12). Cf. below, comm. on 13:3 where I.E.'s remark implies the acceptance of this view. Perhaps the text in I.E. should be emended to read: ומלת משכים כמו משכים היו שמשכים היו כל אחד וכו' (= [for the meaning of] the word *mashkim* compare *mashkim hāyū* [Jer. 5:8], i.e., each one of them rose early [in the morning, etc.]).

16 Most translators render the phrase *ḥaṣab̲tī baneb̲ī'im* as "I hewed them (viz., the people) by the prophets." However, there is nothing in the text that corresponds to

"them." Moreover, the object in the following clause, "I have slain them," may indeed refer to the prophets, i.e., I cut into the false prophets and "I slew them by the words of my mouth." I.E. takes the *beth* in the phrase *ḥōṣeḇ bāhār* (I Kings 5:29) to be partitive, and, by comparison, the *beth* in *ḥāṣaḇtī baneḇī'im* likewise to be partitive, viz., I hewed some of the prophets.

17 Sharim (p. 28a) reads literally in I.E.: "Because they speak falsely by claiming they are the words of My mouth." Thus he divides the Hebrew word פיהם (= their mouth) into two (פי הם). However, such a reading is found neither in the printed editions nor in our mss.

18 I.e., by decree. Cf. comm. on Ps. 33:4; "The word of God is his decree."

19 According to I.E.'s last remark, "your judgment" is compared by the prophet to the "light that goes forth." Thus the verb *yēṣē* (lit., "will go forth") is designed to modify the juxtaposed "light" and not the antecedent (viz., "and your judgment"). I.e., your judgment will become as the light that goes forth, the idea of which is in apposition to "as the going forth of the dawn" mentioned in v. 3. Rashi and Qimhi, ad loc., both interpret the last clause as a rhetorical question: How can your judgment go forth as the light? – meaning how can I pardon you after all the crimes you have committed? However, by quoting from Ps. 37:6, I.E. seems to indicate that the prophet is speaking in terms of an encouraging judgment by which the people will be vindicated. That is to say, first the Lord will slay the false prophets that led the people astray, and then the people will be able to return to God and their judgment will become as bright as the light that goes forth, i.e., they will be declared innocent.

20 R.S.V. renders the opening phrase as "for I desire steadfast love," whereas A.V. and J.P.S. both translate it "for I desire mercy."

21 A.V. translates our verse as "Gilead . . . is polluted with blood," taking *'aqūbāh* to mean "polluted"; and J.P.S. renders it "Gilead . . . is covered with footprints of blood."

22 J.P.S. renders it thus: "Jehu did it in subtlety."

23 For an interpretation similar to that of I.E.'s, cf. Yefet, p. 102; Menahem, *Mahberet*, p. 136; and Ibn Janah, *Dictionary*, p. 382. Cf. also Bab. Talmud, *Makkot*, 10a where Gilead is described as a city in which "they conspired to kill people," i.e., they ambushed innocent people.

24 I.E. regards the word *ūkeḥakēy* with a *yod* at the end as equivalent to *ūkeḥakēh* where the original *hē* is retained.

25 In the first case the three radicals of the verb are *ḥet*, *kaf*, and *hē* and in the second, *kaf*, *lamed*, and *hē*. Hence, the *yod* (in *ūkeḥakēy*) and the *aleph* (in *leḵalē'*) both replace the third radical of the verb respectively.

26 Friedlaender (*Essays*, p. 167, note 1) includes the last passage concerning these rare words, among a series of passages whose authorship is uncertain. However, when discussing elsewhere the construct form of the verb *ḥyh* (= to live, Ex. 1:16), I.E. uses

almost the same terminology (e.g., משפט זרה בסמוכים). Similarly, the adjective "two" which is used here in the absolute form (השתים instead of שתי) is indeed characteristic of I.E.'s style. Cf. comm. on 5:11, 7:4; *Ṣaḥot*, p. 48a. For the term וכחכי, construed as an infinitive construct, cf. also W. Gesenius, *Gesenius' Hebrew Grammar*, ed. by E. Kautzsch and A.E. Cowley (Oxford, 1910), par. 75 *aa*.

27 Lit., "with one shoulder." It should be noted that A.V. translates the entire passage of our verse "So the company of priests murder in the way by consent," thus agreeing with I.E., who interprets שכמה in the sense of שכם אחד (= one consent). Cf. also Targum, Rashi, Qara and Qimhi, ad loc., for a similar interpretation. However, in Bab. Talmud, *Makkot*, 10a, as well as in J.P.S. and R.S.V, שכמה is rendered as a proper name, viz., the city of Shechem.

28 The Hebrew text of I.E. reads "to the calves," in plural; cf. Targum, ad loc. In reality there was only one golden calf erected in Bethel, comp. I. Kings 12:29. According to Qimhi (comm. on Hosea 10:5), Bethel was considered the main place of worship "as if both [of the golden calves] were [placed] there." However, in I.E.'s commentary on 10:15 and Am. 5:5 "the calf" (singular) in Bethel is mentioned.

29 The translation given here conforms to I.E.'s interpretation, but is evidently not found elsewhere. For the J.P.S. rendition of v. 11, see the following note.

30 J.P.S. renders our verse: "Also, O Judah, there is a harvest appointed for thee! When I would return the captivity of My people." Thus the phrase "there is a harvest appointed *for thee*" refers to the tribe of Judah itself. According to I.E., however, the prophet reprimands Judah in the aforementioned phrase for helping Ephraim in their idol worship; and the phrase "for thee" refers to Ephraim. Note also I.E.'s interpretation of the verb שוב (= to return) as being equivalent in sense to the Hiphil form השב. as in Deut. 30:3; Ps. 14:7; Job 42:10. Cf. also *Sāphā Berūrāh*, p. 26b; ". . . the word *shāḇ* (= returned) is sometimes intransitive and sometimes transitive."

31 By quoting verse 1, I.E. may have had in mind to prove that the prophet begins and concludes this prophecy with the same idea of returning to God. For a similar remark, cf. below, comm. on 14:10.

32 Cf. Qimhi, ad loc., where the closing clause of our chapter is similarly interpreted as meaning: "When I *intended* to restore the captivity of my people; for not all of them were yet unanimously worshiping the idols – but after Judah also began worshiping the idols, I abandoned them to their enemies."

Chapter VII

(1) **When I would heal Israel, [then is the iniquity of Ephraim uncovered]:** Because [the people] said: "He hath smitten, and He will heal us" [6:1], He [now] says: When I attempted to cure them, the [deep-seated] iniquity in their hearts confronted Me, i.e., they have not forsaken it until now, *for they commit falsehood*; at night they steal and during the day bands of robbers roam the outskirts of the cities.[1]

(2) **[But they do] not [consider in their hearts.]:**[2] They imagine that I do not see them, not knowing that *their own doings have surrounded them* and that those [deeds] *are before My face.*

(3) **By their wickedness they make glad the king,** as well as the *princes* who enthrone him.[3]

(4) **They are all [adulterers]:** Viz., including their king.[4] *Tannur* [= oven] is masculine, and thus the accent in the word *bo'ērāh* [= heated] is penultimate; compare *lay̋lāh* [= night], *náḥlāh* [= stream].[5] This is an inverted verse and its meaning is as follows: [*They are all adulterers*] as a baking oven that burns from the [time of] kneading of the dough until it is leavened,[6] when [lit., "until"] the baker ceases to stir [it].[7] For [this] he has to keep kindling and heating [the oven] continuously.

(5) **On the day** that they enthrone their king, i.e., the day that is called *the day of our king*, they intoxicate him[8] with wine, and he joins the mockers. This word [viz., *lōṣeṣim* (= mockers)] belongs to the class of geminate verbs.[9] i.e., [its root] is *lṣṣ*. However, if the word were *melōṣeṣim* [instead of *lōṣeṣim*] it would then belong to the class of [weak] verbs in which the second radical is missing, and would be etymologically derived from *lṣ*, its actual root being *lyṣ*[10] Therefore, [*lōṣeṣim*] belongs to the class of verbs in which the second radical is doubled. Hence, *tōfefőt* [= timbers (Ps. 68:26)] and *metōfefōt* [= drumming (Nah. 2:8)] are two different verbs.[11]

The word *heḥelū* [is derived] from *ḥōlī* [= sickness][12] and is similar [in form] to *her'ū*[13] [= they showed]; for *our king* is the object and the *princes* the subject,[14] viz., *the princes have made sick* the king by intoxicating him.[15] Compare "[hope deferred] maketh the heart sick" [*maḥalāh lēb* (Prov. 13:12)], i.e., [hope deferred] is the active [cause] making the heart to become sick; [in this latter passage the word *maḥalāh* is a verb in] the Hiphil form and is [derived] from *heḥelāh* [= he made sick]. [In the phrase] *bottle of wine*, a prepositional *beth* [= with] is missing, i.e., [the princes have made him sick] *with* a bottle full of wine. For the meaning [of the word] *ḥamat*] compare *min haḥēmet* [= "from the bottle," (Gen. 21:15).[16] The word *ḥamat* (= the bottle of)] in the construct form [is irregular]; as is *delet* [= door] in the phrase "and shut thy door [*delātḵā*][17] about thee" [Is. 26:20]. The phrase *mesapēaḥ ḥamātḵā* [(Hab. 2:15)[18] in which the word, *ḥamātḵā* (= thy bottle)] has a similar inflection, proves the correctness of this interpretation.[19]

(6) **For [they have made ready their heart like an oven, while they lie in wait]:** The word *be'orbām* [= while they lie in wait] signifies their evil designs in which they conspire all night; thus their hearts may be likened unto a [burning] oven [*katannur*]. However, whereas every baker sleeps at night and heats up the oven in the morning only, their hearts do not sleep, but rather [each of them] conspires all night.

(7) **They all [are hot as an oven, and devour their judges]:** The meaning is that they devour one another, including their judges. They also conspire against their kings.[20] Therefore, [the prophet] continues:

(8) **Ephraim, he will become mixed [among the people]:** [For the meaning of the word] *yitbōlāl* [= he will become mixed], compare *bālul* = mixed [Ex. 29:40]; that is to say, [they will become mixed among the peoples] by virtue of having sought help from outside nations for [their internal struggles] against one another;[21] this is also [the meaning of the phrase] "they all call unto Egypt, they go to Assyria" [v. 11]. Therefore, will they become assimilated among the people; the object [in verse 11] is Egypt.[22] The figure of a *cake not turned* [is designed to emphasize] that [just as] a cake when unturned is destroyed by fire, [so is] their [evil] design.[23] [Furthermore,] because [the prophet] compared their impulse and their heart to an oven [v. 6], he compared the [evil] design to a cake.

(9) **[Strangers] have devoured [his strength]:** The reference [here] is to the tribute they [viz., the people of the Northern Kingdom] paid to Assyria and Egypt, as it is written with respect to their kings.[24] The phrase *also gray hairs*[25] signifies that they became weak and poor[26]

[and the subject of the phrase] *zārqāh bō* [= she has thrown upon him] is nature, that sprinkled upon him gray hairs,[27] for [the stage of] becoming gray is the result of man's [physical] nature.

(10) I have already explained [the meaning of the word] *we'ānāh.*[28] **But they have not returned unto the Lord**, [even] in their penury, when they have nothing else to offer to [foreign] nations in return for their help.[29]

(11) **And Ephraim has become [like a silly dove, without understanding]:** I.e., by virtue of his [viz., Ephraim's] frivolity and lack of knowledge. For they were continuously going to Egypt and Assyria to seek help, but did not realize that "even as they go [there], I will spread my net upon them" [v. 12] – that is to say, I will seize them so that they will be unable to escape.[30] Hence, the expression "upon them" and not "unto them."[31] Similarly, because of [the parallel between Ephraim and] the dove [v. 11], the figure "I will bring them down as the fowl of the heaven" [v. 12] is appropriate.

(12) [The verb] *'aysīrēm* is like *'ayasrēm* [in the Piel form, meaning I will chastise them], but it is [here] in the Hiphil form even though the [initial] *yod* has not been changed into a *waw.* Compare "let their eyelids look straight [*yayshīrū*] before you" [Prov. 4:25].[32] The form *'ōsīrēm,*[33] with which compare *'ōshīḇēm, 'ōrīdēm*, was not here used, but rather the word [viz., *'aysīrēm*] was preserved on the basis of the original form [of its root], for the [three letter] root is *ysr* [יסר] and the [third person masculine] future *yeyasēr* [ייסר = he will chastise]. The meaning [of the whole phrase accordingly] is I will chastise those who go to Egypt, after which they will become as a message for their community that remained in their land.[34]

(13) [The phrase] *nādedū mīmennī* means they were escaping from Me[35] and [therefore] will meet with *destruction.* **I would [redeem them:**[36] That is to say], I indeed intended to redeem them, but they [erroneously] thought that My entire intention was [rather] to harm them.

(14) **And [they have] not [cried unto Me]:** When they wailed upon their beds, bemoaning their fate on account of the calamity that befell them, they did not plead with Me as a sick man pleads with his doctor. The phrase *they assemble themselves* [*yitgōrārū*] *for corn and wine* implies that they would join together during the day to eat and drink. Compare "the barns [*mammgūrōt*] are broken down" [Joel 1:17].[37] [The phrase] *yāsūrū ḇī* means they speak rebelliously against Me. Thus [the meaning of the entire verse is that] they do not plead with

Me at night, while during the day they rebel against Me by telling lies [v. 13].[38]

(15) **I have chastised**[39] them–not to their detriment, but rather in order to strengthen their arms. Compare "I taught Ephraim to walk; [taking them on his arms, but they knew not that I healed them" (11:3)][40]

(16) **They return, but to no purpose:** They return to Egypt for no [other] purpose than to slander their princes.[41] Hence, the figure *they are like a treacherous bow.*[42] [The passage *their princes shall fall by the sword*] *for the rage of their tongue* proves the correctness of this interpretation.[43] **This is their derision [in the land of Egypt]:** The [pronominal suffix] *mem* [= their, viz., *their derision*] can probably be ascribed to the slanderers.[44]

Notes

1 Cf. Targum, ad loc., for a similar interpretation.

2 A.V. renders our phrase as "and they consider not in their hearts."

3 I.e., the force of the word *yesammḥū* (lit., "they will make glad") is carried over from the first clause of the sentence. Thus, "by their wickedness they make the king glad and by their treachery [they make glad] the princes." For the princes enthroning the king, cf. below comm. on v.5.

4 The king mentioned in the preceding verse also practiced adultery.

5 Viz., *naḥálāh* as in Ps. 124:4. Cf. comm., ibid.: "The accent of the word *náḥlāh* is on the first syllable, the (cantillation) sign being on the *nun*; the [final] *hē* is superfluous as is the *hē* of [the word] *láylāh*." Similarly, the apparently feminine form *bō'ērāh* should really be considered as equivalent to *bō'ēr*, in consonance with the masculine noun *tannur* (= oven). Cf. *Sāphā Berūrāh*, p. 45b and *Ṣaḥot*, p. 19b. For a discussion of the significance of the accents in I.E.'s commentaries on the Bible, cf. Bacher, *Abraham Ibn Esra als Grammatiker*, p. 67, note 2.

6 According to Qimhi, ad loc., the baker heats up the oven to its highest degree during the period in which the fermentation of the dough is taking place, i.e., "from the kneading of the dough until it is leavened." Hence, it is to the heat of this period that the passion of the people is compared.

7 The method of explaining difficult passages in the Bible by rearranging their words is implemented by I.E. also in other places of his commentary, e.g., 8:12; 10:9; Ex. 4:57; Lev. 4:22; Amos 9:12. It should be noted that while A.V. translates *mē'ir* as "from rising," J.P.S. and R.S.V. render "to stir." However, it is difficult to ascertain how I.E. actually explains this word. Sharim (p. 28a) conjectures that I.E. interprets: "From the

time the baker directs the one who kneads the dough until he ceases to do so" (*mē'ir*). Perhaps, rather, "until the baker ceases to fan [the fire]," which indicates the fire is extensive and needs no additional heating.

8 I.E. construes *heḥelū* as meaning "to make ill" and thus by extension "to intoxicate". See his extended comment below.

9 Heb. *po'olēy hakāful*, i.e., verbs in which the second root letter is repeated.

10 I.E. is of the opinion that triliteral verbs of which the second radical is a *waw* or *yod* had originally consisted of only two consonantal letters with the *waw* or the *yod* missing. Cf. comm. on 8:4; Ps. 4:7; *Moznayim* p. 41b; *Sāphā Berūrāh*, p. 27b. On the difference between the terms *gizrāh* and *shōresh* in I.E.'s writings, cf. Prijs, op. cit., pp. 39, 102.

11 Lit., "are (of) two different roots." In the first instance the radicals are, according to I.E., *taw*, *phe*, and *phe*, and in the second, *taw*, *waw*, and *phe*.

12 See above, note 8. The LXX renders *heḥelu* "they began." Cf. also Abravanel, ad loc. I.E. evidently rejects such a translation. Cf. Wynkoop, ad loc.

13 *Heḥelū*, *her'ū* both with a *segol* under the *hē* instead of *hiriq*, and thus both Hiphil verbs, which are as a rule transitive. See next note.

14 Rashi and R.S.V. interpret *heḥelū* as an intransitive verb, i.e., "the princess became sick." However, according to I.E., the Hiphil form makes the verb transitive. Thus, "the princes have caused [him] (viz., the king) to become sick." So also A.V.: "The princes have made him sick."

15 See above, notes 13-14

16 Rashi interprets *ḥamat* as "heat." So also J.P.S. and R.S.V.: "With the heat of wine." However, I.E. maintains that the word *ḥamat* denotes a flask. Cf. comm. on Gen. 21:14.

17 I.e, the noun חֲמַת is irregular, for it should be חֵמֶת (comp. Gen. 21:15). Similarly, the inflection of the segolate noun דלת (= door) with a possessive pronominal ending, is also irregular, for it should be not דְלָתְךָ but דַלְתְּךָ (= thy door) which would be analogous to the change of מלך (= king) to מַלְכְּךָ (= thy king). See note 19, below.

18 A.V. renders the entire passage thus: "That puttest *thy bottles* to him [and makest him drunken also]."

19 I.E. indicates that *ḥēmet* with a possessive pronominal ending (viz., חֲמָתְךָ) is similar in form to *delet* (viz., דְלָתְךָ) which is irregular, for it should follow the declension of חֵלֶק (= portion) to חֶלְקְךָ. Hence, the construct form *ḥmat* is also irregular. For a similar remark, cf. comm. on Ex. 7:28 (short rec.) and *Ṣaḥot*, p. 38a.

20 I.e., with the result that, as this verse continues, "all their kings have fallen." I.E.'s interpretation alludes to the unstable conditions in the Northern Kingdom and to the frequent dynastic changes after the death of Jeroboam II.

21 According to Ibn Janah, *yitbōlāl* connotes destruction, i.e., "Ephraim . . . he will be destroyed." Cf. *Dictionary*, p. 64. I.E. maintains the verb should be interpreted in

the sense of "will become mixed," i.e., Ephraim will become assimilated among the people from whom it seeks to obtain help in domestic struggles.

22 The remark "the object . . . is Egypt" (lit., "Egypt are the ones being called") may be directed against the comment made by Qara on the same phrase (in v. 11), which suggests that Israel followed Egypt and Assyria whenever *they* (viz., Egypt and Assyria) *called on it* to do so.

23 At first glance, I.E. would not appear to have explained adequately what is meant by the metaphor of "a cake not turned." Qimhi evidently had this problem in mind in explaining that their stubborness in worshiping the idols was one-sided and thus they never considered altering their evil designs for the better.

24 Comp. 12:2: "They make a covenant with Assyria, and oil is carried to Egypt." Comp. also II Kings 15:20: "And Menachem exacted the money of Israel, . . . to give to the king of Assyria."

25 I.e., they turned gray. Heb. *sēḇāh* more literally signifies old age.

26 Lit., "their strength has been weakened and they lost their wealth."

27 Qimhi interprets the Hebrew *zārqāh* as "was thrown," thus making the verb intransitive. I.E. holds that *zārqāh* is a transitive verb that requires a (missing) subject as well as the direct object; hence, "nature sprinkled upon him gray hairs" (*sēḇāh*). For I.E.'s opinion on this grammatical subject, cf. above, comm. 2:7, note 11.

28 "And . . . shall be humbled." According to I.E., *we'ānāh* is derived from *'anî* (= humble) which connotes misery. Cf. above, comm. on 5:5.

29 Lit., "so that they (viz., the outside nations) should help them."

30 I.e, they will be unable to escape My punishment by calling on other nations. Cf. Ibn Janah, *Hariqmah*, p. 111, where "even as they go" (v. 12) is interpreted in the sense of "wherever they go".

31 It is not clear what I.E. means by his remark on the word *'alēhem* (= upon them), since the preposition "upon" is frequently used in the Bible with respect to the figure of "spreading the net." Comp. above 5:1; Ez. 12:13; Prov. 29:5. Perhaps the text in I.E. should be emended to אוי (= woe) in place of ולא (= and not), with the omission of the preceding word עליהם (= upon them) which is missing in ms. R (viz., על כן אמר אוי). According to this conjecture, I.E. may have wanted to explain that in v. 13 the prophet continues the assertion of the inevitable results of Ephraim's conduct (v. 11); Ephraim is like a silly dove, for the people go to Egypt and Assyria to seek help, without knowing that even then "I will spread my net upon them" (v. 12), so that they will be unable to escape Him. Therefore, the prophet continues: *"Woe unto them* for they fled from Me" – that is to say, because they have attempted to flee they will ultimately meet destruction; cf. comm. on v. 13.

32 I.e., the third person Hiphil plural יַיְשִׁירוּ (lit., "they will look straight") is similar in form to the first person singular אַיְסִירֵם (= I will chastise them), with a *yod* rather than a *waw* before the *shin* and the *samek*, respectively. Cf. comm. (attrib. to I.E.) on

Prov. 4:25, where our passage is communicated. It should be noted that Menahem (*Mahberet*, p. 128) interprets *'aysīrēm* as "I will bind (or 'shackle') them." However, I.E.'s, as well as Rashi's interpretation (viz., "I will chastise them") agrees with that of the Targum and Dunash (*Teshūḇōt*, p. 34). For a discussion of this controversy between Menahem and Dunash, cf. Joseph Qimhi, *Sepher Hagālūy*, p. 25, and Hayyug, op. cit., p. 49, note 1.

33 I.e., *'ōsīrēm* instead of *'aysīrēm*, for the *yod* which is the first radical of the verb (יסר) is generally replaced by a *waw* (e.g., ישב = אושיבם, יסר = אוסירם).

34 I.e., the fate of those who escaped to Egypt will serve as a message of failure to the remaining community in Israel, cf. above, note 31.

35 A.V. renders the phrase as "they have fled from Me," while J.P.S. and R.S.V. translate "they have strayed from Me," which means, according to I.E., that the people were attempting to escape from God.

36 So R.S.V.; J.P.S. renders "shall I redeem them?"

37 According to I.E., the words *yitgōrārū* (יתגוררו = they assemble themselves) and *mamgūrōt* (ממגורות = barns, Joel 1:17) are both derived from the root *gur* (גור = to gather together). For a similar comment, cf. comm. on Is. 54:15, in the name of Ibn Janah, which is rejected by I.E.

38 I.e., at night when they wail on their beds, they do not cry out to Me; and during the day, when they assemble to eat and drink, they rebelliously carry out their treacherous designs against Me.

39 A.V. renders: "I have bound"; J.P.S., "I have trained."

40 Verse 11:3 is, according to I.E., parallel in meaning to our verse: "And I have chastised them in order to strengthen their arms and yet concerning Me thay think (only) evil." Cf. also I.E.'s remark on v. 13: "I indeed intended to redeem them, but they [erroneously] thought that My entire intention was [rather] to harm them." For a similar interpretation, cf. Eliezer of Beaugency, ad loc.

41 Cf. above, comm. on v. 8, and below, note 43.

42. So. R.S.V.; J.P.S. translates: "They are become like a deceitful bow."

43 According to I.E.'s interpretation, the prophet concludes that the purpose of the people's mission to other nations is none other but to defame and slander their own princes. These princes will die by the sword as a result of these rivalries and treacherous intrigues.

44 Rashi and Qara refer "their derision" to the Egyptians who scoffed at the people for asking for their help. However, I.E. explains the phrase with respect to those who went to Egypt to deride and slander their own princes.

Chapter VIII

(1) **[Set the horn] to [thy mouth]:** These are the words of God to the prophet: *Set the horn to thy mouth* and swoop *like an eagle to the house of the Lord.*[1] [However], Yefet said [that the prophet was told]: Render your mouth [as] a horn, for the enemy will swoop as a vulture *upon the house of the Lord.*[2] His interpretation is a good one by virtue of the [following] word *because.*[3]

(2) **To Me [they shall cry]:** I.e., to Me shall the children of Israel cry.[4] Or else [the phrase] "house of Israel" is missing.[5]

(3) **[Israel] has spurned the good:** [The term *the good*] is [an epithet for] God, who was good to them.[6] [For the meaning of the word] *yirdefō* [= he shall pursue him] compare *yiqre'ō* [= he shall call him (Jer. 23:6)].[7]

(4) They **[have set up kings but not through Me]:**[8] For they have not consulted God with respect to making Jeroboam king [although] it is stated: "[Thou shalt ... set him king over thee] whom the Lord thy God shall choose" [(Deut. 16:15), which includes] also the kings of [Northern] Israel.[9] [The word] *hēśīrū* [(= they have made princes) is a verb in which] the second radical [*waw* or *yod*] is missing, as in the case of the verb *qm* [= to rise], *shb* [= to return] and *shr* [= to sing].[10] Thus the idea is repeated.[11] However, Yefet said [that the *sin* should be treated] like a *samek*, as in the phrase *besūrī mēhem* [= when I turn away from them (9:12)].[12] Hence the idea is reversed, i.e., if *they have set up kings* [it was not through Me]: or else if they turned them away [(viz., if they removed the kings), *I knew it not*].[13] [The subject of the phrase] *that they may be cut off* [is *their silver and their gold*, i.e., they made idols] with the result that the silver and the gold will be cut off from them.[14]

(5) **[Thy calf] hath spurned thee, O Samaria:**[15] [The object is] repeated as if it were written: *Thy calf has spurned you*, viz., you Samaria[16] – as if [that idol] has rejected you; for the city [viz., Samaria] will be destroyed and its people will go into captivity. **Mine**

anger is kindled against them: Viz., against the calf–[idol] and against Samaria.[17] **How long** will my anger have to endure against them before they become innocent.[18] For they will be unable to attain innocence from it[?].[19]

(6) **For** as a result of the design of Israel and the design of the king was the calf of Samaria made.[20] *Shebābim* means the same thing as *shebībim* [= flames].[21] Yefet said [*shebābim* means rebels], i.e., the calf of Samaria will make Israel become rebels;[22] but this [interpretation] is incorrect.

(7) **For [they . . . shall reap the whirlwind]:** The *taw* in the word *sūfātāh* [= whirlwind] is not essential; compare *ēmātāh* [= terror (Ex. 15:10)].[23] **Were [it to yield]:** I.e., and if you were to claim that [*the bud*] will [nonetheless] yield [some *meal*], you should know that *strangers shall swallow it up.*[24]

(8) **[Israel] is swallowed up:** That is to say, they [viz., the strangers] will swallow up your harvest as well as [the people] that spread the seeds. **[They became among the nations] as a useless vessel** that a man throws out of his house.

(9) **For [they are going up to Assyria like a] wild ass [alone (*pere' bōdēd*)]: Compare** *pere' 'ādām* [= a wild ass of a man (Gen. 16:12)]. The word *bōdēd* [= lonely] signifies that they were not unanimous in their plans.[25] The word *hitnū* [in the phrase *hitnū 'ahābim*] is derived from the same root as *etnan* [= hire (Deut. 23:19)]. [The phrase means] that each one gave gifts of friendship to the princes of the nations.[26]

(10) **Though [they hire among the nations I will soon gather them]:** Meaning, I will gather them into Egypt.[27] Then they shall [indeed] *begin* [*yāḥēllū*] to grumble and complain a *little* [under] the heavy *burden of the king*[s] of Egypt and Assyria and of their princes.[28] Hebrew grammar makes it impossible to explain [the word] *wayāḥēllū* other than as in the word *tāḥēllū* [= you shall begin (Ez. 9:6)].[29]

(11) **For [Ephraim] hath made many [altars]:** The meaning of the [second clause] *altars have been unto him to sin* is that since he [viz., Ephraim] already had [altars], viz., those he had inherited from his forefathers, why did he make many additional [ones].[30]

(12) **I have written [to him** (*'ektōb lō*)]: [That is to say,] I have reproved him [viz., Ephraim] and my laws were [always] written out for him.[31]

(13) **The sacrifices of *[habhabay]*:** R. Moses Hakkohen said that the word *habhabay* is related [in meaning] to the rabbinic expression

"[the wick] that did not char" [*hibhabāh* (Mishnah, *Shabbat* 2:3)].[32] Yefet said [the word] is derived from the verb *yhb* (= to give) as is the phrase] *hab hab* [= give, give, (Prov. 30:15)],[33] with an additional [*nōsāf*] *yod*, just as is the *yod* in the word *sādāy* [= field (10:4, Deut. 32:13)];[34] this is the correct [explanation]. **He will remember their iniquity:** Namely, that they [viz., the people of Northern Israel] will return to Egypt in defiance of His [injunction]: "Ye shall henceforth return no more that way" [Deut. 17:16].[35]

(14) **[For Israel] hath forgotten [his Maker, and builded] palaces,** for protection,[36] ... [but a *fire*] **shall devour the castles thereof:** [Meaning, the castles] of each city.[37]

Notes

1. Similarly, Eliezer of Beaugency, ad loc., explains that the prophet was ordered to act like an eagle by going up to the height of the mountain and to reveal there the sins of the people who come to worship in the "house of the Lord" (viz., the Temple). Hence, the second clause of the verse is a further command to the prophet to go swiftly to the "house of the Lord."

2. Cf. Yefet, pp. 119, line 23-120, line 3: אמר אללה ללנבי אן ירפע צותה מתל צות אלסאפור . . . וקל הודא עלעדו נבוכדנצר יסרע באלמגי אלי בית רב אלעאלמין כמא יסרע אלנסר (= God said to the prophet that he should raise his voice like that of a horn . . . and say: Behold the enemy Nebuchadnezzar will go in haste to the house of the Lord as an eagle goes swiftly."

3. I.E. sanctions Yefet's explanation since there follows in the text the words "because they have transgressed My covenant." This passage indicates that the aforementioned נשר (= "eagle" or "vulture") represents the enemy (viz., Assyria) who is about to descend upon the house of God because of the transgression of the covenant. For a similar explanation, cf. Ibn Janah, *Hariqmah*, p. 270; Rashi and Qimhi, ad loc. Cf. also Targum and Qara. It should be noted, however, that according to Yefet's explanation, "the house of the Lord" signifies the land of Israel (as in 9:15, "from My house") rather than a house of worship as interpreted in the Targum and by I.E.

4. I.E. evidently interprets v. 2 by referring the word "Israel," which appears at the end of the verse, to the first clause. Thus, "to Me [Israel] shall cry: 'My God, we know Thee.'" For a similar view, cf. Ibn Janah, *Dictionary*, p. 359; Rashi and Qimhi, ad loc. So also A.V.: "Israel shall cry unto me, My God, we know Thee." For I.E.'s method of reversing biblical passages, cf. above, comm. on 7:4, note 7.

5. I.e., "to Me [the house of Israel] shall cry: 'My God, we Israel know Thee.'" This interpretation ("my God, we Israel know Thee") is evidently followed by the transla-

tion given in J.P.S. and R.S.V. Cf. also Cheyne, p. 87, footnote, and Harper, p. 309. Filwarg (p. 3b) suggests that by adding *benēy* (= the children of) or *bēyt* (= the house of) I.E. aims to explain the discord between the plural ("they shall cry") and the singular (Israel). However, comp. 9:7 where "Israel" is preceded by the verb *yēde'ū* (= they shall know). Comp. also I Kings 12:19 and II Kings 3:24. These references seem to indicate that "Israel" as a collective noun may be conjoined with either a singular or plural verb.

6. Comp. Ps. 73:1: "Surely God is good to Israel." Cf. Qara, Qimhi and *Commentary of Rabbi Isaiah da Trani the First on Prophets and Hagiographa*, ed. by Abraham Joseph Wertheimer (Jerusalem, 1965), ad loc. For the attribute of "good" with respect to God, cf. *Pesikta Rabbati*, p. 143b, where our passage is cited.

7. The last word of our verse is יִרְדְּפוֹ (= he shall pursue him, viz., the enemy shall pursue Israel) with the unusual pronominal ending וֹ- instead of הוּ- (i.e., יִרְדְּפֵהוּ = he shall pursue him, as in Jud. 9:40). In quoting the passage from Jeremiah, I.E. adduces a similar verb with the same pronominal suffix. For a similar comment, cf. comm. on Num. 23:13, *Ṣaḥot*, pp. 23a, 47a, and Ibn Janah, *Hariqmah*, p. 90. In his commentary on Ex. 1:9, I.E. acknowledges that such endings are indeed few.

8. So R.S.V. ("but not through me"); J.P.S. renders it as "but not from Me."

9. According to Qimhi and Abravanel, ad loc., the people of Northern Israel never consulted the prophet with regard to the choice of their king Jeroboam I. Cf. also Eliezer of Beaugency, ad loc.: "The people were never aware of the divine sanction [to the prophet Ahiyyah (I Kings 11:31)]. Thus, by choosing Jeroboam as their king without consultation, they rejected the Kingdom of David which I have chosen through the prophets."

10. I.E. maintains that the Hiphil form for the word *hēsīrū* is derived from the two consonantal radicals *sin* and *resh* as, e.g., *hēqīmū* (= they established) is derived from *quf* and *mem*. For I.E.'s opinion on verbs having a *waw* or a *yod* as their second radical, cf. above, comm. on 7:5, note 10.

11. The phrase "they have made princes and I knew it not" is a repetition of the idea contained in the former line. I.e., "they have set up kings" without consulting Me and appointed princes without My approval. For a similar view with regard to the word *hēsīrū*, cf. Menahem, *Mahberet*, p. 181; Ibn Janah, *Dictionary*, p. 531; and Isaiah da Trani, op. cit., p. 74.

12. *Besūrī* is also written with a *sin*, but is translated "when I turn away" as if the word were written with a *sameḵ*. Similarly, according to Yefet, the *sin* in *hēsīrū* is also substituted for a *sameḵ* and the word is to be translated "they removed." See following note.

13. For the change in the word *hēsīrū* from a *sin* to a *sameḵ*, cf. comm. on Lam. 3:8. Cf. also Rashi (second interpretation), Qara, ad loc., and Joseph Qimhi, *Sepher Zikkārōn*, ed. by Wilhelm Bacher (Berlin, 1888), p. 71. However, the comment quoted

here by I.E. in the name of Yefet is not found in his published commentary on Hosea. Cf. above, comm. on 4:3, note 8.

14. R.S.V. renders the phrase thus: "With their silver and gold they made idols for their own destruction." However, according to I.E., the implied subject is the silver and gold which had been made into idols; cf. Cheyne, p. 88. For a similar interpretation, cf. *Bereshit Rabbah*, 28:7; Rashi; Qara; and Eliezer of Beaugency, ad loc. According to this explanation, למען may be treated here as conveying a result (i.e., with the result that the silver and gold will be cut off), rather than in its usual sense of purpose. For a similar interpretation of the term למען, cf. Nachmanides on Deut. 29:18, where our passage is cited.

15. According to I.E., *zānaḥ* (= he spurned) is here a transitive verb. Cf. Qimhi, ad loc. Hence, the first two words of v. 5 (viz., *zānaḥ 'eglēḵ*) would have been sufficient to imply "your calf has spurned you." Therefore, the additional name "Samaria" has to be taken as repetition in sense of the implied object, i.e., "you the calf has spurned, you Samaria." This interpretation is close to the rendering given in A.V.: "Thy calf, O Samaria, hath cast thee off." For other translations of the phrases, cf. Harper, p. 315.

16. For a similar interpretation, cf. Isaiah da Trani, op. cit., p. 74. It is not clear, however, whether I.E. means to explain the prophet's condemnation by saying that the calf has rejected the people and can no longer protect them, or else that the calf has been the cause of the people's rejection from their land. Cf. below, note 21.

17. I.e., against the golden calf and against the people of Samaria who worship it. For "the calf," in singular, cf. above, comm. on 6:10, note 28.

18. I.e., how long will it take until they purge themselves of their tarnished life of idolatry.

19. The Hebrew reading of the last line in the text of I.E. is dubious, and the slight changes in our mss. make it no more intelligible. Consequently, it becomes doubtful what I.E. means by his last remark, particularly by his lack of explanation of the cause of the people's inability to attain innocence. Cf. Sharim, p. 29a, where the intention of I.E.'s remark is treated as uncertain.

20. The opening clause of the verse reads literally: "For out of Israel and [out of] it the craftsman made it," which means, according to I.E., that the craftsman was instigated to make the golden calf by the people as well as the king whom they set on the throne. Cf. comm. on v. 4. According to Qimhi, ad loc., the first two words in v. 6 are to be taken separately, viz., "for from Israel [is the calf]," and the phrase means that Israel did not learn to make a golden calf from the other nations, but rather that the cult originated in the molten calf Israel worshiped in the desert. Thus, according to Qimhi, the prophet continues by saying: "And it (the calf)–a craftsman made it"; he thus joins the third word (והוא = and it) with the following phrase ("a craftsman made it"). However, Rashi (ad loc.) interprets the first three words of the verse by dropping

the conjunction *waw*: "For it is out of Israel," i.e., the calf was made out of Israel's own silver and gold. So also A.V.": "For from Israel *was* it also." According to I.E., the *waw* retains its original meaning, i.e., for due to the incentive of Israel as well as of his (viz., the king's), the calf of Samaria was made. For a similar interpretation, cf. Ibn Janah, *Hariqmah*, p. 266, and Schroeter, *Archiv*, II, 169, note 1.

21. I.e., the term *she<u>b</u>ā<u>b</u>im*, so spelled (in the phrase "*she<u>b</u>ā<u>b</u>im* shall the calf of Samaria be"), is a hapaxlegomenon, but equivalent in sense to the almost identical *she<u>b</u>ī<u>b</u>im*, for which comp. Job 18:5 (*she<u>b</u>ī<u>b</u>*) and Dan. 7:9 (*she<u>b</u>ī<u>b</u>in*). This is the view of Dunash (*Teshū<u>b</u>ōt*, p. 36), which is shared by Qara (ad loc.) and Joseph Qimhi (*Sepher Hagālūy*, p. 26), as opposed to the Targum ("splinters," "shivers") and followed by Rashi and others. According to this explanation, the prophet wished to indicate that not only would the calf be unable to protect its worshipers, but it would be destroyed by flames together with them. Cf. above, note 16.

22. The comment attributed here to Yefet is not found in his commentary on Hosea. Cf. above, comm. on 4:3, note 8. However, Jacob Tam (*Teshū<u>b</u>ōt*, p. 36) has an explanation of this term and the surrounding phrase that is closely similar to the one attributed by I.E. to Yefet. Cf. also Eliezer of Beaugency, ad loc.: "The calf of Samaria represented for them an adulterous and rebellious heart."

23. I.e., the Hebrew term for whirlwind is סופה and for terror, אימה. Consequently, the *taw* is unessential in either noun. For the poetical ending תָה-, cf. the list in Gesenius-Kautzsch, par. 90 g.

24. J.P.S. translates the second part of the verse thus: "It hath no stalk, the bud that shall yield no meal; if so be it yield, strrangers shall swallow it up." I.E. suggests that with the last clause, the verse means that even if Ephraim succeeds in producing a harvest, it will be seized by the enemy. Cf. comm. on Gen. 24:5 where our passage is cited.

25. Eliezer of Beaugency, ad loc., ascribes the figure of the lonely wild ass to Assyria. That is to say, Assyria acted like a wild ass in hiding while preparing to ambush the people of Northern Israel. However, I.E. holds that the application is more appropriate to Israel, who was confused like a wild ass and sought the alliance of Assyria in a mood of dissension. I.e., "they are going up to Assyria like a wild ass," each one by himself.

26. Ibn Janah in his *Dictionary*, p. 545, lists *hitnū* under *taw, nun* and *hē* (*tnh*, a verb meaning "to stipulate"). Cf. above, comm. on 2:14, notes 40-41. This view is evidently shared by Qara and Qimhi, ad loc. However, I.E. maintains that *hitnū* and *etnan* are both derived from *ntn*, a verb meaning "to give." Thus Ephraim "gave gifts of friendship to the princes of the nations." Comp. above, 7:9: "Strangers have devoured his strength," a phrase that, according to I.E., describes the tribute the people of Northern Israel paid to Assyria and Egypt. However, J.P.S. translates *hitnū 'ahā<u>b</u>im* as "hath hired lovers."

27. I.E. explains the word *'aqabbṣēm* (= I will gather them) in a punitive sense. Comp.: "Egypt shall gather them" (9:6), which means there, according to I.E., those who left Israel for fear of violence will die in Egypt.

28. The continuation of the verse is *wayāḥēllū me'āṭ*, which J.P.S. translates as "they begin to be minished," whereas I.E. interprets the phrase: "Then they shall begin . . . a little."

It should be noted that by translating מלך שרים (lit., "king princes") as "king of princes," A.V. construes these two words as a construct phrase, which does not require the assumption that a *waw* is missing; cf. Jacob b. Reuben: "'The king of princes,' this is the king of Egypt." However, a (hypothetically) missing *waw* (= and) in front of the word *sārim* (= princes) evidently did not prevent I.E., Qara and Qimhi from interpreting it as "and princes." For I.E.'s opinion on the missing conjunction *waw* in a different context, cf. above, comm. on 6:3. It should also be noted that in Bab. Talmud, *Baba Batra*, 8a, ושרים (= and princes) with a conjunctive *waw* is quoted but later corrected by Solomon Norzi in *Minḥat Shay* (printed in the traditional Bible *Miqraot Gedolot*), ad loc., to שרים.

29. I.E. is of the opinion that the word *wayāḥēllū* (in the last clause of our verse) as well as the word *taḥēlū* (Ez. 9:6), both in the Hiphil form, can be derived only from the radicals *ḥet*, *lamed* and *lamed*, a verb meaning "to begin." This view is supported by the existence, in the Masoretic text, of a *Dagesh* in the extant *lamed*, which *Dagesh*, according to the grammatical principle, makes up for the one that is missing. For a similar remark, cf. Qimhi, ad loc.

30 The comment is designed to explain the redundancy in v. 11, viz., "Ephraim hath made many (J.P.S., "multiplied") altars to sin, altars have been unto him to sin." I.E. evidently explains v. 11 as follows: "Ephraim has made many (new) altars to sin [even though] he already had many altars to sin." For a similar explanation, cf. Yefet, p. 129; Qimhi and Abravanel, ad loc.

31 J.P.S. translates the first clause of the verse as "I write for him so many things of My Law." However, A.V. renders it as "I have written to him great things of my law." Similarly, I.E. interprets *'ekṯoḇ* as indicating the past tense, i.e, the laws of God were always written and available for Ephraim. Thus v. 12 is here linked with the preceding verse as well as with the following one, i.e., they have built additional altars to offer there pagan sacrifices (v. 11); even though there were always before them written laws and prohibitions which they ignored (v. 12). They rather sacrifice flesh and eat it, something the Lord does not accept (v. 13). For a similar remark, cf. Rashi, ad loc.

32 I.e., they offer charred (roasted) sacrifices. [they offer] meat and eat it, meaning that their main purpose in offering sacrifices is to eat the meat. This explanation is similar to the one given by Ibn Janah, *Dictionary*, p. 125, who also compares *haḇhāḇay* with the Arabic هبهبي (i.e., the cook who roasts the bread).

33 The phrase *haḇ haḇ* (= give, give) thus signifies a process in which people kept

on calling repeatedly "give us more sacrifices," but only for the purpose of eating more meat. Cf. Solomon Parchon, *Mahberet He'āruk̲* ed. by S. G. Stern (Pressburg, 1854), sec.2, p. 17a. s.v. הבהב, where De Rossi's explanation of our phrase is quoted as "Sacrificia Continua."

34 Cf. Yefet, p. 131, lines 203 and Schroeter. *Archiv*, II, p. 171. It is not clear whether I.E., by using the term *nōsāf*, means (1) that the *yod* is not essential and could be dropped completely (viz., הבהב instead of הבהבי) or (2) that the *yod* is not indicative of the possessive plural which it generally designates, but rather it takes the place of the *hē* (e.g. שדי instead of שדה). For his use of the term *nōsāf* in the second sense, cf. *Moznayim*, p. 8a: ויש אלף נוסף שהוא במקום הא (= there is an additional *aleph* which takes the place of a *hē*). It should be noted that in addition to *sāday*, Yefet (ibid.) as well as I.E. (in comm. on Ps. 8:8, and *Ṣaḥot*, p. 26a) also list *yāday* (lit., my hands," Ez. 13:18) as a strange form for *yādayim* (= hands). Schroeter (ibid.) evidently failed to identify the biblical source for the word *yāday*, and thus remarks (note 6) erronenously: "ידי is wohl ein Fehler. Solte er ידי Esra 10:43 Keri meinen?"

35. R.S.V. renders the closing passage of our verse thus: "Now he will remember their iniquity, and punish their sins; they shall return to Egypt." However, according to I.E., the last line in the verse is to be taken as a reason for their punishment. Hence, "He will remember their iniquity and punish their sins, [for] they returned to Egypt"; cf. comm. on 7:11, 16. Cf. also Qimhi, ad loc.: "Soon, He will remember their sin, when they will return to Egypt. . . thereby transgressing My words. Then shall I remember their sins, etc."

36. Lit., "to fortify (themselves) in them," i.e., against the enemy. See following note.

37. Cf. Qimhi, ad loc.: "I.e., they have forgotten God their protector and secured themselves in their palaces and strongholds but to no avail; for I will send 'a fire against his cities,' that is to say, the enemy will assail them with My consent in order to burn down his cities and castles with fire." By adding the remark "of each city," I.E. aims to conjoin the singular feminine suffix in the final word of the verse (*'armenōtehā*) with the preceding city. For a similar remark cf. above, comm. on 4:11 et passim.

Chapter IX

(1-2) **[Rejoice] not [O, Israel]:** That is to say, it is [only] proper for all [other] nations to rejoice when gladness befalls them; for there is none among them who commits harlotry while serving his god as you have done.[1] You have loved to give gifts to the Baalim in place of your God's tithe[2] – this is [your] harlotry. Therefore, *the threshing-floor and the wine press* [*shall not feed them*], for strangers will seize them.

(2) **[And the new wine] shall fail them**, as if [to say that] it did not recognize them.[3]

(3) **They shall not dwell [in the Lord's land] . . . and they shall eat unclean food in Assyria:** For in the same [manner] they used to eat [their food] *in the Lord's land,* insofar as they withheld the hallowed contributions from Him, rather than giving gifts [to the Baalim].[4]

(4) **They shall not [pour out wine-offerings**, etc.]: **Those who remain [in the land shall no more pour out wine-offerings to God]; and if [they were to have [some offerings]** *they shall not be pleasing to Him.*[5] **[Their sacrifices shall be unto them] as the bread of the mourners** [*keleḥem 'ōnim*]: Compare "I have not eaten thereof in my mourning" [*be'ōnī* (Deut. 26:14)]. This [word (viz., *'ōn* = mourning)] is a noun and its plural is *'ōnim.*[6]

(5) **What [will ye do . . . in the day of the] feast of the Lord:** [This verse is] in apposition to "their sacrifices" [v. 4].[7]

(6) **For, behold they are gone [away from destruction** (*mīshōd*), **Egypt shall gather them up, Memphis shall bury them**: Out of fear of destruction that may befall them, some of them will die in Egypt, and [others] on the roads. Therefore, [the prophet continues to] say: *Their precious treasures of silver* [*nettles shall possess them*] etc., i.e., they will [ultimately] be destroyed.[9]

(7) **The days of recompense have come:** That [is to say], God will punish you. For you have been saying about *the prophet* of God that he is *a fool* and that *a man* [truly] inspired [by God] is *mad.*[10] [In the

final phrase, the last word,] *masṭēmāh,* [means "enmity," which] exists in everyone's heart.[11]

(8) **[Ephraim is a] seer** [*ṣōfeh*]: I.e., [Ephraim] said that the prophet of God is a fool [v. 7], and has set himself up as a seer, claiming to be like a prophet who foresees what may happen. This false prophet is as a *fowler's snare.* The meaning of [the following phrase] *enmity in the house of his god* [can be explained] by way of a previous [phrase], "therefore shall thou stumble and the prophet also shall stumble" [4:5].[12]

(9) **They have deepened** to do evil,[13] **as in the days of Gibeah,** when the Benjamites rebelled.[14]

(10) **Like grapes [in the wilderness I found Israel]:**[15] Compare "He found him in a desert land" [Deut. 32:10].[16] The meaning of the phrase *like grapes in the wilderness* is that there are no inhabitants there, so that anyone who finds them [viz., grapes] is pleased thereby.[17] The same [idea is expressed in the phrase] *like the first fruit on the fig tree.*[18] [However], My pleasure was meager, it did not last, because they bowed to Baalpeor [Num. 25:2-3] and separated themselves from Me *unto boshet.*[19] [For the name *boshet,*] compare "the boshet hath devoured the labor [of our fathers]" (Jer. 3:24), where [boshet] is the name of an idol.[20] **They became detestable [like the thing they loved]**: I.e., they became defiled because of [their] love [for] the Midianite women.[21]

(11) **Ephraim, [their glory shall fly away like a bird]:** The *bird* signifies swiftness, meaning they will not rejoice.[22] Similarly, they will have no honor from the birth [of children], neither *from the womb* [i.e., from pregnancy], viz., when the womb of a pregnant woman will be seen swelling, [nor] *from conception,* i.e., when the woman ceases to menstruate. That is to say, conception will diminish and it will not [even] reach [the stage] of being noticed; while, if it does reach [that stage], the child will die before its birth.[23] [The word *lēdāh* (= birth)] is a noun, as *dē'āh* [= knowledge].[24] Hence, the subsequent verse [states that] if they shall [indeed] give birth and "bring up their children I will bereave them," so that they will not reach manhood.[25]

(12) **When I depart** [*besūrī*] **from them:** The *sin* [in the word *besūrī*] is in place of a samek̲.[26]

(13) **Ephraim** will be like Tyre, which was [once] *planted in a pleasant place,* but then waters covered her. Similarly, I [Hosea] have seen by way of prophecy that the father will hand over his children to the slayer.[27]

(14) **Give them [a miscarrying womb and dry breasts]:** The prophet here prays [to God]: Since You have decreed upon them that each one shall hand over his children to the slayer (v. 13), perhaps they should rather die young so that their anguish shall not be great; and this is why [the prophet continues]: *Give them a miscarrying womb,* i.e., so that [the unborn] shall die in the womb and the [born] children shall die from lack of milk [in the mother's dry breasts].[28] For *ṣōmqim* [= dry breasts],[29] compare *ṣīmūqim* [II Sam. 16:1], i.e., dry [raisins].

(15) **All [their wickedness is in Gilgal]:** I.e., in Gilgal, which is the place where [the people] remained after crossing the Jordan.[30] [Thus] it would have been fitting for them to remember My kindness [during the time] their forefathers were there, namely, that I brought them into My land–but now *I will drive them out of My house.*[31]

(16) **[Ephraim] is smitten, [their root is dried up]:** The sense [of the passage] is that the tree *is smitten.*[32] [This phrase] is a metaphor for the fathers and for the children.[33].

(17) **[My God] will cast them away:** The prophet said: "[My] God has told me that he is no longer their God."[34]

Notes

1 I.e., rejoice not, O, Israel as other nations do when gladness comes to them; for unlike them you have not been loyal to your God. Comp. Jer.2:11: "Hath a nation changed its gods which yet are no gods? But my people hath changed its glory for that which doth not profit."

2 I.e., you have preferred to present gifts to the Baalim rather than to bring tithes to the house of God. Comp. Deut. 14:22-23.

3 I.e., the wine "which cheereth God and man" (Jud. 9:13) shall fail to exhilarate them; as if the wine were alienating itself from those who come to drink it. I.E.'s comment was prompted by the verb *kḥsh,* which literally means "to deny" rather than "to fail." It should be noted that I.E. reads יכחש בם (= shall fail them, instead of יכחש בה = shall fail her), in consonance with the Targum and the suggested reading in the Rabbinic Bible.

4 Cf. above, comm. on v.1: "You have loved to give gifts to the Baalim in place of your God's tithe."

5 Harper (p. 328) and Wynkoop (ad loc.) interpret v. 4 as a continuing thought from v 3, i.e., after the people will be exiled to Egypt and Assyria (v. 3) they will be unable to pour out their wine-offerings to God (v. 4). However, I.E. implies that v. 4 is to be

taken as a threat to those who remain in the land after the rest of the people are exiled. Those are the people who will no longer be able to fulfill their ritual demands; but even if they were able to do so, their offerings would not be accepted by God. For the wine that accompanied the burnt offering and the peace-offering, comp. Num. 15:5.

6 This remark is evidently directed against those who take אונים to be the plural of אָוֶן (= sin); cf. al-Qumisi, p. 15; Jacob Mann, "Early Karaite Bible Commentaries," *JQR* (N.S.), XII, 483, note 8; and Poznanski's note (47) to Ibn Bal'am's commentary, ibid., XV, 20. However, I.E. maintains that the word is a noun that signifies mourning (or mourners). Cf. also comm. on Gen. 35:18 and Deut. 26:14 where our passage is communicated. For "the bread of the mourners," comp. Jer. 16:7.

7 Lit., "your sacrifices." The translation follows here the emendation suggested by Filwarg (p. 4a) which makes the reading more intelligible. This rhetorical question is thus addressed to the Israelites who remained in the land after the exile, i.e., why do you need to make sacrifices on the day of your feast if they are no longer accepted by God.

8 I.E. apparently construes Egypt and *mōf* (= Memphis) as the goal of the exiles, on the way to which they will die.

9 Lit., "and behold they go toward destruction," i.e., they want to escape destruction, but in so doing run toward destruction. According to I.E., the prophet portrays the people of Northern Israel as seeking to escape to Egypt because they feared their oncoming destruction by the Assyrians. As a result of this escape some of them would die either in Egypt or on their way. Moreover, I.E. apparently interprets the word *shōd* (= destruction) in the sense of the people being despoiled by the enemy of their belongings. Hence, by using the phrase מחמד לכספם the prophet meant to indicate, according to him, that by putting their trust in Egypt, "their precious treasures of silver" (viz., their belongings) would not be saved, but would be ruined ("nettles shall possess them, thorns shall be in their tents"). For a similar interpretation, cf. Eliezer of Beaugency, ad loc. and Wynkoop, p. 19b.

10 So also Jacob b. Reuben and Qara, ad loc. The full passage reads: "The prophet is a fool, the man of the spirit is mad."

11 I.e., the people called their true prophets "fools" or "madmen," because of their great iniquity and out of the contempt they had in their hearts for the prophets. I.E.'s remark is evidently designed to reject the explanation given by Rashi whereby the "enmity" is ascribed to God.

12 In his commentary on 4:5, I.E. interprets "the prophet" to be a false prophet who will stumble together with the High Priest. I.E. does not specifically explain the meaning or function of the term "enmity" (*masṭēmāh*) repeated here in verse 8. Perhaps he meant to imply that the enmity mentioned above (v. 7) against the true prophet will ultimately result in Ephraim's hatred against their false prophet who speaks to them "in the house of his (own) god." Cf. Qimhi, ad loc.

13 A.V., J.P.S., and R.S.V. all translate the first two words in v. 9 as a syntactic unit:

"They have deeply corrupted themselves," adding the direct object ("themselves") to the verb *shiḥētū* (= they have corrupted). However, by adding the remark "to do evil" to the first word of the verse, I.E. explains the Hiphil form of the verb *he'emīqū* as not having an object. Hence, "they have deepened to do evil," i.e., they have done profound evil. For an earlier remark on the same verb in Hiphil, cf. above, comm. on 5:2 et passim.

14 The "days of Gibeah" are cited again by Hosea in 10:9 and are similarly interpreted by I.E. (cf. Qimhi, ad loc.) as the period of warfare between the Benjamites who lived in Gibeah and the rest of the tribes; comp. Jud. chaps. 19-20. However, according to Rashi, ad loc., the name Gibeah may here refer to the institution of the monarchy under Saul, when the people demonstrated their faithlessness in God. Comp. I Sam. 8:7.

15 All through v. 10, we follow the translation given in R.S.V.

16 I.e., God found His people in the desert.

17 I.e., as one who unexpectedly finds grapes in the desert and is pleased with them, so has God greeted the people in the desert with pleasure.

18 The first ripe fig was considered a delicacy "which when one looketh upon it . . . he eateth it up" (Is. 28:4).

19 A.V. renders it as "unto that shame," and J.P. S., "unto the shameful thing."

20 According to Qimhi, ad loc., the idol is called boshet (viz., "embarrassment") because those who worship it will be embarrassed.

21 I.e., by virtue of the close relationship in which they engaged with the Midianite women they became eventually defiled themselves. Comp. Num. 25:16-18. This explanation is similar to that given by Rashi, but is in marked contrast with the one quoted by Qimhi in the name of his father, who interpreted the entire last phrase as meaning "they became detestable (in my eyes), to the same extent that I formerly loved them."

22 I.e., the glory shall depart from Ephraim as swiftly as a bird in flight. The departure of glory signifies their future inability to rejoice. Comp. v. 1: "Rejoice not, O Israel."

23 According to I.E., the phrase moves from end to beginning rather than from beginning to end, i.e., women will not conceive; if they do, their pregnancy will not be noticeable, for the fetus will never develop to reach a lasting stage; if it should survive the embryonic period, the child will die before the time of its natural birth arrives.

24 The Hebrew term *lēdāh* is also referred to by some grammarians as the infinitive (to give birth), e.g., Qimhi, quoting the Targum, on II Kings 19:3. The same holds true for the term *dē'āh-*, cf. ibid., *Dictionary*, s.v., ידע and S. Poznanski, *Mose B. Samuel Hakkohen Ibn Chiquitilla*, (Leipzig, 1895), pp. 127–128. I.E. maintains that all three words in the second clause of v. 11 are nouns, including *lēdāh* (= birth).

25 After having established that the climax in v. 11 is the abortive birth, I.E. attempts further to conjoin the two verses (11-12) by adding that in v. 12 the prophet continues to say that even if the children will survive birth and infancy they will not live to reach the age of manhood.

26 The radicals of the Hebrew verb "to depart" are *swr*, spelled usually with a *samek̲*. Hence, the *sin* in the word *besūrī* is in place of the *samek̲*. Cf. above, comm. on 8:4 (where a similar remark is ascribed to Yefet) and *Ṣaḥot*, p. 24a; cf. also comm. on Is. 19:10 and Qimhi's interpretation of vs. 11-12, which is almost identical with that given here by I.E.

27 I.e., Hosea has seen prophetically that Ephraim's end will be as tragic as that of Tyre's. I.E. evidently had in mind Tyre's end as described in Ez. 26:19: "When I shall make thee a desolate city, . . when I shall bring up the deep upon thee, and the great waters shall cover thee."

28 Rashi, I.E., Qara, Qimhi, and Eliezer of Beaugency all agree that v. 14 is to be considered as a plea in which the prophet asks for mercy for his people. Cf. also *Pesiqta Rabbati*, p. 183. However, the Targum renders: "Give them retribution for their deeds," as if the prophet in v. 14 calls for judgment upon his people. Cf. also Harper, p. 339: "To understand that this ejaculation is born of a sympathy . . . is farfetched."

29 I.e., give them "dry breasts" so that the sucklings will have no milk to drink. Consequently, they will die in infancy.

30 Comp. Josh. 4:19: "And the people came up out of the Jordan, . . and encamped in Gilgal on the east border of Jericho."

31 I.E. maintains that the prophet deliberately mentioned Gilgal here in order to make the people aware that by making the place a center for Baal worship (comp. above 4:15) they failed to remember the kindness God had bestowed upon their forefathers when they arrived there after crossing the Jordan. This is, according to him, the meaning of the phrase "all their wickedness is in Gilgal, etc.," for which reason "I will drive them out of My house" (i.e., out of the land of Israel, in punishment). For the phrase "the house of God" as a figure for the land of Israel, cf. Yefet's comment as quoted by I.E. in comm, on 8:1.

32 The Targum, ad loc., explains: "The house of Israel (viz., Ephraim) is comparable to a palm tree with roots beneath, whose branches became dry from above." The phrase "Ephraim is smitten, etc.," thus means Ephraim is like a withered tree unable to bear fruit.

33 I.e., the first clause of the verse implies that Ephraim will be barren with no hope of having children.

34 According to Abravanel, ad loc., v. 17 is taken as a plea to God for the rejection of the people by making them "wanderers among the nations" in exile instead of slaying "the beloved fruit in their womb" (v. 16). However, I.E. interprets the words of the prophet as a prediction that God will spurn the people by disavowing them.

Chapter X

(1) **[Israel is] an empty vine** [*gefen bōqēq*]: Empty [in the sense] it has no strength to produce fruit, and [so] it has no fruit.[1] The phrase *perī yeshawweh lō* means he [viz., Israel] thinks that he will be fruitful;[3] or else [the meaning of the phrase is that] his fruit will be as a vine that is empty.[4] For when I increased his fruit *he increased the altars.*[5]

(2) **[Their heart] is divided**: For they have no one god.[6] **Now they shall be desolated**, [*(ye'shāmū),* **it will break down** (*ya'arōf*) **their altars**]: *Ye'shāmū* is derived from *shemāmāh* [=desolation]; compare "Samaria shall become desolate" [*te'sham* (14:1)], which is similar in meaning to the phrase "and that land be not desolate" [*tēshām* (Gen.4:19)]. It is their divided heart that will cause their altars to break down whose number they have multiplied.[8] [For the word *ya'arōf* (= will break down)] compare *wa'araftō* [= thou shall break its neck (Ex. 13:13)], implying destruction.[9]

(3) **For** when their hearts became divided, they desired that *no king* should rule over them, nor did they fear God.[10] Consequently, they had no fear [at all] and each one could do as he pleased.[11]

(4) **They have spoken [words] swearing falsely . . . [thus justice springs up like bitter weeds]**:[12] [*'Ālot* (= swearing)] is of a rare grammatical formation, as if the word were a combination of the infinitive in the construct and in the absolute state.[13] Or else it is so vocalized due to the guttural letter [*aleph*].[14] For the figure of *justice* being sweet and turning bitter [*kārō'sh*], compare "ye who turn justice to wormwood" [Am.5:7]. That is to say, their justice, which is not honest, will grow *like bitter weeds*[15] *in the furrows of* [*the field (talmēy sādāy)*]. [For the word *talmēy* (= furrows of)] compare "watering her furrows [*telāmehā*] abundantly" [Ps. 65:11]. The word *sādāy* [= field] is equivalent to *sādeh*; [the phrase] "let the field [viz., *sādāy*] exult" [Ps. 96:12] attests [this interpretation].[16]

(5) **For the calves [of Beth-aven]**: These are the golden calves that

were [erected] in Bethel.[17] [The phrase] *yāgūrū* [*shekan shōmrōn* means] those who dwell in Samaria shall fear.[18] **[For its people] shall mourn over it**: I.e., [they will mourn] over each calf in Bethel when it will be destroyed.[19] **And the priests thereof**, who **rejoice** [*yāgîlū*][20] **over it** [i.e., over the idol] today, will [instead] mourn in the future [*over its glory*] *that* [*has departed from it*]. The idea is [here] repeated.[21]

(6) **[It] also**: Viz., the calf of Samaria, *shall be carried unto Assyria*, for it is gold.[21] **[Ephraim shall receive shame** (*boshnāh*)]: The *nun* in *boshnāh* is not essential. Compare *shib'anāh bānim* [= seven sons (Job. 42:13)].[23]

(7) **[Samaria] is cut off**: The force of the word *nidmeh* [= is cut off] is carried over to the second noun, i.e., Samaria is cut off and *her king* is cut off[24] *as a chip* [(*keqeṣef*) *upon the water*]. Compare "[he hath laid my vine to waste,] and my fig tree to chips" [Joel 1:7].[25]

(8) **[The high places of Aven] shall be destroyed**: I.e., the high places of Baal [worship will be destroyed], when the calfs will be removed.[26] **And they shall say [to the mountains]**: R. Moses Hakkohen said that the phrase *and they shall say* etc. is a figurative expression, because [it follows] the [aforementioned] *altars*. Compare "for it [viz., the stone] hath heard" [Josh. 24:27]. That is to say, they [viz., the altars] will not be seen again.[27] Yefet said the [meaning of the phrase is] that their worshipers will call out to [the mountains: *Cover us*, etc.], out of their distress.[28]

(9) [The phrase] *mîmēy* [*hagib'ah* means] more [than in the days of Gibeah]. Compare "I understand more than elders" [Ps. 119:100]; ["Thy commandments] *make* me wise, more [i.e., wiser] than mine enemies" [ibid., v. 98].[29] [The phrase] *there they stood* is to be explained with respect to the sins of his (viz., the prophet's) generation, as if they were standing [in Gibeah] together with the Benjamites who are [called here] *the children of iniquity*.[30] [The Hebrew word] *'alwāh* [= iniquity] is a transposition of *'awlāh*. Compare "and thou shalt be a horror" [*zā'wāh* (Deut. 28:25)], "it shall be sheer terror" [*zewā'āh* (Is. 28:19)].[31] [The prophet thus continues to say that] today they [viz., the people of the Northern Kingdom] are no longer afraid that war will overtake them as war [conducted by the other] tribes overtook the Benjamites.[32] [The distribution of the words in the second clause of] this verse is similar to [the one in the phrase "see, the smell of my son is] as the smell of a field [which the Lord hath blessed" (Gen. 27:27)], whose real meaning is "see, the smell of my son whom God hath blessed, is as the smell of the field."[33]

(10) **When it is my desire I will chastise them**: [The word *we'essārēm* (= and I will chastise them)] is derived from [the verb *ysr*, connoting] chastisement. However, the first radical [of the verb (viz., the *yod*)] is assimilated by intensification of the second radical of the verb [viz., the *samek̲*]. Compare "before I formed thee [*'eṣṣārk̲ā*] in the belly" [Jer. 1:5], "for I will pour [*'eṣṣāq*] water" [Is. 44:3][34]. [The meaning of the phrase] *and* [*nations*] *shall gather against them*, etc. is designed to explain how will I chastise them? – by means of [other] nations that will gather against them; and I will yoke them as one yokes oxen. **[When they have bound themselves] in their two furrows** [*lishtēy ōnōtām*]:[35] [For *ōnōtām* (= their furrows)] compare "within as it were half a furrow" [*ma'anāh* (I Sam. 14:14)], "they made long their furrows" [*ma'anitān* (Ps. 129:3)]. *Two* [*furrows*] is [a figure of speech] for Judah and Ephraim [v. 11].[36]

(11-12) **And Ephraim [is a well-trained heifer**: Meaning,] I trained him at the beginning[37] to bear the burden of My precepts. **And I have passed** the law **[on the good portion of her neck]**: I.e., on every plowman by virtue of having benefited her [viz., the heifer's] neck (?). [Furthermore], I have put Ephraim together with Judah [to the yoke of plowing[38] so that] all of *Jacob* [*shall harrow*] My field. This [viz., the field] is a figure [which is designed] to represent the law.[39] Similarly, I have instructed them:[40] *Sow* [*to yourselves according to righteousness*] *and reap* [*according to mercy*] as a consequence.[41] *Niru* [is the imperative of a verb which means] to remove the thorns, to clear the paths.[42] For at the *time* you *seek the Lord* to water the seeds, there will descend a latter rain and a righteous early rain [*yōreh ṣedeq*] unto you.[43] [For the meaning of the word *yōreh*] compare *yōreh ūmalqōsh* [= former rain and later rain, (Deut. 11:14)]. However, all [other] commentators say that the meaning [of the second clause] is: Seek [to understand] His law, and [then] He will come and teach you.[44]

(13) **You have plowed [wickedness,** etc.**]:** I.e., you have continued all this[45] insofar as you have not borne the yoke [of] My [precepts], but rather you trusted in *your mighty men*.

(14) Therefore, **[a tumult] shall arise . . . as Shalman spoiled [Beth-arbel]**: [The name Shalman] may [stand for] Shalmaneser.[46] **Beth-arbel** is the name of a place,[47] where *the mother was dashed in pieces with her children*.[48] [The explanation that *'arbēl*] is to be considered a derivation from *'ōrēb̲*[49] [= ambush] makes no sense.

(15) **So [hath] Bethel [done unto you]**: For there was placed the calf that was the cause of their greatest wickedness,[50] as most of the kings

of Israel had not turned away from Jeroboam's sins.[51] [By the word] *basḥahar* [(= at daybreak) the prophet] meant to say that they [viz., the people] would be spoiled at night, whereas at daybreak their king would be cut off.[52]

Notes

1 According to Rashi's first explanation, ad loc., the word *bōqēq* is taken to be a transitive verb, i.e., "Israel is like a vine that empties all of its good fruit." By adding the remark "empty [in the sense] that it has no strength to produce fruit," I.E. evidently holds that *bōqēq* remains here intransitive; cf. comm. on Nah. 2:3 where *bōqēq* is described as a verb that may be at times transitive and at times intransitive. However, in comm. on Is. 24:1 our passage is adduced as proof that *bōqēq* is transitive.

2 A.V. renders this phrase as "he bringeth forth fruit unto himself," and J.P.S. translates it as "which put forth fruit freely."

3 The remark "he thinks that he will be fruitful," indicates that I.E. takes the word *yeshawweh* in the sense of "putting forth." Comp. Ps. 16:8 *shīwwītī* (= I have put). I.E. thus interprets the first clause in v. 1 to mean that Israel is an empty vine that still hopes to put forth fruit for itself. A different explanation of I.E. is encouraged by Qimhi's remark that the phrase פרי ישוה לו means "how (איך) will he produce fruit." It lends itself to conjecture that the reading ואין פרי, which has here been translated "it has no fruit," should likewise be read ואיך פרי, meaning, with the following two words, how will he (Israel) think to produce fruit?.

4 So in mss. B. L . N. According to this reading, *yeshawwe* is taken here in its more general sense (to be equal), i.e., Israel's fruit will be equivalent to that of an empty vine.

5 I.e., the more prosperous they became, the more altars they erected for idol worship - and for this reason, according to I.E., Israel will become like "an empty vine."

6 R.S.V. renders the phrase as "their heart is false." Cheyne (p. 101) favors the rendering "their heart is slippery." However, I.E.'s comment lends itself to the translation given in A.V. and J.P.S.: "Their heart is divided." According to Abravanel, ad loc., I.E. does not mean to say that the prophet depicts here only the divided loyalty in their heart between God and Baal, but rather that their heart was divided even in their idol worship, "for not all of them had the same god" (viz., the same idol).

7 R.S.V. renders *ye'shāmū* as "they must bear their guilt," deriving the word from the root *'shm* (= to bear guilt). Cf. also Qara, ad loc. However, I.E.'s interpretation that *ye'shāmū* signifies desolation is closer to that given in the LXX: "Now shall they be utterly destroyed." For the root of this verb, according to I.E.'s explanation, cf. above,

comm. on 5:15, note 50.

8 This remark is designed to explain the Hebrew *hū'* (= "it" or "he") referring quite necessarily to the preceding "heart." Cf. Rashi, Qara and Qimhi, ad loc. By this explanation I.E. rejects the notion that the word *hū'* means "he," viz., the enemy, as suggested by Jacob b. Reuben, ad loc.

9 The verb *'rf* means to break off the neck of an animal and is used here metaphorically as a term for the destruction of the altars. Cf. Ibn Janah, *Hariqmah*, p. 330. Cf. also comm. on Is. 5:30, where our passage is cited.

10 Lit., "they did not want a king to be over them." J.P.S. translates the entire passage thus: "Surely they say: We have no king, for we feared not the Lord."

11 The remark on v. 3 is evidently designed to maintain that verse's connection with the preceding and the following verses. That is to say, subsequent to their divided heart (i.e., their internal squabbles mentioned in v. 2) they denounce the monarchy and abandon their faith in God (v. 3). Consequently, each one acted as he pleased, either by uttering empty words, by swearing falsely, or by making separate bargains and distorting justice (v. 4). The result was anarchy.

12 A.V. and J.P.S. translate the latter phrase as "thus judgment springeth up as hemlock."

13 The infinitive absolute is generally vocalized with a *qamaṣ* under the first letter of the verb. However, the ות ending in the word אלות indicates, according to I.E., that the infinitive is here in the construct state and should therefore be vocalized with a composite *sheva*, rather than with a *qamaṣ*. Cf. above, comm. on 4:2, note 3.

14 I.e., because the first letter of the verb is guttural (viz., *aleph*) and does not take a *sheva*, the *qamaṣ* has been retained. However, the grammatical formation of the word *'ālōt* remains rare, for the *aleph* should be vocalized with a composite *sheva* rather than with a *qamaṣ*. Cf. comm. on Ex. 14:11 and on Is. 47:10 where I.E. maintains that the *aleph* in the words ראני, להוציאנו have a *qamaṣ* instead of a *ṣere* because it is a guttural letter.

15 I.e., the bitterness of injustice takes the place of the sweetness of justice. Cf. also comm. on Am. 6:12: "For you have turned justice, that is sweet, to gall" (לרוש).

16 The *yod* of שָׂדָי, which is generally considered to be a possessive suffix, is here, according to I.E., a replacement for the interchangeable *hē*. For a similar comment, cf. comm. on 8:13 and on Ps. 80:14; cf. also comm. on Deut. 32:13 where he once again refers to *sāday* of Ps. 96:12. However, Qimhi, ad loc. and on 12:12, maintains that the *yod* in שדי indicates the plural, viz., fields.

17 On the view identifying Beth-aven with Bethel, cf. Targum, ad loc., and above, comm. on 4:15, note 48. Cf. also comm. on 6:10, note 28, with respect to calves (in plural) in Bethel.

18 I.e., the inhabitants of Samaria will be in fear when the idols will be destroyed or carried off by the enemy. Cf. Rashi, ad loc. It should be noted that the LXX takes

יגורו to mean "they shall dwell," a word derived from the root גור and meaning "to dwell." I.E. also maintains that יגורו is derived from the same root, but by adding the verb יפחדו he indicates that he construes the root here to signify "fear." Cf. *Ṣaḥot*, p. 54b. According to Qimhi, ad loc., the prophet here refers to Samaria because Samaria was the capital of the Northern Kingdom, which practiced idol worship.

19 The remark "[they will mourn] over each calf" is designed to reconcile the use of the preceding plural ending of the word לעגלות (= for the calves) with the singular pronominal ending of the preposition עליו (= over it). For a similar remark, cf. above, comm. on 4:11 et passim.

20 The verb *yāgīlū* here means, according to Ibn Janah (*Dictionary*, p. 88), "they will move under stress," and is a term which signifies that the priests will move about under the stress of sorrow. Similarly, R.S.V. renders *yāgīlū* as "shall wail." However, I.E. takes *yāgīlū* in its usual sense ("they will rejoice"), which agrees with the rendering given in A.V.: "For the people thereof shall mourn over it, and the priest thereof that rejoiced on it." For an interpretation similar to I.E.'s, cf. Menahem, *Mahberet*, p. 13, Rashi, Qara and Qimhi, ad loc.

21 According to I.E.'s explanation, the force of the preceding phrase "for its people shall mourn" is evidently carried over to the last line of the verse. Hence, the idea of their desperation is repeated, i.e., the people shall mourn over the destruction of the calf, and will also mourn over the glory that departed from it.

22 I.e., also the gold of the destroyed calf shall be carried unto Assyria.

23 I.e., the *nun* in *boshnāh* as well as in *shib̲'anāh* is not essential. By dropping the *nun* from *boshnāh*, I.E.'s interpretation evidently follows here that of Menahem in *Mahberet*, p. 49 (shame). However, cf. Ibn Janah, *Dictionary*, p. 60: *Hariqmah*, p. 92, where *bōshnāh* is identified with *bōshet* (Jer. 3:24). Cf. also comm. on 9:10, where *bōshet* is interpreted as "the name of an idol."

24 I.E. interprets the word *nidmeh* to mean "is cut off." Cf. above, comm. on 4:5, 6, notes 12, 14. However, Qara evidently follows here Menahem's interpretation (*Mahberet*, p. 65) by explaining that "Samaria and its king will become like foam that moves on the face of water." Thus *nidmeh* is taken to mean "being like." Cf. also above, comm. on 3:3 for I.E.'s method of interpreting elliptical passages by applying the force of one word a second time.

25 J.P.S. renders our phrase as "as a foam upon the water," thereby following the rendering of the Targum (cf. Marcus Jastrow, *Dictionary* [New York, 1967], p. 1503, s.v. רתחא). In his commentary on Joel 1:7, I.E. also indicates that the word *qeṣef* is taken to mean "a useless foam." However, R.S.V. (following the LXX) translates thus: "Like a chip on the face of the waters." Cf. Qimhi (ad loc.) and Cheyne (p. 103) where both interpretations are quoted. Cf. also Abe Lipshitz, "Pērush R. Abraham Ibn Ezra 'al Yō'ēl", *Jubilee Volume in Honor of Rabbi Joseph B. Soloveitchik* (Jerusalem, 1984), vol. 2, p. 1004, note 13.

26 I.E. evidently takes *'āwen* to be a synonym of Baal, rather than a name for Bethel (see Targum), i.e., "all high places of the Baalim will be destroyed when the calves will be removed."

27 R. Moses Ibn Chiquitilla interprets the figure as an expression of shame and embarrassment on the part of the altars, i.e., "and they (viz., the altars), shall say to the mountains: Cover us, etc." so that they may be hidden from view.

28 According to Yefet (p. 157, lines 15-17), the idol worshipers petitioned the mountains and the hills to bury them in order to put an end to the sufferings they endured.

29 Most translators render the first clause of the verse as "from the days of Gibeah, etc.," as if to say, Israel's sins go far back to the days of Gibeah. However, I.E. construes the *mem* of *mīmēy* as a comparative (= more than). Hence, the interpretation "*more than* in the days of Gibeah, you have sinned, O Israel," just as the initial *mems* in the words מזקנים (= more than elders [Ps. 110:10]) and מאויבי (= more than mine enemies [ibid., v. 98]) are interpreted. Cf. Yefet, p. 158, line 3, אכתר מן איאם אלגבעה אכטאת ישראל. For the meaning of "the days of Gibeah," cf. above, comm. on 9:9, note 14.

30 I.e., by the phrase "there they stood," the prophet describes the sinful attitudes of his generation, as if people stood together with the children of iniquity (viz., the Benjamites) in support of their unrighteousness. Comp. Jud. 19:22. This explanation involves the transfer of the last three words of the Hebrew text from the end of the verse to follow the phrase "there they stood," i.e., "there they stood (together) with the sons of iniquity." I.E. thus interprets v. 9 as follows: More than in the days of Gibeah you have sinned, O Israel; the people's present behavior is such as if they were joining in the unrighteousness of the sons of iniquity with a sense of confidence that a war like the one that took place in Gibeah will not overtake them. Cf. Qimhi, ad loc., where the last clause of the verse is also explained with respect to the people of the prophet's generation who "think in their heart that a war similar to the one that overtook the transgressors in Gibeah will not overtake them," but without transposing the last phrase of the verse. For I.E.'s method of explaining difficult passages in the Bible by rearranging the order of their words, cf. above, comm. on 7:4, note 7.

31 Rashi interprets the word עלוה as "conceited." However, I.E. is of the opinion that the Hebrew word זעוה ("horror" or "terror," with the *waw* following the *ayin*) has the same meaning as זועה (in which the *waw* precedes the *ayin*). Cf. comm. on Deut. 28:25; similarly, the word עלוה is to be taken as עולה (= iniquity), despite the fact that in the former the *waw* follows the *lamed* instead of preceding it. Cf. Hayyug, op. cit., p. 85, and Ibn Janah, *Hariqmah*, p. 352. It should be noted, however, that in his commentary on Is. (ibid.), I.E. rejects the idea that the words זעוה and זועה are both of the same meaning.

32 I.e., in their present conduct the people of the Northern Kingdom have displayed

an even higher degree of arrogance and shown an even greater sense of confidence than the Benjamites had. For the fate of the Benjamites in Gibeah, comp. Jud. 19:22-30.

33 This last remark is absent from I.E.'s commentary on Gen. 27:27. However, cf. Saadya Gaon (as quoted by Abraham Maimonides in his *Commentary on Genesis and Exodus*, pub. by Sulaiman David Sassoon [London, 1959], p. 76) and Nachmanides (ibid.) for a similar interpretation.

34 I.e., the word *'eṣṣārk̲ā* (lit., "I will form you") is derived from a verb consisting of the radicals *yod*, *ṣade*, and *resh*, meaning "to form," and the word *'eṣṣāq* (= I will pour) is derived from a verb consisting of *yod*, *ṣade*, and *qof*. However, in each case, the missing *yod* is assimilated to the second radical (a process indicated in the Masoretic text by a *Dagesh forte* in that radical). Similarly, the *yod*, which is the first radical of the verb meaning "to chastise," is also assimilated in the *Dagesh* of the second radical (viz., the *samek̲*).

35 The translation follows the first of several interpretations quoted by Harper, p. 353. I.e., just as oxen are yoked and bound by their master, so will God bind the people by subjecting them to the yoke of other nations, thereby chastising them. I.E. probably takes the word *be'osrām* to mean "when they are bound" or "when I bind them," a derivation from the verb *'sr*, meaning "to bind." This interpretation is similar to that given by Ibn Janah, *Dictionary*, p. 378, but different from Isaiah da Trani's interpretation (p. 77) in which the word *be'osrām* is derived from *ysr* (to chastise).

36 Cf. Ibn Janah (ibid.): "I interpret the phrase 'to two furrows' [to mean] to two plows (or 'two plowings'), for the furrows come as a result of plowing and is included in it. . . . [Reference is here made] only to their unanimity in two false ideas, i.e., the idea of Judah and the idea of Ephraim in regard to the disobedience of God." Cf. also Qimhi, ad loc.

37 I.e., when the people left Egypt; cf. below, comm. on 11:1.

38 I.E.'s comment on the phrase "and I have passed the law etc." is ambiguous and uncertain; e.g., his remark "the law on every plowman" hardly tells us how he would wish to explain the second clause of the verse *'ōhab̲tī lādush*. It is equally unclear how I.E. interprets the word *'arkib̲* (= I will put to yoke). Accordingly, the thought expressed in v. 11 may be as follows: At the beginning, when God yoked the people to the observance of His commandments, He did not burden Ephraim's neck alone, but rather He taught Ephraim together with Judah how to carry the burden of His precepts in order that all of Jacob (i.e., Ephraim and Judah) should be engaged in the performance of God's precepts. For a similar interpretation, cf. Jacob b. Reuben, ad loc. Comp. also below 12:3 where the name Jacob represents, according to I.E., Ephraim and Judah.

39 I.e., the phrase "Jacob shall harrow" means all of Jacob shall harrow God's field, which, according to I.E., is an implied figure of speech employed here to express Jacob's adherence to the commandments. The missing object ("My field") is evidently,

according to I.E., implicit in the verb ישדד (= shall harrow). Cf. above, comm. on 2:7, note 11. It should be added that according to Qimhi (*Dictionary*, s.v. שדד), שדה and ישדד both derive from the same root.

40 I.E. evidently takes v. 12 not as a plea by the prophet to the present generation but rather as a thought continuing from v. 11 ("Ephraim is a well-trained heifer"), with regard to the instructions that were given to the heifer (viz., Ephraim) in the early days.

41 According to I.E., the reaping is to be taken as a reward for the preceding "sowing with righteousness," i.e., sow, etc., and as a consequence "reap according to mercy." comp. "this do and live" (Ex. 42:18), meaning if you do this you shall live. The figure employed here by the prophet apparently relates to the promise: "If you will walk in My statutes and keep My commandments and do them, then I will give your rains in their seasons, and the land shall yield her produce and the trees of the fields shall give their fruit" (Lev. 26:3-4).

42 The phrase *nīrū lāḵem nir* is identical with that in Jer. 4:3, which is generally rendered as "break up for you a fallow ground" or "break up your fallow ground." However, I.E.'s interpretation here follows the explanation given by Ibn Janah in *Dictionary*, p. 294.

43 I.E. evidently interprets עד (lit., "until") in the sense of "then"; cf. Rashi, ad loc. (second interpretation). However, in relating here the Hebrew ויורה with מלקוש (= latter rain) I.E. follows the explanation given by Menahem in *Mahberet*, p. 84, in which ויורה is taken to be a noun and translated "former rain" (omitting the conjunction *waw*) rather than as a verb ("and will rain" or "and will teach"). Hence, according to I.E., the meaning of the second clause in v. 12 is as follows: When you realize that the success of your prosperity depends on God, then He will respond by sending autumn rain and spring rains in due time (viz., in order that you may reap the aforementioned abundant harvest). For a detailed discussion on I.E.'s view regarding the Hebrew יורה, cf. above, comm. on 6:3, note 11. Cf. also I.E.'s remark on מורה ומלקוש (Joel 2:23).

44 Cf. Rashi, ad loc. According to Qimhi, ad loc., this latter explanation quoted by I.E. in the name of the commentators rests on the Rabbinic expression "Heaven helps him who would be improved" (Bab. Talmud, *Yoma*, 38b). Cf. above, comm. on 2:19, note 54 and below, comm. on 12:7. For the basic difference between I.E.'s interpretation and the one quoted here in the name of the commentators with regard to the term *yōreh*, see the preceding note.

45 I.e., instead of obeying the early instruction given to Ephraim, "you have plowed wickedness," "reaped iniquity," and "eaten the fruit of lies."

46 I.E. had probably in mind the Assyrian king Shalmaneser IV who besieged Samaria (c. 724-722 B.C.). comp. II Kings 17:3. This view is shared by Samuel b. Hofni (cf. Abraham E. Harkavy, "Extracts from the Books of Ben Hofni," *Ozar Tob*, Supplement to *Magazin für die Wissenschaft des Judenthums*, VI [1878], 56) and after him by Ibn Janah (*Hariqmah*, p. 288). However, Rashi, Qara, Eliezer of Beaugency

and Isaiah da Trani, ad loc. all follow the Targum where Shalman is taken to be a substitute for *shālōm* (= peace, i.e., כשד שלמן "as the spoil of a peaceful people.) "

47 Dunash and after him Jacob Tam agree that *Arbel* is the name of a city the identity of which was to them uncertain. Cf. *Teshūḇōt*, p. 48. See note 49.

48 The reading in the printed editions as well as in our mss. of I.E.'s commentary is: "*Rūtāshā* is a noun," or "is a noun of the mother with the children" (sic), which makes no sense. Our translation is based on the emendation suggested by Filwarg (p. 4a), whereby the word *dāḇār* is dropped from the text of I.E. and the word *shēm* (= name) is to be taken as *shām* (= there, where). The literal reading in I.E. thus becomes: "Beth-arbel is the name of a place, where the mother was dashed in pieces with her children."

49 For the opinion that *'arbēl* is derived from *'ōrēḇ* (= ambush) cf. Rashi and Qara, ad loc.

50 I.e., the idolatry of Bethel was the main source of their evil. For the "calf" or the "calves" in Bethel, cf. above, comm. on 6:10, note 20.

51 I.e., most of the kings of Israel continued to worship the idols Jeroboam had set up in Bethel.

52 I.e., the tumult described in v. 14, by which the fortresses would be spoiled "as Shalman spoiled Beth-arbel," is to take place during the night, when such activity is common, while the king would perish during the day.

Chapter XI

(1) **When Israel was young** [(*na'ar*) **I loved him**]: This is [the sense of the phrase] "a well-trained heifer" [10:11], viz., trained by Me.[1] For when he [viz., Israel] was young, i.e., at [the time of] his departure from Egypt,[2] I began to train him, because I loved him.

(2) **They called [unto them so they went because of them]**: That is to say, "out of Egypt I called My son" (v. 1) to serve Me,[3] but now *they called unto them*, viz., unto the Baalim. And the more they called unto the Baalim the more they would wander from their [own] land because of them.[4] Some say that [the meaning of the phrase is] My prophets called on them [to instruct them], but they slid backward.[5]

(3-4) **And I taught [Ephraim] to walk** [(*tirgaltī*), **taking them by their arms]**: The [first] *taw* in [the word] *tirgaltī* [= I taught him to walk] replaces a *hē*; there is no parallel case in Scripture.[6] The meaning [of the phrase] is that I have trained him [viz., Ephraim] to walk on his feet, just as a child being trained [to walk] is taken by his arms.[7] This is like a medical practice, being [designed] to strengthen the child until he is able to walk. Because [the prophet] had compared Israel to a "trained heifer" [10:11] he now states: *I drew them with cords of a man, with bonds of love*, [which are] unlike the bonds that pull the neck of the toiling heifer.[8]

(4) **I was to them [as those who take off the yoke from upon their jaws]**: I.e., [I was to Ephraim] as people who have compassion upon a heifer by lifting the yoke which is placed on her jaw, time after time.[9] For [the meaning of the term] *we'aṭ* [in the phrase *we'aṭ 'ēlōw 'o̱kil,*] compare *'aṭeh* [= I will extend (Jer. 6:12)]. The word *'ōḵil* is a common noun [viz., food] similar to [*'ōḵel* in the phrase] "food [*'ōḵel*] for money" [Deut. 2:28]. Hence [the meaning of the last clause is] "I have extended to him [viz., to Ephraim] food."[10] However, R.Marinus said that *'ōḵil* should [indeed] be taken as *a'aḵil* [(= I will feed)] and as for the missing *aleph* in *'ōḵil*], compare "and David gathered together [*wayōsef*] all the chosen men of Israel" [II Sam.

6:1].[11] Thus he interprets *we'aṭ* literally, i.e., I fed him gently.[12]

(5) **He should not have returned [unto the land of Egypt**; but having done this] he [viz., Ephraim] will appoint Assyria as *his king*, as I have remarked [on the phrase] "they shall appoint themselves one head" [2:2].[13] **Because they refused to return** to Me: I.e., those who went to Egypt [refused] to return to My land.[14]

(6) [For the meaning of the word] *weḥālāh* [= and it shall fall], compare "let them fall [*yāḥūlū*] upon the head of Joab" [II Sam. 3:29], "no hands fell [*ḥālū*] upon her" [(Lam. 4:6)[15], meaning] the hands of the enemy.[16] [The **sword**] . . . **shall consume its branches**: [*Badāw* means] its branches. Compare "and [the vine] brought forth branches" [*badim* (Ez. 17:6)].[17] All this evil happened to them because of *their* own *counsels*.[18]

(7) **My people are suspended** [*telū'im*) **in My backsliding]**: [The word *telū'im* ("suspended," "hung") has here] an *aleph*; compare "where the Philistines had hanged them" [*telā'ūm* (II Sam. 21:12)].[19] The *yod* in the word *limshūḇātī* is not a sign of the subject[20] – compare "I shall make them joyful in the house of prayer directed to Me" [*beḇēyt tefīllātī* (Is. 56:7)], "I will bow down toward Thy holy temple in the fear of Thee" [*beyir'āteḵā*, (Ps. 5:8)] – insofar as the term *meshūḇāh* (= backsliding) is always used in a negative sense. Thus the meaning [of the sentence] is that they behave toward Me by way of backsliding, as a man suspended [*tālūy*] in the air who moves neither up nor down [i.e., who is uncertain].[21] **[Though they call them] to the Most High**, etc.: [For the meaning of the phrase *we'el 'al* (= and to the Most High)] compare "the saying of the man raised on high" [*'al* (II Sam. 23:1)] where [*'al*] is an adjective equivalent [in meaning to] *'elyōn* [= Most High]. Hence the meaning [of the phrase] is that the prophets of God call [the people] *to the Most High*, but *none of them raise* [their] heads [to listen to them].[22]

(8) **How [shall I give thee up, Ephraim? How] shall I deliver thee?**: [The term] *'amaggenḵā* [= I shall deliver thee] is similar [in meaning] to [the term] *'ettenḵā* [= I shall give thee].[23] Compare "who hath delivered (*miggēn*) thine enemies" [Gen. 14:20]; "a crown of glory will she [viz., wisdom] give thee" [*temaggeneḵā* (Prov. 4:9), which latter may be] compared with "for that thou hast given me [*netattānī*] the South-land [Josh. 15:19].[24] [The sense of the term] *niḵmerū* is they [viz., My repentings] were kindled and grew hot; compare "our skin is hot [*niḵmerū*] like an oven." [Lam. 5:10].[25] [The word] *nīḥūmāy* [(= My repentings) is derived] from the root [*nḥm* (a verb

meaning "to repent"),[26] as is the verb *wāyînāḥem* in the phrase] "and the Lord repented" [Ex. 32:14]. This is an anthropomorphism.[27]

(9) **[I will] not [execute the fierceness of Mine anger, for I am] God**, and [thus] able to endure anger. Moreover, it was *in your midst alone that I have been hallowed* [28] – **for I am God, . . . even if I will not enter into the city**. [The idea in this passage] is similar to [that in the phrase] "but will God [truly] dwell with men on the earth?" [II Chron. 6:18].[29] [However, R. Saadya] Gaon said the meaning [of the phrase in Hosea] is "I will not enter into any other city except into Jerusalem alone."[30]

(10) **[They shall walk] after [the Lord]**: I.e., if they will repent by following God – compare "after the Lord your God shall ye walk [Deut. 13:5][31] – then *will He roar like a lion.*[32] **And the children shall come trembling [from the west]**: I.e., [the people of] Israel who went to the west, viz., to Egypt [shall return trembling].[33] For Egypt is located to the southwest as is Assyria.[34]

(11) [The phrase] *and they shall come trembling as a bird* [derives its sense from the fact] that a bird trembles at the roar of a lion; [thus, the prophet means to say], I shall make them fly [swiftly] as a bird [does].[35] [The figure] *and as a dove [out of the land of Assyria]* is in contrast to what [the prophet] had said [before]: "Ephraim is become like a silly dove without understanding" [7:11].[36] [The clause] *I would make them dwell in their houses* means: I would have made them return [from] their captivity.[37]

Notes

1 Comp. above, 10:11: "And Ephraim is a well-trained heifer," which is interpreted by I.E. as meaning: "I trained him at the beginning to bear the burden of My precepts."

2 I.E. maintains that the term *na'ar* connotes the days of Israel's youth, i.e., the period of Israel's national inception after the exodus from Egypt. Comp. above, 2:17: "As in the days of her youth, and as in the days when she came up out of the land of Egypt."

3 By quoting here the phrase "out of Egypt I called My son" (v. 1) with the additional remark "to serve Me," I.E. aims (1) to conjoin the first two verses of our chapter, i.e., I called My son out of Egypt, but they called unto the Baalim, and (2) to emphasize that the prophet meant to say that God called out to his son to serve him. Comp. Ex. 4:24 : "Let My son go that he may serve Me." However, the Arabic commentary pub-

lished by Schroeter (*Archiv*, I, 43) paraphrases: "And from Egypt I called him My son." Cf. also Targum, ad. loc.: "And from Egypt I called them My sons."

4 Viz., because of the Baalim. However, it is not clear if I.E. means to interpret v. 2 by saying that because Ephraim called unto the Baalim they (viz., the people) were exiled from their land as a punishment or if the prophet simply spoke of the people who worshiped the Baalim and even followed them from their own land into Egypt.

5 According to this latter explanation, the subject (viz., the prophets) of the verb *qār'ū* (= they called) is understood, i.e., the more the prophets kept calling Israel in order to guide them, the more Israel kept going away from them. For a similar interpretation, cf. Targum; Jacob b. Reuben; Ibn Janah, *Dictionary*, p. 50, and Rashi, ad loc.

6 *Tirgaltī* (in the Taphel form) is derived from the root *rgl*; the Hiphil form, which generally means "I taught (or "I trained") to walk," would be *hirgalti*, with a preformative *hē*, instead of a *taw*. This replacement of the Hiphil by the Taphel is, according to I.E., not found elsewhere in Scripture. In *Ṣaḥot*, p. 19a, I.E. agrees with the view of R. Moses Chiquitilla that *tirgaltī* "is a rare word," for as a rule no *taw* can replace a *hē* at the beginning of a word. The same view is also expressed in comm. on Deut. 33:3. For a further discussion on this matter, cf. Menahem, *Mahberet*, p. 43; Dunash, *Teshūḇōt*, p. 96; and Ibn Janah, *Hariqmah*, pp. 83, 342.

7 However, Menahem (ibid.) and Qimhi, ad loc. explain the word as meaning that when the child grows weary the trainer or the parent lifts him up and carries him in his arms until he gains enough strength to walk again. According to Ibn Janah (*Hariqmah*, p. 328: *Dictionary*, p. 468) and Qimhi (ad loc.) *zerō'ōtaw* (lit., "his arms") should be taken in the sense of "My arms," thus conjoining the beginning of the verse ("and I taught") – which is in the first person singular – with "My arms." This latter explanation is closer to that of the LXX ("I took him on My arm") and R.S.V. ("I took them up in My arms"). On the other hand, J.P.S. and A.V., in consonance with I.E., both render the phrase as "taking them by their arms," depicting parental guidance of a child by holding on to his arms until he is able to walk by himself. Thus the Hebrew preposition *'al* is to be taken as "by" rather than "on." For a similar usage of the preposition *'al* in the same sense, cf. Rashi on Gen. 27:40.

8 The figure thus signifies the idea that Ephraim has always been guided and protected by God with bonds of love and compassion, unlike the toiling heifer, which is burdened or mistreated by the driver pulling the reins that are placed on her neck.

9 Qimhi, ad loc., interprets the phrase as meaning "like those who have compassion upon the heifer . . . and hang it (viz., the yoke) upon her jaw," in order to afford relief to the animal. However, I.E. evidently maintains that the preposition על (=on) should be taken in the sense of מֵעַל (= from upon), i.e., "as those who remove the yoke from upon their jaw." Cf. Abravanel, ad loc., and Harper, p. 364, both of whom prefer the rendering "from upon" over "on."

10 The term *we'aṭ* is derived, according to I.E, from *nṭh* a verb meaning "to stretch

out," "to extend." Cf. comm. on Ex. 9:15, where our passage is adduced as evidence for verbs in which only one radical (e.g., *teth*) is retained. Furthermore, I.E. takes *'ōḵil* in the sense of *'ōḵel* (= food); so also Joseph Qimhi in *Sepher Hagaluy*, pp. 103, 161. Thus the meaning of the closing phrase in v. 4 is as follows: And I have extended to him food, i.e., God always provided for Ephraim in times of need. For a similar explanation, cf. *Bereshit Rabbah*, 86:1.

11 There is evidently an *aleph* missing in the word *wayōsef* (= and he gathered). According to Hebrew grammatical principles, it should be *waye'esōf*, with an additional *aleph* after the *yod* as the first radical of the verb (*'sf*). The verb *'ōḵil* may similarly be taken in the sense of *'a'aḵil* with one *aleph* missing. It should be noted that the explanation quoted here by I.E. could not be located in Ibn Janah's writings. As a matter of fact, in *Hariqmah*, p. 136, Ibn Janah seems to treat *ōḵil* as a noun in the Po'il form.

12 According to the interpretation ascribed here to Ibn Janah, *'aṭ* is an adverb ("gently," "softly"); comp. I Kings 21:27: "And (Ahab) went softly (*'aṭ*)." However, the preposition *'ēlaw* (lit., "to him") would in this interpretation have to be construed as a direct object; cf. Rashi on Gen. 37:18, where *'ōtō* (= him) is indeed translated as *'ēlāw* (= to him).

13 The "one head" mentioned in 2:2 is, according to I.E., to be identified with Sennaherib king of Assyria. See following note.

14 According to I.E., the prophet here continues describing Ephraim's failure to remain loyal to its land by saying that Ephraim was not supposed to return to Egypt in the first place (comp. above, v. 1: "And out of Egypt I called My son"); however, since they went there and refused to return to their own land (comp. above, 7:11), they will have to submit to the Assyrian conqueror as a punishment. For a similar interpretation, cf. Rashi and Qimhi, ad loc.

15 The verb *ḥul* may also connote "to begin," and the anonymous Arabic commentary (Schroeter, *Archiv*, I, 43) and al-Qumisi (p. 19) both translate the first line in v. 6 thus: "The sword shall begin in his (or "in their") cities." However, I.E. evidently agrees with Ibn Janah (*Dictionary*, p. 146) who interprets *weḥālāh ḥereḇ* as "and the sword shall fall."

16 I.e., the iniquity of the people of Judah referred to in this passage from Lamentations was even greater than the sin of Sodom, which was overthrown by God rather than by the hands of a mortal enemy.

17 According to I.E., the term *badāw* does not denote "its princes" (as rendered in the Targum) nor does it mean "its bars" (as translated in R.S.V.), but rather "its branches." Thus the phrase "and (the sword) shall consume its branches" would evidently signify, according to I.E., the destruction of the different areas and settlements of Ephraim which constitute, as it were, "branches" of the cities.

18 I.e., because of the ill advice they received to worship the idols.

19 A reference to Saul and Jonathan, who were hanged by the Philistines in Beth-shan. The three radicals of the Hebrew verb "to hang," "suspend" are *taw, lamed* and *hē*. However, in the present passive participle (*telu'im*) the *hē* (which is generally changed into a *yod*) is here replaced by an *aleph*, as is the case (according to the *Qeri*) in *telā'um* (II Sam. 21:12). For a similar view, cf. Ibn Janah, *Dictionary*, p. 422. In his commentary on Num. 11:5, after citing our passage, I.E. remarks: "And there are many such cases."

20 Cf. Gesenius-Kautzsch, par. 135, m (= p. 439): "The possessive pronouns are . . . expressed by the suffixes of the noun (in the genitive), which may represent either a subjective genitive or . . . an *objective genitive*, e.g., חמסי the wrong done against me . . . ." See the various examples of the objective genitive cited by G-K (ibid.). For the term סימן הפועל and its concomitant סימן הפעול, cf. *Moznayim*, p. 30b.

21 The pronominal ending ִי generally denotes "mine." The expression בית תפילתי (Is. 56:7), which might be construed as meaning "the house of My prayer," really means "the prayer of others directed toward God." Furthermore, the proper rendering of the word ביראתך (Ps. 5:8), which literally means "in Thy fear," is "in the fear of Thee," viz., the fear of others directed toward God. I.E. maintains that the *yod* in *limshūḇātī* connotes an objective rather than a subjective genitive. Accordingly, the meaning of the sentence would be: My people are as those suspended in midair (viz., undecided), by virtue of their backsliding and unruly behavior toward Me. For since the term *meshūbā* in Scripture always denotes ill behavior (cf. below, comm. on 14:5), it is unthinkable that the word *limshūḇātī* should be construed as denoting an action executed by God rather than an action against Him.

22 By adding the term ראש (= head) to the words לא ירומם (= they will not raise), I.E. evidently aims to explain the verb רום (= to raise), which is transitive and would thus normally require a direct object; hence, "they will not raise *their head*." It should be noted that Yehuda Kil in his commentary on Hosea, *Da'at Miqra* (Jerusalem, 1973), p. 87, takes I.E.'s remark (they shall not "raise their heads") in a rebellious sense, i.e., the people will not raise their heads in order to listen to the prophets who call them to return to the Most High. A different suggestion is offered by Qimhi, who identifies I.E.'s comment with that of the Targum, which latter paraphrases this passage in the text as "they shall not walk with erect posture," i.e., proudly. Abravanel, ad loc., quotes I.E. as interpreting the passage to mean that "they shall not raise their heads nor be successful." Cf. also Eliezer of Beaugency, ad loc.: "They will no more raise the head from under [the yoke of] the King of Assyria."

23 According to I.E., the prophet here uses two different words, but of a similar meaning (אתנך, אמגנך), to express the same idea, i.e., how can I surrender you, how can I deliver you into the hands of the enemies?

24 The reason for this additional remark appears to be the following: According to Hebrew grammatical principles, the pronominal suffix attached to a transitive verb is

generally designed to express the object pronoun, e.g., אתנך = I will give you; אמגנך = I will deliver you. However, the verb תמגנך (Prov. 4:9), which has a similar suffix, is taken to mean "[wisdom] will give *to you* (or "bestow upon you") [a crown of glory]" – i.e., the pronominal suffix is construed as an indirect object. Similarly, the verb נתתני (Josh. 15:19) with its ending is also interpreted by I.E. as "you have given to me" instead of "thou hast set me" (J.P.S.) or "you have given me away." For a similar remark, cf. Ibn Janah, *Dictionary*, p. 253.

Cf. also *Sephat Yether*, p. 17a, where I.E. favors Dunash's explanation that תמגנך denotes "giving" over the one given by Saadya in the sense of "protection."

25 For a similar remark, cf. Rashi, ad loc., and comm. on 13:14 and on Gen. 43:30. However, Ibn Janah (*Dictionary*, p. 233) differentiates between the sense of the verb נכמרו in the Hosea passage and its meaning in the passage in Lamentations. Here (v. 8) the phrase נכמרו נחומי is taken by him as meaning "My compassions *moved* Me," i.e., I yearned, whereas the phrase in Lam. 5:10 is interpreted as "our skin became dry like an oven." For Ibn Janah's complete interpretation of v. 8, cf. ibid., p. 298.

26 I.e., God's compassion for Ephraim was kindled and reached such proportions that He regretted the idea of its total destruction.

27 Lit., "Scripture speaks in human terms" (Bab. Talmud, *Berakot*, 31b), i.e., the action of repentance as applied to God is an anthropomorphic concept. In his comm. on Ex. 32:14, I.E. cites four additional biblical expressions which are considered by him to be anthropomorphic. Cf. also above, comm. on 4:6 and on Is. 43:24. This talmudic dictum has already been used by R. Hai Gaon as a means of explaining corporal expressions in the Bible ascribed to God, in an anthropomorphic sense. Cf. *Teshūbōt Hageōnim*, ed. and pub. by Jacob Mussafia (Lyck, 1864), p. 30a and the subsequent note by S.J. Halberstam in *Jeshurun* (Heb. ed.), V (1866), 44.

28 According to I.E.'s interpretation, the sympathy for Ephraim expressed in v. 8 continues with v. 9 by adding the thought that God will not execute the fierceness of His anger against the people, for, not being human, He is able to restrain those emotions that are considered passionate in men. Furthermore, God's presence is closely related to the people of Israel (with emphasis on the term בקרבך = within you) and needs no geographical dwelling place (see following note). It is thus unlikely that He would destroy the very people in whom God's holiness inheres. It may be noted that to arrive at this interpretation I.E. partially inverts the word order of the verse.

29 The quote referred to here is part of King Solomon's prayer made after the building of the Temple was completed and is usually thought to mean that a dwelling place (viz., Temple) for God among men is indeed impossible; for "behold heaven and heaven's heaven cannot contain You; how much less this house I builded" (II Chron., ibid.). Similarly, when the prophet represents God by saying: "[I am] the Holy One in the midst of thee, and I will not enter into the city," he means according to I.E., that God and the people are interrelated in the sense that He had established His presence

in their midst, even without entering the city, i.e., even without finding a dwelling place among them, for no place can contain Him. For a similar interpretation, cf. Ibn Janah (quoting his teacher Isaac b. Shaul), *Dictionary*, p. 366. Cf. also Qimhi, ad loc., and his *Dictionary*, p. 263. It should be noted that J.P.S. renders the closing phrase of our verses: "I will not come in fury," instead of: "I will not enter into the city."

30 Cf. Rashi, ad loc.: "I have already promised to maintain My presence among you, [but only] in [the city of] Jerusalem and I will no more maintain it in any other city." For a similar explanation in which בעיר is taught to refer to cities other than Jerusalem, cf. Targum, ad loc., and Yefet, p. 177, lines 3-4. Cf. also Saadya as quoted by Qimhi, ad loc.

31 Maimonides (*Guide*, part I, chap. 58, p. 87) explains the passages both in Deut. and Hosea in the sense of "following in obedience to Him, imitating His acts and conducting life in accordance with His conduct," a remark similar to I.E.'s in his commentary on Deut. (ibid.).

32 Lit., "now will He roar." Our translation is based on the explanation given by Sharim (p. 30a) in which I.E.'s "now" (עתה) is taken in the sense of "then" (usually, in a result clause, expressed by Heb. אז).

33 I.e., if they will repent of their ill behavior and renew their faith in God, then those who went into Egyptian or Assyrian captivity will return to their land in a mood of contrition.

34 The LXX renders מִיָּם as "from the waters." However, I.E. evidently agrees with the Targum, Rashi, and others that מִיָּם means "from the West" (viz., *mīyyām*). In accepting this rendering, I.E. attempts to conjoin vv. 10-11 by saying that Egypt and Assyria (v. 11) are both located southwest of the land of Israel. This erroneous statement occurs repeatedly in his commentaries (Ex. 25:18, Zech. 8:7, Is. 43:5; 49:12) and it has long ago been challenged by Joseph Bonfils (*Ṣophnat Pa'anēaḥ*, I, p. 119), stating that Assyria is to the east of the land of Israel and not to the west. Fleischer conjectures that in all the above-mentioned places of I.E.'s commentary מים points to Tunis, which, according to him, was at one time called "Aschir." Cf. "R. Abraham Ibn Ezra be'africa," *Mizraḥ Uma'arab̲*, III (1929), 88, note 3; but on this view how would I.E.'s remark fit in with v. 11, which speaks of Israel's return from captivity? We find no implication anywhere in the Bible that the people of Israel were ever exiled to Tunisia.

35 The remark "a bird trembles at the roar of a lion" is merely designed to explain that the figure of the "bird" (v. 11) is in apposition to the figure of the "lion" (v. 10); but at the same time the figure also represents, according to I.E., the process of the people's return from captivity, which would have been as swift as the flight of a bird when it hears the roar of a lion. Cf. above, comm. on 3:5, where our passage is cited.

36 I.e. Ephraim had been compared by the prophet to a "silly dove without under-

standing," but if they would have repented "by following God" (comm. on v. 10), their homecoming would have been as swift as that of a dove that immediately returns to its nest in response to its caller.

37 The verb והושבתים is derived from the root ישב, meaning "to settle," "to dwell," "to sit." However, for the concept of "return from captivity" one would expect to read in v. 11 והשיבותים, a Hiphil form derived from the root שוב, meaning "to return." By his remark "I would have made them return from captivity," I.E. may have wished to imply that the prophet promised the people the restoration to their houses by way of bringing them back from captivity. By this token, the verb והושבתים would retain its original meaning, viz., "I will make them dwell," or "I will restore them."

In I.E.'s view the ensuing chapter XII is a direct continuation of the thought expressed in this passage.

Chapter XII

(1) [However, **Ephraim] has encompassed Me with lies [and deceit]**: I.e., [the people] do not follow God, but rather [they walk] deceitfully, and not in truth.[1] This is also the case with Judah, who claimed that *he ruled with God*.[2] [The term *rad* (= ruled) is similar] in form to [that of *tām* (= "ended" or "finished") in the phrase] "that our money is all spent" [*tām* (Gen. 47:18)].[3] [By the phrase *and Judah would rule with God* the prophet implies] that he [viz., the tribe of Judah], by virtue of its king having been the descendant of the Davidic family, thought that it was the [chosen] kingdom of God.[4]

(2) **Ephraim** does not follow God, but [adheres instead] to his [own] ways, for indeed [Ephraim] *feeds the wind*[5] – as in "shall windy words have an end?" [Prov. 16:3]. [The phrase] *"they make a covenant with Assyria"* proves [this contention].[6] **And oil is carried into Egypt**, [as] a tribute to the Egyptian king.[7]

(3) **[The Lord hath a] quarrel [with Judah]**: A [certain] interpreter said that *Judah* is [here] considered to be the "faithful" [v. 1],[8] and [so] he shall be an arbitrator.[9] He [viz., the interpreter] further said that Scripture does not state "the Lord quarrels against [על] Judah," but rather with [(עם) *Judah*], meaning that God together with Judah will contend against Ephraim.[10] However, [this interpreter] erred contextually as well as grammatically. For it has been stated above: "[When Ephraim saw his sickness], and Judah his wound" [(5:13), and] "I will make Ephraim to ride, Judah shall plow" [10:11]. [Subsequently, the prophet] said with respect to both of them [viz., with respect to Ephraim and Judah]: "You have eaten the fruit of lies [ibid., v. 13].[11] [This interpreter] has also forgotten the phrase "and the herdsmen of Gerar strove against [עם] Isaac's herdsmen" [(Gen. 26:20), and] "wherefore the people strove against [עם] Moses" [Ex. 17:2][12] and many other such passages. [It is] therefore [my view that] the prophet [here] linked Ephraim with Judah, adding *to punish Jacob according to his ways* – for this name [viz., Jacob] includes both of them [viz., Ephraim and Judah].[13]

(4) **In the womb**, etc.: [Were I to believe] the interpreter's claim that [this passage means that while Jacob was] in the womb, God decreed the matter of the birthright and the blessing,[14] I would not know [the significance of the term] *in the womb*; for Scripture states: "*Before* I formed thee in the belly I knew thee" [Jer. 1:5].[15] It is my opinion that the passage is [to be taken] in its literal sense, i.e., *in the womb he took his brother by the heel.* This is obviously expressed [in the phrase] "and his [Jacob's] hand had hold on Esau's heel" [Gen. 25:26].[16] Thus the passage means: Why should the children of Jacob not have remembered that I chose their forefather and made him superior to all [other] human beings? – for when he had been in the womb I gave him the strength to hold on to Esau's heel. This is something of a miraculous act, for [a fetus both] within the membrane and when the latter breaks open has no strength to hold on to anything, until it emerges from the uterus into the light of the [outside] world; and yet when [Jacob] was [still] in the womb I had given him [such] strength.[17] Afterward he wrestled with the angel and the latter "was unable to prevail against him" [Gen. 32:26], notwithstanding the fact that one angel slew the whole Assyrian army,[18] and that people become frightened [only] by beholding [such a sight] – as happened to David[19] – let alone by wrestling with him [viz., an angel]. Thus this event [viz., Jacob grasping Esau's heel] was meant to demonstrate to all people that his [Jacob's] children would persevere forever and that at the end they would defeat their enemies.[20] However, Ephraim thought that he [alone] had found such strength.[21]

(5) **He strove**: [The prophet now] explains how [Jacob] strove with a God-like being[22] at which time *he prevailed* against that angel who almost *wept*[23] and [then] pleaded with him to send him away before daybreak[24] – which is prior to [the time] when daylight becomes strong – in order that Jacob should not be stricken with fear.[25] [By the phrase] *he found him in Bethel [and there he spake with us*, the prophet] implies that when [Jacob] returned to his father, he there met the angel [once more];[26] and because the angel appeared twice in Bethel, the place was [considered to be] the gate of heaven. It is for this reason that I [Hosea] and Amos prophesied concerning Jeroboam in Bethel,[27] which is [also] his royal seat, as I shall explain.[28]

(6) [The verse] **but the Lord, [the God of hosts, the Lord is His remembrance]** means that it was the angel who spoke with their forefather, whereas God, who is the God of the angels, revealed His name to Moses [to proclaim Himself] to be their God.[29] Hence, the phrase *the Lord is his remembrance.*[30]

(7) **So you**, if you would have returned to your God, He would have assisted you in order to bring you back to Him.[31] This is the [true] meaning of the phrase *you return to your God . . . and wait for* Him. [That is to say], you should not rely either on your own wealth or your own strength, for you have attained that strength as well as wealth from Him.

(8-9) By the term *'aḵ* [(= yet) in the passage] *Ephraim said* [*yet I am become rich*, the prophet] implies that [Ephraim claimed]: God did not give me wealth, but rather I became rich through my own effort.[32] For I am not like "Canaan" [v. 8] viz., a merchant; compare "and there shall no longer be a Canaanite [(viz., merchant or trader) in the house of the lord" (Zech. 14:21)]. That is to say, why should [the prophet] caution: "Keep mercy and justice" [v. 7] so that there shall be no exploitation of [others] like that done by a Canaanite, [at a time] when *in all my labor* people do not find that I [Ephraim] have sinned.[33]

(10) **And I am [the Lord thy God from the land of Egypt]** etc.: This means: Do you not remember that I brought you up from Egypt with an abundance of wealth – for which you did not toil, that I sustained you in the desert when you were [dwelling there] *in tents* and that I am again able to act on your behalf "as in the days that you came forth out of Egypt"? [Deut. 16:6].[34]

(11) **I have spoken [unto the prophets]**: I.e., I have already spoken repeatedly [about these things][35] unto the prophets, in order that they should ask you to abandon [your] falsehoods.[36] **I gave parables through the prophets**[37] [means,] I have used similes [and] parables, so that you might [readily] understand.[38]

(12) And now – *if* the people of *Gilead* were *iniquitous* before the prophets,[39] *they surely came to naught* afterward.[40] **In Gilgal they sacrifice bullocks** to Baal,[41] [*their altars are*] *as heaps* [*in the furrows of the field*] – a figure [indicating] that they [viz., the altars] were numerous and conspicuous.[42]

(13) **[Jacob] fled [into the field of Aram]**: I.e., you were supposed to consider [the fact] that your forefather [Jacob], when he fled to Aram, was poor.[43] Thus he said: "[If God will be with me] . . . and give me bread to eat, etc." [Gen. 28:20]. **And [Israel] served for a wife**: This term [viz., *waya'aḇōd* = and he served] refers back to the phrase "did not I serve with thee [*'aḇadetṯīḵā*] for Rachel?" [Gen. 29:25], while [the meaning of the phrase *and for a wife he kept* is that] for a wife he [viz., Jacob] became a shepherd, and it was I [God] who enriched him.[44]

(14) **By a prophet [the Lord brought Israel up out of Egypt]**: [That is to say,] I also brought up his [Jacob's] children [out of Egypt] *by a prophet* – meaning Moses; [subsequently,] Israel turned out [to be] like sheep, and Moses guarded them.[45] Israel, however, has forgotten all this.[46]

(15) **[Ephraim] hath provoked** God **[overtly[**:[47] [The word] *tamrūrim* signifies overtness. Compare "set thee up waymarks" [*tamrūrim* (Jer. 31:20), "and he became lofty" [*wayitmamar* (Dan. 8:17)].[48] **[Therefore] his blood** – viz., the innocent blood that [Ephraim] spilled[49] – **He will spread**[50] [(*yittōsh*) **upon him[**: Compare "and behold they were spread" [*netūshim* (I Sam. 30:16)].[51]

Notes

1 I.e., if the people had followed God earnestly, He would have "roared like a lion" in order to restore them to their own land (comm. on 11:10-11); but Ephraim has shown no deference to the call of the prophet. Instead it has surrounded God with falsehood and deception. (See last note of preceding chapter.) We here follow the reading in ms. L; cf. the variants in the notes to the Hebrew text.

2 Rashi, Qara, and Eliezer of Beaugency all interpret verse 11:1b in a complimentary sense. So also R.S.V. (based on the LXX): "But Judah is still known by God (A.V.: "Judah yet ruleth with God") and is faithful to the Holy One." However, according to I.E.'s explanation, the whole verse is taken to be an expression of contempt against Ephraim as well as against Judah, i.e., Ephraim has acted deceitfully, and Judah, who claimed to rule with God (cf. below, note 4), has also been disloyal to Him.

3 I.e., our money has come to an end (the treatment of the verb *rad* in the text of I.E. must be construed as a parenthesis). It should be noted that most early Hebrew grammatical sources list רד under the root רוד, a verb in which the second radical is a *waw*. Cf. Hayyug, p. 91; Ibn Janah, *Dictionary*, p. 472, and Qimhi, *Dictionary*, p. 691; by this interpretation the verb רד (= he ruled) properly retains a *qamaṣ* (as in שב, קם, quoted in *Moznayim*, p. 9a). However, I.E.'s analogy here between the two verbs רד and תם, the latter of which is derived from the root תמם, seems to suggest that, according to him, the verb רד is derived from רדד. This interpretation is open to question, for why is רד vocalized with a *qamaṣ* instead of a *patah*, as is generally the case in the third person perfect singular masculine of double-*ayin* verbs?

4 I.e., by merely belonging to the royal family of David, Judah's king felt that he was the only one privileged to rule by the power of God.

5 According to I.E., the prophet continues in v. 2 to depict the people's misconduct, the nature of which he began to describe in v. 1; i.e., not only had Ephraim surrounded

God with falsehood (v. 1), but it also abandoned its faith in Him by pursuing windy (viz., empty) alliances with Assyria (v. 2).

6 I.e., the reference to the covenant made with Assyria proves I.E.'s contention that the prophet meant to say that Ephraim relied upon their useless alliance rather than upon the salvation of God. It is clear that by comparing the words "feeds the wind" with the phrase of Prov. 16:3 "windy words," I.E. evidently had in mind a figurative expression for the trivial agreements and empty words upon which the people based their relationship with other nations. Cf. Rashi, ad loc., where the opening phrase of our verse is interpreted in the sense of "Ephraim is an alliance with the wind."

7 I.e., the oil that was given to the Egyptian king represented still another kind of dependency – viz., a tribute either for protection or for help which the last king, Hosea, expected from Egypt against Assyria; comp. II Kings 17:4. Cf. also above, comm. on 7:9.

8 According to this interpretation, the last word in v. 1 (viz., נאמן = faithful) becomes the predicate of the aforementioned subject, Judah; i.e., Judah "is faithful to the Holy One," as rendered in R.S.V. and already quoted above in note 2.

9 I.e., Judah the faithful shall become the arbitrator in the controversy between God and Ephraim. This interpretation, quoted here by I.E. in the name of an anonymous interpreter, resembles the one given by Qara, ad loc., who also uses the term מוכיח in the sense of "arbitrator." With regard to the possible literary relation between I.E. and Qara, cf. Introduction, note 49.

10 I.e., God will be assisted by Judah in the presentation of charges against Ephraim, with God as the plaintiff and Judah as an arbitrator.

11 By quoting the passages from Hosea 5:13 and 10:11 (comp. 5:6), I.E. aims to establish the prophet's hostile attitude to Judah as well as to Ephraim, thus making it unlikely that Judah should be able to sit in judgment as an arbitrator between God and Ephraim. Of even greater significance to him is the phrase "you have eaten the fruit of lies" (10:13), which is reminiscent of the lies mentioned in 12:1. Hence I.E. concludes that the accusation in v. 1 is designed to stigmatize Ephraim and Judah alike.

12 According to the anonymous interpreter, the preposition עם is taken in its literal sense (viz., with) of assistance, i.e., God is being helped out by Judah in His quarrel with Ephraim. However, the two passages quoted here by I.E. establish that following the verb ריב (= quarrel, strife) the preposition עם should be taken in the sense of "against", i.e., the herdsmen of Gerar argued against the herdsmen of Isaac (Gen. 26:10); the people argued against Moses (Ex. 17:2). Consequently, v. 3 of the present chapter must represent the thought that God has an argument against Judah (rather than *with* Judah against Ephraim), who followed the evil example of Ephraim.

13 After attempting to establish the interpreter's error, I.E. continues to explain the second clause of v. 3 by saying that in view of his own interpretation, the name of

their ancestor "Jacob" applies to both Ephraim and Judah. Thus he renders v. 3 as follows: God has a quarrel (even) with Judah, (i.e., an argument against Judah), with the intention to punish Jacob (viz., Ephraim and Judah) "according to his ways, etc." For a similar remark regarding the name "Jacob," cf. above, comm. on 10:11 and *Yesōd Mōrā*, ch. 5.

14 I.e., when Jacob was still in his mother's womb God had already designed the plan whereby Jacob might supplant his brother Esau with regard to the birthright and the blessings. Thus the verb *'āqab̲* is taken to mean "to supplant"; comp. Gen. 27:36: "Is not his name Jacob? For he hath supplanted me (*waya'aqb̲ēnī*) these two times: he took away my birthright; and behold, now he hath taken away my blessing." For a similar interpretation, cf. Eliezer of Beaugency, ad loc.

15 I.E. maintains that since God knows the people before they are formed (Jer. 1:5), there would be no significance in the fact that God's decree to supplant Esau took place when Jacob was in the womb.

16 The verb *'aqab̲* thus signifies Jacob's grip on Esau's heel.

17 Until now I.E. attempts to explain the first clause in v. 4 by referring it to the account of Jacob's and Esau's birth; comp. Gen. 25:25-26. Cf. also comm. on Is. 44:2 where our present biblical passage is cited with the remark: "There (viz., in my commentary on Hosea) I shall explain it." From here on I.E. deals mainly with the second clause of the verse, "and by his strength he strove with a God-like being", which alludes to Jacob when he confronted an angel and prevailed (ibid., 32:25-26). By his remark "afterward he wrestled with an angel, etc." I.E. evidently aimed to underscore the juxtaposition of allusions to these two accounts (Gen. 25:25-26, 32:25-26) in the present verse, viz., the prophet had in mind to emphasize the superhuman strength (ובאונו) that God gave to Jacob when he was still in the womb (בבטן), which enabled him to prevail in his confrontation with the angel. See note 21, below.

18 Comp. II Kings 19:35: "And it came to pass that night, that the angel of the Lord went forth, and smote in the camp of the Assyrians a hundred four score and five thousand.

19 Comp. II Chron. 21:30: "For he [David] was terrified because of the sword of the angel of the Lord." By citing the last two incidents, I.E. implies that by man's strength alone he is unable to strive against an angel, and that Jacob was only able to withstand his angelic opponent because of his God-given strength.

20 According to Qimhi, ad loc., the heel signifies the distant end (or distant future), the idea of which marks the ultimate triumph of Jacob's descendants over their enemies.

21 Lit., "Ephraim thinks that Ephraim, he found the strength" – where the second occurrence of the term "Ephraim" may be an explanatory scribal gloss. In making this remark I.E. evidently had in mind the prophet's admonition followed in v. 9 : "And Ephraim said: Surely I am become rich, I have found wealth" (or "strength,"), thereby

underscoring Ephraim's claim to have attained his position by himself, which is in contrast with Jacob's fortune that rested on God's strength.

22 I.E. here indicates that in v. 5 the prophet describes the God-like being of v. 4 (*'elōhim*) as an angel, and begins to explain how the struggle between the two combatants turned out at the end, i.e., who prevailed.

23 The feature of weeping mentioned here by the prophet is not found in the Gen. 32:27 narrative. Thus I.E. takes the word בכה (= he wept) in Hosea to mean only that when pleading with Jacob: "Let me go, for the day breaketh," the angel almost wept.

24 The term עלות השחר (Gen. 32:25), which is generally rendered "daybreak," is explained by I.E. (ibid.) as meaning when darkness (of the night) is lifted (Heb. שחור = "darkness" or "black").

The printed editions of I.E.'s commentary on Hosea as well as our mss. all have the reading וטעם עלות השחר (= and the meaning of the term עלות השחר), which marks a sudden break in I.E.'s interpretation of our text by turning to Genesis in order to explain the quoted term. We thus read here טרם (= before) in place of וטעם (= and the meaning of), i.e., the angel pleaded with Jacob that he should send him away *before* (טרם) dawn, so that Jacob would not see him in daylight. For this reading in I.E., see the following note.

25 We here give the excerpt from I.E.'s commentary on vv. 4-5 as quoted by Joseph Bonfils in *Ṣoḇhnath Pa'anēaḥ*, I, p. 140: והנה מלאך אחד הרג מחנה אשור ומראותו יפחדו בני אדם כמו דוד שנבעת ואף כי להתאבק עמו ואיך שרה את האלוהים: ויוכל. למלאך וכמעט בכה ויתחנן לו שישלחנו טרם עלות השחר לפני שיתחזק האור שלא יבעת יעקב. (= Behold a single angel slew the Assyrian army and people become frightened [only] from seeing him [the angel] – as was David stricken with fear – let alone by wrestling with him; how then could [Jacob] have striven with a God-like being. *And he prevailed* [means Jacob prevailed] against the angel, who almost wept and pleaded with him [with Jacob] that he should send him [the angel] away *before daybreak*, in order that Jacob should not be stricken with fear). Such a reading in I.E. could not be found either in our printed editions or in any of the mss. at our disposal. therefore, we have only adopted the emendation essential to making our translation intelligible, as indicated in the preceding note.

26 I.E. appears to make reference to the vision which occurred to Jacob when he returned home from Laban (Gen. 35:1-7).

27 Bethel had already been called by Jacob the "gate of heaven" after he woke up from his dream in which he encountered the angels for the first time (Gen. 28:17). However, I.E. maintains that by the word ושם (= and there) the prophet evidently referred to Bethel as a place of distinction, i.e., "and *there* he spoke with us," meaning the angel spoke "with us" (with Hosea and Amos) in Bethel by way of prophecy, after he appeared there twice to Jacob, thereby giving the place the distinct quality of being a veritable "gate of heaven" and thus becoming the appropriate place to perform their

own prophetic activity with respect to Jeroboam II and his royal residence. It should be noted that by interpreting the word עמנו (lit., "with us," so also in comm. on Gen. 28:11) I.E. appears to reject any notion of taking the word in the sense of עמו (= with him, viz., with Jacob) as suggested by Jacob b. Reuben (ad loc.), Ibn Janah (*Hariqmah*, p. 93), and others (R.S.V. renders: "And there God spoke with him"). This rejection becomes even more apparent in *Sephat Yether*, p. 28a, where I.E. insists that עמנו should be taken literally, after he ascribes the same view of treating the word in the sense of עמו (= with him) to Dunash (cf. *Kritik des Dunash ben Labrat*, ed. by Robert Schröter [Breslau, 1866], p. 50) and rejects it.

28 Bethel was originally designated by Jeroboam I as one of two places to worship the golden calf (I Kings 12:20). However, comp. Amos 7:13 where Bethel is later quoted as the "royal house" of Jeroboam II. This royal house may, according to I.E. (ibid.), be traced back to Jehu, the founder of the new dynasty in Israel, himself a resident of Bethel, who subsequently established his headquarters there.

29 I.e., to be also the God of the people of Israel who will be subjected to His exclusive supervision rather than to the influence or direction of the heavenly bodies. For I.E.'s view on the concept of God directly supervising the people of Israel, cf. comm. on Deut. 4:20 and A. Lipshitz, *Pirqēy 'Iyyun Bemishnat R. Abraham Ibn Ezra* (Jerusalem, 1982), pp. 127-129.

30 I.E. appears to interpret v. 6 as a continuation of the thought expressed in the preceding verse, in which the prophet may imply that God has generally manifested Himself to the patriarchs by way of angelic revelation, without actually disclosing the Tetragammaton (v. 5, comp. Ex. 6:3; "their forefathers" in I.E.'s comment is evidently an allusion to Abraham). This name was later revealed to Moses (the revelation of which is evidently implied, according to I.E., in the phrase "the Lord is His remembrance" [*zik̲rō*, v. 6]; a phrase which corresponds in essence with Gods' response to Moses: "This is My name forever and this is My remembrance [*zik̲rī*] unto all generations," [Ex. 3:15]) and it represents God's supremacy over the angels, the constellations, and other heavenly bodies (v. 6). I.E.'s interpretation of the name אלהי הצבאות (= God of the angels) is consistent with a similar remark made in his commentary on Ex. 3:15 and on Ps. 24:10, in which Saadya's interpretation – which corresponds to a statement made by R. Jose in Bab. Talmud, *Sheb̲ūot*, 35b – of this name as "God of the hosts of Israel" is rejected.

31 R.S.V. translates the opening clause of the verse as "so you, by the help of your God, return." However, I.E. interprets this to be a conditional clause. He also seems to take the prepositional *beth* in the second word (באלהיך) in the sense of a *lamed* (= to, cf. Qimhi, ad loc.) – i.e., if only you had turned to your God by keeping "mercy and justice" and by waiting for Him continually. I.E. then supplies the missing conclusion to this protasis, viz., then He would have helped you find how to draw nearer to Him. Cf. above, comm. on 10:12, note 44.

32 The continuation of this verse reads thus: "I have found wealth" (און). I.E. apparently took the word און in the sense of חיל (= wealth, Deut. 8:17, 18) which also means strength. The strength (און) Ephraim claimed to have attained by himself thus may be contrasted with Jacob's (v. 4). See above, note 21.

33 According to I.E., the first and second clauses in v. 9 are in apposition to vv. 7 and 8 respectively. In the first clause the prophet implies that Ephraim boasted of having obtained riches by means of its own effort, thereby rejecting the idea of dependence on God rather than on its own strength (v. 7). Similarly, in the second clause the prophet describes Ephraim's claim that in all efforts to attain wealth its transactions were honest and legitimate. Hence there is no reason for comparing Ephraim with the Canaanite trader, who desires to oppress people by means of exploitation (v. 8), nor was there a need for the prophet to exhort the people by calling on them to "keep mercy and justice."

34 Cheyne (p. 116) is inclined to support the view that the second clause, "I will again make you dwell in the tents, etc.," is a prediction in which the people are threatened to be driven into the wilderness to live in tents, rather than a promise of restoration (as suggested by Jerome, Qimhi, and others). I.E. evidently holds that our verse is neither a threat nor a promise, but rather a rhetorical expression of amazement in which the prophet ponders Ephraim's insensitivity both to God's performance at the early stages of its history and to His ability to repeat the same acts again; i.e., how could you forget the God who brought you out of Egypt with an abundance of riches, the One who is able to maintain you in the future as He did in the past during your tent life in the desert?

35 Lit., "I have already spoken such and such." It should be noted that the LXX renders the verb ודברתי as "and I will speak." However, I.E. maintains that the word should be taken literally, viz., "I have already spoken repeatedly." In his commentary on Lev. 10:19, I.E. indicates that the present verb *inter alia* should be construed as implying the past tense because of its penultimate accent.

36 Lit., "words of lies," evidently a reference to Ephraim's false claims to have obtained its wealth all by itself (v. 9).

37 The translation is based on R.S.V.; J.P.S. renders the phrase thus: "And by the ministry of the prophets have I used similes."

38 According to I.E.'s explanation, the prophet continues here to speak in historical terms (see above, note 34) by saying that God constantly conveyed His will to the people by means of many prophetic parables, in the hope that the message would be readily understood – but to no avail. Qimhi, who adopted here I.E.'s interpretation, points to Is. 5:1 and Ez. 16:3 et passim as salient examples of such parables. Cf. also Maimonides, *Guide* (Introd. to Part I), pp. 10-11: "Know that the key to understanding of all that the prophets . . . have said, and to the knowledge of its truth, is an understanding of the parables . . . .You know what God . . . has said: 'And by the ministry

of the prophets have I used similes,' " (see preceding note).

39 The Hebrew words of our phrase in Hosea, viz., אם גלעד און may be literally translated as "If Gilead [is] iniquity." R.S.V. renders the phrase as "if there is iniquity in Gilead."

40 I.e., if the people of Gilead were formerly iniquitous, they surely came to naught afterward. Comp. 6:8: "Gilead is a city of them that work iniquity." However, I.E. fails to point out which historical event in Gilead the prophet here had in mind. It should be noted that Saadya conjoins the last word of v. 11 (אֲדָמָה) with the following verse, interpreting the words to mean "I have considered the people of Gilead to be either iniquitous or fraudulent"; cf. Zucker, p. 250. By the remark "if the people of Gilead were iniquitous before the prophets" (lit., "and behold if the people of Gilead, etc."), I.E. evidently insists that v. 12 should be taken as an independent statement with respect to the historical deterioration of the people of Gilead, thereby rejecting Saadya's interpretation. In *Moznayim*, p. 4b, I.E. considers Saadya's interpretation unrealistic, "because the word אם (= if) interrupts [the connection] between them" (viz., between vv. 11 and 12). For an earlier objection to a similar interpretation by Saadya, cf. above, comm. on 4:10, note 30.

41 J.P.S. renders this portion of the verse as "in Gilgal they sacrifice unto bullocks." However, A.V. takes the word שורים (= bullocks) to be a direct object of the phrase (i.e., "they sacrifice bullocks") which is equivalent in meaning to the interpretation given here by I.E. ("they sacrifice bullocks to Baal"). Cf. Rashi, Qara, and Qimhi, ad loc.

42 Eliezer of Beaugency, ad loc., takes the correspondence between the heaps and the altars to be a sign of destruction, i.e., their altars have become like heaps of stone. However, Jacob b. Reuben, Rashi (ad loc.), and I.E. together believe that the figure represents the numerous altars they have erected; cf. also Bab. Talmud, *Sanhedrin*, 102b.

43 Comp. Deut. 26:5: ארמי אובד אבי, which is traditionally (e.g, in the Passover Haggadah) taken to mean "[Laban] the Aramean sought to destroy my father [Jacob]." However, in his commentary on Deut. (ibid.) I.E. interprets the phrase thus: "When my father was an Aramean (i.e., when Jacob stayed in Aram) he was poor."

44 By the quotations from Gen. 28:20 and 29:25 and by the remark that Jacob "became a shepherd" for a wife, I.E. explains that the prophet, whose present account of Jacob is based on the narrative given in Gen. 27:45 and 29:20, attempted here to remind the people of their forefather's miserable condition at the time he fled to Aram; i.e., he had to plead with God to provide him with bread, he became subservient to Laban the Aramean and tended his sheep in order to marry Rachel. However, when God rescued him, Jacob became a successful and wealthy man. Cf. Qimhi, ad loc., where I.E.'s interpretation is closely followed almost until the end of this chapter.

45 According to I.E., v. 14 should be taken as a reminder by the prophet of the protection God extended to Jacob's children when they came out of Egypt. This reminder is emphasized by the repetition of the word ובנביא (= and by a prophet),

which indicates that Hosea speaks here only in terms of the people of Israel being cared for by God's chosen prophet (Moses) when he redeemed them from Egypt, rather than in terms of wealth, which they brought with them (cf. comm. on v. 10). I.E. also appears to point out the parallel between the verbs שמר (= he kept, v. 13) and נשמר (= was kept) by explaining the prophet's assertion that Israel turned out to be like the sheep Jacob had cared for (or "guarded," שמר) and that they were likewise cared for (or "guarded") by Moses (נשמר) in later days.

46 The remark "Israel, [however], has forgotten all this" is evidently designed to serve as a link between vv. 14 and 15, i.e., Ephraim has forgotten the preservation of Jacob and the protection of his descendants, instead behaving in a mood of provocation (v. 15).

47 The verb הכעיס (lit., "he has provoked") in its Hiphil form requires a direct object. According to I.E., the missing object is implied in the verb and should be supplied. Hence "Ephraim has provoked *God.*" For the method of supplying the missing object of a transitive verb, cf. above, comm. on 2:7, note 11. The translation "overtly" is based on the interpretation given by I.E. on the following word *tamrūrim.*

48 I.E. evidently takes the term תמרורים in the sense of "waymarks" that are set up on high places in order that they become visible to all bypassers. Similarly, the verb ויתמרמר (Dan. 8:7) also connotes the idea of becoming high and conspicuous. Cf. Qimhi on Jer., ibid., and Ibn Janah, *Dictionary,* p. 273. Hence the phrase means that Ephraim has overtly and conspicuously provoked God. Cf. above, comm. on v. 12: "They (the altars) were numerous and conspicuous." Cf. also Qimhi, ibid.

49 Comp. above 4:2: "And blood toucheth blood". Cf. also below, comm. on 13:2, where our passage is cited.

50 Ibn Janah (*Dictionary,* p. 110) interprets the word יטוש as an intransitive verb, i.e., his blood (viz., Ephraim's lewdness) will be revealed (or reflected) upon himself. However, Qimhi, ad loc., takes the last word of the phrase (אדוניו = his Lord) to be the subject of the two preceding verbs (ישיב, יטוש), thus interpreting both of them in a transitive sense, i.e., and the Lord will spread (or thrust = יטוש) upon him (upon Ephraim) his blood-guilt (viz., his guilt for the acts of bloodshed, cf. Rashi, ad loc.) and He will likewise turn His reproach back upon him (viz., the reproach Ephraim brought upon God by worshiping the idols). From the remark "the innocent blood that Ephraim spilled" and from the quotation "behold they were spread," (I Sam. 30:16) it becomes apparent that Qimhi has substantially adopted I.E.'s overall interpretation, including that of the verb יטוש (= He will spread).

51 The words יטוש (= He will spread) and נטושים (= they were spread) are both derived from the root נטש, a verb meaning "to spread", "to extend."

Chapter XIII

(1) **When [Ephraim] spoke, [there was trembling** means that other] nations [once] were fearful of his [Ephraim's] utterance[s].[1] The word *retēt* [= trembling] is a hapax legomenon [appearing otherwise] only in Aramaic.[2] R. Moses Hakkohen interpreted this [phrase] with respect to Jeroboam [I],[3] who was [of the tribe] of Ephraim as was that [other] Jeroboam the son of Joash, as I shall yet explain.[4] **He was exalted** [means] that [Ephraim's] kingdom was exalted in Israel, for he ruled over the ten tribes; *but when he became guilty . . . he died*, i.e., he was considered as being dead.[5] Furthermore, Abijah slew all of his [Jeroboam I's] troops.[6]

(2) **And now they continue** [*yōsīfū*]:[7] Viz., the present generation continues *to sin.*[8] [The word] *kitb̲ūnām* [(= according to their understanding) is an irregular form for] *kitb̲ūnātām*. Compare *weṣūrām* [(= and their form), in the phrase] "and their form shall be for the netherworld to wear away" [(Ps. 49:15), which similarly is an irregular form for] *weṣūrātām*.[9] **To them they say: [Sacrificers of men kiss calves]**: I.e., people [say it] to them [viz., to the idol worshipers] sarcastically, for they kiss the Baalim which are images of calves. Compare ["yet I will leave seven thousand in Israel] . . . and every mouth which hath not kissed him" [viz., the Baal (I Kings 19:18).[10] Similarly], they shed innocent blood, the idea of [which is expressed in] the [phrase] "his blood He will spread [or "thrust"] upon him" [12:15].[11] They thus act in a way contrary to [the normal actions of] people in general; for normally a man kisses his fellowman who is his friend, and slaughters calves for consumption.[12]

(3) **Therefore [they shall be . . . as the dew of the morning** (*kaṭal mashkim*) **that passeth away**; consequently, they [viz., the worshipers of the idols] will not last. [The term] *mashkim* I have [already] explained.[13] [The figure itself signifies that Ephraim will disappear, as does the dew in the morning], for in the heat of the sun it [viz., the dew] cannot be found.[14] [The word] *kemōṣ* depicts the thin straw

[that is driven] by the whirlwind.[15] [However, the following verb] *yesō'ēr* [= will be swirled] should normally be vocalized with a *patah.* thus [as it stands] it is a rare word [if judged] by [the rules of Hebrew] grammar.[16]

(4) **Yet I am [the Lord thy God . . . and beside Me there is no savior]**: That is to say, how could you turn back to kissing the calf [v. 2] which can neither save nor satiate[17] and abandon God [who was] yours from early days and who has [always] saved you.

(5) **I did know thee [in the wilderness, in a land of *tal'ūbōt*: Meaning,]** He was aware of all your needs.[18] Compare "a righteous man is aware [(*yōdē'ā*) of the life of his beast" (Prov. 12:10)].[19] *A land of tal'ūbōt* signifies a dry and thirsty ground.[20] In Arabic [the root] is the same.[21] [To claim] that it is [a combination of] *kol telā'ōt bō*[22] would be a homiletic explanation, not a literal one.[23]

(6) **[When they entered the land of] their pasture [they became full]:**[24] The prophet here tells [the people] the good things God had done for their forefathers when they came [out] of the wilderness into the land of Canaan.

(7-8) **[And I have become** (*wā'ehī*) **unto them as a lion; as a leopard on a trodden way** (*derek 'āshur*)]: *Wa'ehī* is a verb [connoting] the past tense,[25] which refers to the punishment that God had [already] brought upon them. [The word] *'āshur* is an adjective similar [in form] to *'aṣum* [= mighty], i.e., [*derek 'āshur* = a trodden way] on which a man treads with his steps;[26] yet more, **I will** [in the future] **meet them as a bear robbed of her cubs** [*shākul*]:[27] Some say [that the word *shākul* signifies a bear] whose cubs have been killed; or else it is a transitive participle.[28] [The phrase] *the wild beast,* etc, is [to be taken in its literal sense, i.e.,] I will devour some of them by [means of] pestilence and famine, and the wild beasts will tear apart some of them.[29]

(9) **It is thy destruction [O Israel],**[30] **for in Me** there is compassion which is like a desire [that serves] to help you.[31]

(10) **I will be** [(*'ehī*) **thy king**]: Some say [that the letters in the word *'ehī* (= I will be)] are transposed [and that they should be taken] as *'ayēh* [= where].[32] [However], the correct [interpretation of the phrase] is that of the one who says [it means] *I will be thy king, where* is he, *so that he may save thee* from Me and from the wild beasts;[33] [by mentioning] *thy judges* the idea is [here] repeated.[34]

(11) **I gave thee a king [in Mine anger]**, like Saul of whom the prophet said: "They have rejected Me, that I should not be king over them" [I Sam. 8:7];[35] now *I will take him away in My wrath.*[36]

(12) **[The iniquity of Ephraim] is bound up** means it is [bound up] in My heart – [that is], I shall not forget it,[37] [which is in opposition to the idea contained in the phrase] "they have forgotten Me," mentioned above [v. 6].

(13) **The sorrows of [a travailing woman shall come upon him** (viz., upon Ephraim)]; while [as for] the son whom he will beget – I know that he [too] will be as foolish and *unwise*[38] as his ancestors. Therefore, *he shall last no time at childbirth,*[39] for he will die forthwith.

(14) **From Sheol** have I [in the past] ransomed your ancestors, but now I will become the plague of your death. I will also *become* [*'ehî*] *your destruction.* [The verse "nor] of the plague that walketh in darkness, nor of the destruction [that wasteth at noonday" (Ps. 91:6)] attests [to this interpretation],[40] as if [the prophet] meant [to decree] destruction. Some say [that the word] *'ehî* [(= I will become) should be treated] as *'ayēh* [= where is],[41] because they claimed: "We have made a covenant with death."[42] **[Repentance shall be hidden from Mine eyes]**: The word *nōḥam* [= Repentance] is a noun derived from [the same root as the verb] *wāyînnāḥem* [= and He repented (Ex. 32:14), so that the closing phrase here] means I will no more repent.[43]

(15) **For though [he be fruitful** (*yafrî'*) **among the reed-plants** (*'aḥim*), **an east wind shall come – the wind of the Lord . . . and his spring shall dry up** (*weyēḇōsh*)]: [The word] *aḥim* [= reed-plants] is derived from the [same] noun [as that in] *bā'āḥū* [= in the reed-weeds, (Gen. 41:2)].[44] [The verb] *yafrî'* is identical in meaning to *yafreh* [= "he may be fruitful," "he may flourish"], just as the verb *heḥelî* [Is. 53:10] is an [alternate form] for *heḥelāh* [= he has put to grief].[45] This verse should be taken figuratively. Just as [the prophet] stated [above]: "When they entered the land of their pasture [they became full" (v. 6)], so he now describes how God will kill them and destroy them [vv. 7-8].[46] [The verb] *weyēḇōsh* is similar [in meaning] to *weyyîḇash* [= and shall dry up].[47] Alternately, its literal sense may be retained, [meaning] that its waters [viz., the waters of Ephraim's spring] shall fail [him];[48] and *the wind* [*of the Lord*] is [here] designed to represent symbolically the enemy,[49] *who will spoil* [*the treasure of all precious vessels*].

Notes

1 I.e., at the early stage of the Northern Kingdom, when it stood high among the nations, the words of its leaders commanded awe and respect. According to this interpretation, the syntactical relation of the word רתת to the first line of the verse is that of an apodosis to a preceding protasis, both of which represent a complete statement with regard to Ephraim's glorious past. R.S.V. similarly translates thus: "When Ephraim spoke men trembled," Cf. also note 3, below.

2 The word רתת does not occur elsewhere in the Bible, except as an Aramaic translation of the Hebrew nouns רעד and רטט (= trembling, Ex. 15:15, Jer. 49:24). So also Jacob b. Reuben, ad loc.; Ibn Janah, *Dictionary*, p. 488; and Ibn Parchon, op. cit., p. 65b.

3 According to Rashi, ad loc., the prophet's rapid résumé of Ephraim's early history includes the first and the second phrase of the verse, i.e., when Ephraim (viz., Jeroboam I) spoke harshly and fearfully against King Solomon, he was exalted to become the king of Israel (comp. I Kings 11:26-27). Thus the word רתת (= fearfully) is taken to be an infinitive (similar in form to שאת = forgiveness, Gen. 4:7) designed to modify the first word of the verse (viz., כדבר = when he spoke, i.e., when Ephraim spoke fearfully [רתת], etc.). A.V. similarly translates thus: "When Ephraim spake trembling, he exalted himself in Israel." By the remark "vgl. Raschi z. St." (= comp. Rashi ad loc.), Poznanski (*Ibn Chiquitilla*, p. 151) seems to imply that Chiquitilla's (= R. Moses Hakkohen's) interpretation of our verse is similar to that of Rashi, rather than to the one given above by I.E. (see note 1, above). This conjecture is open to question. For Ibn Chiquitilla may very well agree with I.E.'s interpretation according to which the term רתת serves as an apodosis to the first phrase of the verse, i.e., when Ephraim spoke, there was trembling (= רתת) among other nations. However, since the prophet may have referred to the general position the tribe of Ephraim occupied in the past (e.g., in the times of Joshua), the comment ascribed to Ibn Chiquitilla stipulates that the prophet here describes the days of Jeroboam I. Furthermore, due attention should be given to I.E.'s final remark, "as I shall yet explain," which denotes a sense of approval of the preceding quotation. Cf. also I.E.'s remark on the word וימת (= and he died), which lends tacit approval to Ibn Chiquitilla's explanation. It is thus fair to conclude that I.E.'s own comment on the opening phrase of the verse is consonant with the one quoted here in the name of Ibn Chiquitilla.

4 Cf. comm. on Am. 7:13: "That Jehu (the founder of the dynasty of Jeroboam II) was from Bethel" (viz., from Ephraim). Cf. also above, comm. on 5:3.

5 I.e., when Ephraim incurred guilt through worshiping the Baalim, they were spiritually as good as dead; cf. Bab. Talmud, *Berakot*, 18b: "The wicked even in their lifetime are reckoned as dead". Cf. also Harper, p. 394: "Each step in this direction was a step nearer death as a nation. Ephraim in Hosea's time, had been dying for a long time."

6 Comp. II Chron. 13:15: "As the men of Judah shouted, it came to pass that God

smote Jeroboam and all Israel before Abijah and Judah," ibid. v. 20: "Neither did Jeroboam recover strength again in the days of Abijah; the Lord smote him, and he died." Hence the word וימת (Lit., "and he died") may be taken either in its spiritual (see preceding note) or in its literal sense.

7 So Harper, p. 394; A.V., J.P.S., and R.S.V. all render *yōsīfū* as "more and more" instead of "continue".

8 I.E. evidently aims here to explain the word ועתה (lit., "and now") as connoting that the present generation of Jeroboam II is no better than the one of Jeroboam I (v. 1).

9 The Targum and Rashi, ad loc., both interpret the word כתבונם in the sense of כתבניתם (= according to their model), a noun which is derived from the verb בנה (= to build), i.e., they have made for themselves idols according to their own model. However, according to I.E., כתבונם should be taken to mean "according to their understanding," a noun which is derived from the verb בון (= to understand), but in the sense of כתבונתם with an additional *taw* between the *nun* and *mem*, as in the case of the noun וצורם, which is also missing a *taw* and is taken in the sense of וצורתם (= and their form, with a *taw*). Cf. Qimhi, ad loc. Cf. also A.V.: "And (they have made) idols according to their own understanding."

10 The passage cited here is designed to show the practice of kissing the Baalim – evidently as a token of homage – elsewhere in the Bible. Comp. also I Kings 18:27: ויהתל בהם אליהו (= And . . . Elijah mocked them), viz., the prophets of Baal, to which I.E. may have also referred indirectly by his remark להתל בהם (lit., "to mock them").

11 Cf. above, comm. on 12:15, note 50, for a comment on I.E.'s interpretation of the phrase in question.

12 The second clause of the verse should, in I.E.'s view, be taken in the following sense: People deride the absurdity of idol worshipers by telling them sarcastically that their sacrificing men and worshiping calves is contrary to human behavior.

13 Cf. above, comm. on 6:4 where the term *mashkim* is treated as a noun (viz., "morning," "dawn"), with the possibility left open that it is also a verb (viz., "to rise in the morning")

14 I.e., as the dew passes away in the morning and is no more, so will the Northern Kingdom vanish swiftly.

15 The phrase reads: כמץ יְסֹעֵר מגרן, which A.V. translates in the passive sense: "As the chaff that is driven with the whirlwind out of the floor," i.e., Ephraim will easily be driven off "like the chaff which the wind driveth away" (Ps. 1:4); cf. comm. ibid., where our passage is cited.

16 R.S.V. renders our phrase: "Like the chaff that swirls," thus taking the verb יְסֹעֵר (= that swirls) in the active sense. However, I.E. considers it to be a passive verb of the Pual form (cf. Qimhi, ad loc.), therefore the proper vocalization should be יְסֹעַר with a *patah* under the *ayin*, instead of יְסֹעֵר with a *sere*, which is indeed rare.

17 By the phrase ולא ישביע (lit., "and will not satiate") I.E. evidently had in mind the words וישבעו and שבעו ("they became full" or "satiated") of verse 6.

18 I.E. interprets the word ידעתיך in the sense of God's "being aware" of the needs of the people when they walked in the wilderness, i.e., you have abandoned your God who helped you come forth out of the land of Egypt (v. 4) and who knew how to supply you with all your needs in the desert (v. 5).

19 In addition to the phrase quoted here by I.E. from Prov. 12:10, cf. Qara, ad loc., who quotes Deut. 2:7: "These forty years the Lord thy God hath been with thee; thou hast lacked nothing," a phrase which is preceded by the verb ידע (= He hath known) in a similar sense.

20 I.E. here quotes a phrase from Ez. 19:13: "And now she is planted in the wilderness in a dry and thirsty ground." However, the Hebrew words translated as "dry" and "thirsty" (ציה, צמא) have no etymological relationship to the Heb. *tal'ūḇōt.*

21 I.E. appears to have had in mind the Arabic translation given by Ibn Janah of the phrase בארץ תלאובות, في بلاد الاب اى المعاطش (= in the land of the Lybians, that is, the thirsty [= dried-out] grounds). Cf. Bacher, *Abraham Ibn Esra als Grammatiker*, pp. 167-168, and Ibn Janah, *Dictionary*, p. 236, s.v. לאב.

22 According to this explanation, the last *taw* would have to be placed after the *aleph* and the order of the *beth* and the *waw* reversed, thus forming two separate words: *Telā'ōt bō* (תלאות בו), lit., "troubles in it," i.e., God knew (or was aware) of the people's needs in the wilderness, in the land of all the troubles. For a similar interpretation, cf. Menahem bar Helbo as quoted by Joseph Qara in *Sokolow Jubilee Volume* (Warsaw, 1904), p. 426.

23 I.E. is essentially not opposed to the method of transposing letters in a difficult word that needs clarification (cf. e.g., above, 10:9), nor does he object in his commentaries (e.g, Gen. 11:9, 30:11; Ps. 116:12) to such interpretations in which the disjunction of a Hebrew word is involved. However, he may have considered the homiletical character of the explanation *tela'ōt bō* (= troubles in it), viz., in the wilderness, to be farfetched, because it involves the disjunction of the word and the additional transposition of its letters at the same time. For I.E.'s view on homiletical expositions, cf. above, comm. on 4:3, note 9.

24 The translation here is based on the interpretation given by Rashi; Qara, ad loc.; and evidently also by I.E., according to which the first word of the verse (כמרעיתם, lit., "according to their pasture") signifies here a place of pasture rather than the act of pasturing, i.e., when God caused their ancestors to reach the place of pasturing, viz., the land of Canaan, they soon became successful. Cf. Qimhi, ad loc., for a similar explanation. J.P.S. renders the opening phrase of the verse as "when they were fed, they became full."

25 The LXX, A.V., and R.S.V. all render the verb ואהי in the future tense ("and I

will be"). So also Qara and Eliezer of Beaugency, ad loc. However, I.E. (as well as Qimhi, ad loc.) evidently construed the copulative *waw* as a *waw* conversive preceding an imperfect conjugation. Hence "and I have become," i.e., after their forefathers have forgotten Me (v. 6) I also rejected them "and I have become unto them as a lion, etc."

26 According to I.E., the word *'āshur* is taken as an adjective which defines the preceding noun (viz., *dereḵ* = way) in the sense that God has become to the people as a concealed "leopard on a trodden way," ready to leap upon the many bypassers there (in addition, when a leopard attacks on a trodden way there is hardly any escape for his prey). So also Ibn Janah (*Dictionary*, pp. 51, 504) who rejects Yehuda Hayyug's view (p. 97, which view is shared by Menahem [*Mahberet*, p. 36], Rashi, and Qara, [ad loc.]) wherein *'āshur* is treated as a verb (viz., "I will look," "I will observe").

27 A bear robbed of her cubs is ferocious and extremely dangerous. R.S.V. renders the opening phrase of our verse thus: "I will fall upon them like a bear robbed of her cubs."

28 תואר יוצא, lit., "transitive adjective," i.e., "I will meet them" (as rendered in A.V., or "I will fall upon them," see preceding note) as a robbing (viz., attacking) bear. Thus the adjective שכול ("robbed," "bereaved"), which is generally considered to be a passive participle, would be taken here in the active sense (viz., שוכל = robbing). For a similar interpretation, cf. Rashi and Qara, ad loc. Cf. also Gersonides on II Sam. 17:8. For a more detailed discussion on the character of the passive as well as the active Hebrew participle (including those commented on here by I.E.), cf. comm. on Ex. 18:10.

It should be noted that the term "transitive adjective" appears also in I.E.'s commentary on Is. 2:21 and in the commentary on Prov. ascribed to I.E. (ed. S.R. Driver [Oxford, 1880]), 17:12. Moreover, both interpretations of the phrase כדב שכול given here by I.E. are also found in the aforementioned commentary on Prov., a significant point of agreement which Driver (ibid. Introd., pp. xiii-xiv) failed to list in his attempt to attribute the work on Proverbs to Ibn Ezra.

29 The Targum renders the closing phrase of the verse as "I will destroy them as the wild beast tears." However, according to I.E. the prophet here implies that in addition to receiving God's natural punishment they will in fact be torn by wild beasts. I.E. evidently has in mind the natural punishment mentioned in vv. 14-15.

30 So J.P.S. However, the rendering of A.V. ("O Israel, thou hast destroyed thyself") agrees with that of Rashi, ad loc. See following note.

31 Rashi interprets v. 9: "O Israel, you have destroyed yourself, [for you have rebelled] against your help" (or "your helper"). However, I.E.'s remark ניחום כמו יצר (lit., "compassion which is like a desire," or "consolation, as an inclination") is not clear in itself (cf. also the variant readings in the ed. of the Heb. text) nor does it explain how he interprets v. 9 as a whole. Cf. Filwarg (p.4b) who also concludes that the present remark by I.E. is obscure and requires further consideration. According to our conjectural translation, v. 9 was construed by I.E. in the sense of "O Israel, the

revolt against Me who has a passionate desire to help you, has caused your destruction."

32 Viz., where is your king? The Targum, LXX, and Menahem (*Mahberet*, p. 18) all render אהי (lit., "I will be") in the sense of איה (= where is). So also R.S.V.: "Where now is your king to save you?" Cf. also below, comm. on v. 14 for the same quotation.

33 According to I.E., the word אהי is to be taken in its literal sense (viz., "I will be"), i.e., that one claiming to be the king who protects you – where is he now when such a calamity (vv. 7-8) is confronting you? For a similar interpretation, cf. Jacob b. Reuben, ad loc. By the remark "from Me and from the wild beasts," I.E. evidently has in mind his comment on v. 8: "I will devour some of them . . . and the wild beast will tear apart some of them."

34 I.e., where is the one who claims to be your king and where are your judges who might save you at this critical juncture? Cf. above, comm. on 5:1, where the term "judges" is also applied to kings.

35 The phrase "I give thee a king in Mine anger" refers, according to I.E., to the establishment of King Saul's monarchy, when the prophet Samuel expressed God's anger ("they have rejected Me"), by virtue of the people's demand "make us a king to judge us" (I Sam. 8:5).

36 By emphasizing "*now* I will take him away, etc." I.E. appears to ascribe the closing phrase of the verse to the days of Hosea, when the kingdom had undergone a disastrous decline which could only be interpreted as being a result of God's anger.

37 Viz., the iniquity of the Northern Kingdom will not be forgotten, but rather it will be remembered by God and produced as evidence against Ephraim on the day of reckoning.

38 By using the terms "foolish" (נבל, according to most mss. at our disposal), and "and unwise" (ולא חכם), I.E. may have aimed to paraphrase the passage "O foolish people and unwise" (Deut. 32:6).

39 J.P.S. renders the second part of the verse thus: "For it is time he should not tarry in the place of the breaking forth of children." According to this rendering, the figure depicts Ephraim's failure to desist from idolatry, which may be compared to a child failing to emerge from the mother's womb. However, I.E. appears to take v. 13 in the sense of an announced punishment which Ephraim will endure on the day of reckoning (see note 37), i.e., Israel will bear children in – or will suffer – great pain; and since God knows that a future generation will not take to heart the reason for the sufferings of their ancestors, the generation will not persevere, but rather its newborn children will die instantly. Cf. above, comm. on 9:12.

40 Rashi takes the word דבריך in its literal sense (viz., "your words") i.e., "I will direct myself to speak with regard to you words of death." Cf. also Qara, ad loc. However, I.E. considers the terms to be derived from דבר (*deb̲er* = pestilence, plague), which

is synonymous with קטב (= destruction). Thus the meaning of our phrase will be "I will be your plague, which will cause your death," "I will be your destruction unto Sheol." This view is adopted by Ibn Parhon (op. cit., p. 2a) and shared by Eliezer of Beaugency, ad loc. Cf. Qimhi, *Dictionary*, s.v. אהי, where our passage is similarly interpreted: "I will be the cause of your plagues resulting in death and the cause of your destruction unto Sheol." Cf. also Schroeter, *Archiv*, II, 190.

41 For the identical suggestion to read איה for אהי, cf. above, comm. on v. 10.

42 According to this interpretation, the prophet attempts here to ridicule their so-called covenant with death by saying sarcastically: Where are your words (איה דבריך) that you have uttered when you made a covenant with death and destruction? The phrase "we have made a covenant with death" (Is. 28:15) is explained by I.E. (ibid.) to mean "we shall not die now." For an interpretation similar to that quoted here by I.E., cf. Poznanski, "The Arabic Commentary of Abu Zakariya Ibn Bal'am", *JQR* (N.S.), XV (1924-1925), 24; Ibn Janah, *Dictionary*, p. 14; Qara (in the name of Menahem bar Helbo), ad loc.; Joseph Qimhi, *Sepher Hagaluy*, p. 68; and Jacob b. Reuben (the disputant), *Milḥamōt Hashēm*, ed. by Yehudah Rosenthal (Jerusalem, 1963), p. 128.

43 So also Menahem (*Mahberet*, p. 122), Rashi, and Qara (ad loc.), all of whom take the closing phrase of the verse as a warning that God will show the people of the Northern Kingdom mercy no more. However, Ibn Janah (*Dictionary*, p. 298) interprets the phrase in the sense that God will not console them.

44 The LXX and A.V. both render the word אחים as "brethren"; cf. also Qimhi, ad loc. However, Menahem (*Mahberet*, p. 20), Ibn Janah (*Dictionary*, p. 22), and I.E. (cf. also *Ṣaḥōt*, p. 23b) all agree that the term אחים is the plural of אחו meaning reed-weeds (or grass-weeds).

45 I.E. is of the opinion that the word *yafrī'*, although with an *aleph* at the end, is derived from the radicals *pe*, *resh*, *hē*, a verb meaning "to be fruitful" (or "to flourish"), rather than from the radicals *pe*, *resh*, *aleph* (= to grow wild, as listed in Ibn Janah's *Dictionary*, p. 410). Similarly, the verb *heḥelī* (= he has put to grief, with a *yod* at the end), which is the apocopated form of *heḥelī'* (with an *aleph* at the end), is in reality derived from the radicals *ḥet*, *lamed* and *hē*. Thus in both cases the *aleph* replaces the *hē*, which is originally the third radical of each verb. Cf. Rashi, ad loc. (first explanation). Cf. also *Moznayim*, p. 50b, for a discussion of the same anomalies.

46 I.E. holds that the opening phrase of the verse is not a promise that the people will prosper and be fruitful, but rather a figure of speech designed to describe the impending punishment; i.e., although they could have been fruitful as is the reed-grass in the midst of water, nevertheless because of their stubbornness, an east wind (viz., the enemy) will destroy them.

47 Most translators who render the word *weyēḇōsh*: "And . . . shall dry up" (LXX, R.S.V., and Harper; A.V. and J.P.S.: "And . . . shall become dry") evidently agree that

the radicals of this verb are *yod*, *beth*, and *shin*. However, according to Hebrew grammatical principles, the proper vocalization of the word should then be *weyyīḇash* with an additional performative *yod* to indicate the imperfect (comp. *wayyīḇash* = and it dried up, I Kings 17:7, with a double *yod*). Since I.E. treats *weyēḇōsh* (with one *yod*) in a sense similar to that of *weyyīḇash* (with a double *yod*), he evidently shares the opinion of Dunash (*Teshūḇōt*, p. 30) that in our case one *yod* is dropped and the remaining one may serve simultaneously as the first radical of the verb as well as a preformative letter to indicate the third person future. For the controversy between Dunash and Menahem with regard to our passage, cf. *Sepher Teshūḇōt Talmīdēy Menahem Wetalmid Dunash*, sec. 2, pp. 38-39.

48 According to this explanation, the word *weyēḇōsh* is derived from the radicals *beth*, *waw*, and *shin*, a verb meaning "to embarrass," "to put to shame" (as above in 10:6, but in a transitive sense; cf. Menahem, *Mahberet*, p. 48); i.e., and his spring (viz., his waters, which are the source of fruitfulness) will fail (or embarrass) Ephraim. I.E.'s remark "that its waters shall fail" seems to be based here on the passage "and thou shalt be . . . like a spring of water, whose waters fail not" (Is. 58:11).

49 Comp. Jer. 18:17: "I will scatter them as with an east wind before the enemy," meaning (according to Qara, ibid.) that the people of Judah will be scattered by a hostile king who is as strong as an east wind.

Chapter XIV

(1) [The verb] *te'sham* [in the opening phrase means] that [Samaria] shall become desolate.[1] **They shall fall by the sword**: Viz., its people;[2] **[and their pregnant women shall be ripped up]**: Since the word *wehārîyōtāw* [= their pregnant women] is in the feminine, [the prophet] did not mind using *yebuqqā'ū* [=they will be ripped up, in the masculine]. Compare "that ye awaken not, nor stir up," [Cant. 2:7, 3:5].[3]

(2) **Return [O, Israel]** a little bit **toward** [*'ad*] **the Lord**:[4] The meaning [of the closing phrase] is *for thou hast stumbled in thine iniquity*, and there is no one who will restore you, except God alone.[5]

(3) **Take [with you words]**: [That is to say], when you go to seek His good will He does not ask you for any payment of money nor burnt offerings, but only words of confession.[6] [The word] *tissā'* [in the second clause of our verse means You shall bear]; compare "the goat shall bear" [Lev. 16:22].[7] R. Marinus said that [the literal order of the words in the phrase] *all bear iniquity* is reversed, [meaning] all iniquity thou shalt bear [(viz., remove).[8] However], the correct interpretation [of the phrase] is that as long as You forgive our iniquities we shall return.[9] [The phrase] *weqaḥ ṭōb* [means] accept that which is better than a burnt offering; or else [it means accept] the *good* words that we are able to offer before you, meaning to confess.[10] R. Joseph said [the term *good*] signifies the scanty good deeds.[11] **And we will render** a rendering of **bullocks [our lips]**: Compare "for Thou hast smitten all mine enemies' cheeks" [Ps. 3:8], which means [with] a blow upon the cheek,[12] or else supply [here] a *kaph.*[13] The bullocks are mentioned [here] because they are the biggest and most expensive [animals] among the burnt offerings.[14] The following is what you should say:

(4) **Assyria [shall not save us]**: Since it is written [above]: "Assyria shall be his king" [11:5],[15] we shall [now by contrast] no longer depend on Assyria nor on our horses that are obtained from Egypt [Is. 31:1]. **Neither will we call any more the work of our hands our**

gods; [for in Thee the fatherless findeth mercy]: [The first part of this passage] is meant to recall "the work of the craftsmen;"[16] for there is no one who can assist the helpless, e.g., the fatherless, except You, as it is written: "A father of the fatherless . . . [is God in His holy habitation" (Ps. 68:6)]. This passage is in opposition to [the statement] "for thou hast stumbled in thine iniquity" [v. 2], and there being no one to help you.[17]

(5) **I will heal [their backsliding[**; The word *meshūb̲āh* [= backsliding] is used in a pejorative sense throughout Scripture.[18] Its meaning is not as [a certain interpreter] claims, namely, that the word equals *mōshb̲ōtām* [= their dwellings],[19] meaning that [*I will heal them*] everywhere I smote them; but rather it means backsliding, which is [as harmful] for the soul as a disease for the body. Hence the terms *erpā'* [=I will heal],[20] which is in contrast to [the expression] "Ephraim is smitten" [9:16]. **I will love them** with *free* love[21] – contrary to [the threat] "my God will cast them away" [9:17]. **For [Mine anger] is turned away** – contrary to [God's warning]: "Mine anger is kindled against them" [8:5].

(6) [The promise] **I will be [as the dew unto Israel]** is contrary to [the prophet's assertions] "their root is dried up" [9:16], and "his [Ephraim's] spring shall become dry" [13:15]. The [simile of the] *lily* is [here appropriate on account of its] quick blossoming;[22] [however], because it has none other than a slender root [the text continues by] saying that its *roots* will [despite this simile] be [as firm as] the root of the trees of Lebanon.[23] [Israel] **shall strike** [*weyak̲*] **his roots** lengthwise and breadthwise. [For the meaning of the verb *weyak̲*] compare "[the border] . . . shall strike [*ūmāḥāh*] upon the slope of the sea of Chinnereth" [Num. 34:11]. In geometry [the terms to describe this are] *sheb̲ārim* and *tab̲rītā* [?].[24]

(8) **[They that dwell within his shadow] shall return**: Yefet said [the meaning of this phrase is] that those who dwell under the shadow of Lebanon [shall return].[25] [However], in my opinion [the prophet spoke here of those] who dwell within the shadow of Israel, namely the servants who will become their farmers and their vine growers; *they shall revive the grain*[26] and the standing grain[27] *shall blossom as the vine*. [The noun] *zik̲rō* [in the closing phrase means Israel's] fragrance; compare "*azkārātāh* [= the incense thereof (Lev. 2:2)].[28] Yefet said [that the noun *zik̲rō* signifies] the fame of their vines,[29] which will be [known] a great distance away as [that of] the wine of Lebanon [par excellence].

(9) When [the prophet] says: *Ephraim, what have I to do any more* [*with idols*, he refers to Ephraim's future declaration]: I have no need for them – *I* [viz., God] *will respond* to him by providing him with all his needs;[30] compare "money answereth all things" [Eccl. 10:19].[31] **I will look after him** by setting My eyes upon him [viz., upon Ephraim] benevolently (until *I will look after him*).[32] Subsequently, he will become *like a leafy cypress tree.*[33] [However], do not be dismayed by the fact that a cypress has no fruit, for *from Me is thy fruit found.*

(10) **Whoever is wise, [let him understand these things; prudent let him know them]**: [The force of the pronoun] *whoever* is carried over to the following [phrase];[34] while [the pronoun] *these* refers to the *ways of the Lord.* The meaning [of this passage and the foregoing prophecy] is interconnected – for when you [will] return to God He will heal you.[35] **[For the ways of the Lord are right, and the just do walk in them; but transgressors do stumble therein]**: [The term] *poshe'im* [(=transgressors) depicts] those who forsake legitimate authority. Compare "for every matter of embezzlement" [*debar pesha'* (Ex. 22:8)], "then did [Libnah] revolt" [*tifsha'* (II Kings 8:22)].[36] Accordingly, the one who perverts himself[37] by [abandoning] the righteous way[38] will stumble. [The prophet thus] concludes [this prophecy] by way of [citing the idea contained in the phrase] "for thou hast stumbled in thine iniquity" [v. 2].[39]

Notes

1 The Targum, R.S.V, and J.P.S. all render the first line of our verse as "Samaria shall bear her guilt." However, I.E. and before him Menahem (*Mahberet*, p. 35) both maintain that the word תאשם here signifies destruction. So also the LXX ("Samaria shall be utterly destroyed") and A.V. ("Samaria shall become desolate. ") For I.E.'s view regarding the verb אשם, cf. above, chap. 5, note 50.

2 The remark "its people" is evidently designed to conjoin the plural in the second clause of the verse (e.g., "they shall fall, etc.") with the preceding singular verbs (e.g., "she shall become desolate," "she has rebelled"), i.e., Samaria shall become desolate and its people shall fall (= יפלו) by the sword. See, however, *Kritik des Dunasch ben Labrat*, p. 52, note 16, where our passage is listed among others to show the promiscuous combination of singular and plural in Scripture.

3 The term הריות (= pregnant women) is a plural formation of the singular feminine noun הרית. Consequently, the following Hebrew verb meaning "they shall be ripped

up" should also be in the feminine (viz., תבוקענה instead of יבקעו). However, I.E. seems to imply that the rules governing the coordination of *feminine* nouns with their verbal predicates are not as strictly followed as those governing the coordination of *masculine* nouns with their predicates. By quoting the example from Cant., he intends to show a similar case, in which the masculine verbs תעירו, תעוררו (lit., "you will awaken," "you will stir up,") appear to be in discord with their preceding feminine subject בנות ירושלים (= daughters of Jerusalem).

4 I.E. evidently takes the preposition עד (which is in striking difference to the preposition in v. 3, אל) in the sense of "until" rather than "unto." Thus, in his view, the prophet here calls upon the people to turn away little by little from apostasy, until they draw nearer to the Lord and reconcile with Him. For a similar interpretation, cf. *Yalqut Hamakiri* on Hosea, ed. by A.W. Greenup (London, 1903), p. 2.

5 Cf. below, comm. on v. 4, where the phrase "for thou hast stumbled in thine iniquity" is cited.

6 Cf. *Pesiqta Rabbati*, p, 198b: "God said to Israel: My children, I will no longer accept from you either burnt offerings or sin offerings, etc., but rather you shall entreat Me . . . by way of confession, supplications, and tears. Hence the phrase 'take with you words.'"

7 Our translation at this point is based on the suggestion of Sharim (p. 31b) that I.E. here begins a new comment regarding the verb. By quoting the phrase "the goat shall bear," I.E. appears to indicate that in his opinion the verb תשא (= You shall bear) should be taken here in the sense of "carrying away" or "removing" (i.e., forgiving), which is similar in meaning to the verb ונשא in the phrase "the goat shall bear" (Lev. 16:22). Cf. above, commentary on 1:6. Thus the prophet urged the people to plead with God so that He might remove iniquity and accept their confession. Significantly, I.E. does not here quote God's attribute נושא עון (lit., "bearer of iniquity," Ex. 34:7) to which a lengthy discourse is dedicated in his commentary (ibid.) in order to define its meaning with respect to forgiveness or punishment.

8 Cf. Ibn Janah, *Hariqmah*, p. 224. However, in his commentary on Ps. 74:3 I.E. attributes this interpretation to R. Moses Hakkohen (= Ibn Chiquitilla). See following note.

9 According to I.E.'s own interpretation, the preposition כל (lit., "all") has the sense of "alongside with" or "in the presence of," which is similar to that given by Saadya in his *Hāʾemūnōt Wehadēʿōt*, sec. V., chap. 5; i.e., by virtue (or "in the presence") of Your forgiveness You shall accept our confession. In his commentary on Ps. 74:3, I.E. explains the second clause of our verse as follows: "[Say unto Him]: Along with Your forgiveness of our iniquities You shall accept the good things we possess; this is our confession. For [the confession of] our lips is even better than to offer bullocks" (viz., sacrifices).

10 In the first instance the term טוב is construed as a substantive, meaning "a better thing," and in the second טוב becomes an adjective in which the noun דיבור (lit.,

"speech") is implied (i.e., "accept our good words"), but in any case the idea here remains that God should accept their confession.

11 I.e., accept our remaining good deeds and count them in our favor. Cf. Rashi, ad loc.; cf. also Isaiah da Trani, p. 84: "Look at our scanty merits rather than at our iniquities." The remark ascribed here to the yet unidentified R. Joseph appears in the printed editions of I.E. as well as in all the mss. at our disposal. However, on the basis of a manuscript of the British Museum (237), Harry Cohen (in the additional notes to his edition of *The Commentary of Rabbi David Kimhi on Hosea* [New York, 1966], p. 129) concludes that the present remark is a gloss which was added to the text of I.E.

12 J.P.S. renders the passage as "for thou hast smitten all mine enemies upon the cheek," but there is nothing in the Hebrew text standing for "upon the." According to I.E., the term לחי (= cheek) is an ellipsis in which the word מכת (lit., "a blow of") should be supplied. Similarly, the word שילום (= a rendering) should be supplied in the closing phrase of our verse, i.e., by confessing with our lips we will render *a rendering* of bullocks, for confession is preferred over sacrifices. Cf. above, note 9, and comm. on 2:20.

13 A.V. renders the closing phrase of our verse as "so we will render the calves of our lips," as though the term for "calves," despite its orthography, were in the construct state. According to I.E.'s second interpretation, the word פרים (= bullocks) is lacking a comparative *kaph* (= as), i.e., and we will render, instead of sacrificial bullocks, our lips (viz., the words of our lips) by way of prayer and confession. For a similar remark, cf. comm. on Is. 26:6 and *Sāphā Berūrāh* (supplement to *The Book of Reasons*, ed. by Naphtali Ben-Menahem [Jerusalem, 1941], pp. 49, 59). Cf. also Saadya (as quoted above in note 9) יתכן להיות כפרים ויתכן שיש בו הסתר (= perhaps read כפרים [with an additional *kaph*] or else the verse may be elliptical).

14 Burnt offerings may also be taken from flock or fowl; comp. Lev. 1:10, 14. The bullock, however, was considered to be the prime sacrifice, because it was the largest and costliest animal offered on the altar. For a similar remark, cf. comm. on Ps. 50:9.

15 I.E. evidently wishes to point out that by the phrase "Assyria shall not save us" the prophet asked the people to renounce their reliance on the Assyrian king to whom they once submitted in return for security and friendship (11:5).

16 I.E. construes the term מעשה ידינו (= the work of our hands) as being similar to מעשה חרשים (= the work of the craftsmen, 13:2), viz., the inert idols in which the people once put their trust, but pledge now to call them gods no more.

17 I.E. here refers to the closing phrase "for in Thee the fatherless findeth mercy." He evidently interprets the preposition בך (lit., "in Thee") as "in Thee alone" (so also Qara, ad loc.), i.e., for only You extend mercy to the fatherless. Similarly, Israel's only hope for restoration rests in their return to God; they had stumbled in their iniquity (v. 2) and He alone can restore them.

18 For a similar remark, cf. above, comm. on 11:7.

19 The printed editions of I.E. as well as our mss. all have *meshūḇātām* (משובתם = their backsliding) for *moshḇōtam* (מושבותם), which makes no sense; our translation is based on the reading cited by Sharim (p. 31b). The source in which משובתם is taken to mean מושבותם (= their dwelling places) could not be ascertained, but the rendering of the LXX ("I will restore their dwellings") lends credence to this interpretation.

20 I.e., backsliding with respect to the soul is like a physical disease that requires healing. Comp. Jer. 3:22: "I will heal your backsliding," and Ps. 41:5: "Heal My soul; for I have sinned against Thee."

21 Most translators (A.V., J.P.S., R.S.V.) render the phrase אהבם נדבה thus: "I will love them freely." However, according to I.E., the phrase should be treated as an ellipsis, in which case the required noun אהבת (lit., "love of") is supplied. Thus, lit., "I will love them a love of generosity" (i.e., with a generous love). For I.E.'s method of interpreting similar elliptical passages in the Bible, cf. above, notes 10,12.

22 I.e. the phrase "he shall blossom as a lily" means Israel shall blossom as quickly as a lily.

23 The closing phrase reads literally thus: "And he (viz., Israel) shall strike his roots as Lebanon." Note that I.E. supplies the word עצי (= trees of) that is indeed required in the text, i.e., "as the trees (viz., the cedars) of Lebanon," instead of "as Lebanon." Cf. Qimhi, ad loc., for a similar interpretation.

24 Cf. Ibn Janah, *Dictionary*, p. 304: "[The phrase] 'and he shall strike his roots' means he shall take roots which will extend a great distance away." Cf. also comm. on Num. 34:11 and Is. 55:12, where *maḥah* is interpreted in the sense of "to break" (תבריתא) or "to strike."

The last comment by I.E. on v. 6 (ובמדות שברים ותבריתא = and in geometry breaking and striking) is vague and ambiguous and the many attempts to explain its exact meaning are to no avail (cf., e.g., Sharim, p. 31b; Filwarg, p. 5a; Eisler in *Beth Talmud*, II [1882], 187). Friedlaender (*Essays*, p. 209, note 1) remarks: "According to I.E. the verbs denoting 'to strike', 'to break' may be used in the sense of 'extending,' and he supports his view by citing שברים and תבריתא, used by mathematicians in the sense of 'surface'," a remark which hardly explains I.E.'s comment adequately. It should be noted that in three of the mss. at our disposal (M,R and V) the three words ובמדות שברים ותבריתא are indeed missing.

25 According to Yefet's explanation quoted here by I.E., the pronominal ending ו (= his) in the word בצלו (= in his shadow) refers back to "Lebanon," mentioned in the preceding verse. It should be noted that in Yefet's commentary on Hosea (p. 223) the noun בצלו is taken to mean "in His shadow" (viz., in the shadow of God), as rendered by Jacob b. Reuben and Qimhi, ad loc., i.e., those who will return from exile will dwell under the shadow (viz., protection) of God. However, the interpretation ascribed here to Yefet may have been quoted by I.E. in view of the fact that the name "Lebanon" is also identified with the Temple, which is considered to be the shadow of God; cf. Targum on Deut. 3:25 and Rashi, ad loc.

26 I.e., the servants who dwell in "his shadow," (viz., the shadow of Israel) shall return to revive the crops and make the grain grow.

27 Note that the subject supplied here by I.E. (קמות = standing stalks of grain), which is in plural, agrees in number with the preceding verb ויפרחו (= and they shall blossom); it may also have been introduced by him to indicate the contrast of the present thought with the expression "the standing grain has no heads" (8:7).

28 It should be added that the identification of *zik̲rō* with *azkārātāh*, which I.E. seems to have adopted here, is quoted in his commentary on Lev. 2:2 and Cant. 1:4 in the name of others, as a subsequent interpretation to that of his own. Cf. also comm. on Is. 66:3 and Friedlaender's note (4) thereon.

29 In his commentary on Hosea (p. 224) Yefet interprets the phrase זכרו כיין לבנון by saying that "the prophet meant their fame and excellent renown among the nations, to the extent that the nations of the world will enter into their religion. It is also possible that the prophet meant by this phrase the fragrance of their offerings included among which was the wine of libation," i.e., Israel's renown would extend as far as that of the wine of Lebanon. This last interpretation by Yefet appears to be closer to I.E.'s own remark on the term *zik̲rō*.

30 For a similar interpretation, cf. Targum, Jacob b. Reuben, and Rashi (ad loc.).

31 I.E. is of the opinion that the verb ענה (lit., "to answer," "to respond") connotes providing for someone in need. Cf. above, comm. on 2:23. Thus "and money provides all things" (instead of "answereth all things"). Similarly here, "I will provide" (instead of "I will respond").

32 After Ephraim will renounce the idols God will respond to their needs, by setting His eyes upon the people, meaning that He will look after them (or "on them") favorably. The final phrase עד שאשורנו (= until I will look after him) appears to be a scribal redundancy. Alternatively, we may read in I.E. with ms. M. עתה (= now) instead of עד (= until), i.e., I will look after him by setting My eyes upon him benevolently; now that I look after him, he will become "like a leafy cypress tree."

33 I.e., as a result of God's providence Ephraim will become as stately as a leafy cypress tree. I.E. evidently takes the pronoun אני (= I) as an ellipsis in the sense of "I *will make him*," cf. Targum, ad loc. Cf. also Isaiah da Trani, p. 84: "I will make him (אשימנו) like a leafy cypress tree."

34 I.e., whoever is wise, on the one hand, and whoever is prudent, on the other, should know and understand the right "ways of the Lord."

35 According to I.E., God's promise of providence, which begins with v. 5 ("I will *heal* their backsliding") and ends with v. 8, will be the result of Ephraim's repentance (v. 2). Subsequently (in v. 10), the prophet reflects upon these last prophecies by saying that these are "the ways of the Lord" (viz., that He heals after repentance), which wise and prudent men shall perceive.

36 The printed edition of I.E. as well as most of our mss. have erroneously: אז תפשע אדום (= then did Edom revolt). However, by reading with ms. N אז תפשע (without

the word אדום) I.E. evidently has in mind the phrase אז תפשע לבנה (= then did Libnah revolt); see below, note 38. It should be added that after a similar remark in comm. on Is. 1:2, I.E. cites the preceding passage of the same verse: "And Edom revolted (ויפשע אדום) from under the hand of Judah."

37 Lit., "the one who perverts his soul," a comment that reminds us of a previous remark by I.E. concerning "backsliding, which is as harmful for the soul as a disease for the body" (comm. on v. 5).

38 I.E. is of the opinion that the term פושעים, which is generally understood to mean "sinners" (or "transgressors"), should be taken here in the sense of those who leave the righteous way, which is in the domain of God, in exchange for a path that is crooked and broken; i.e., those who pervert themselves by abandoning the domain of God and by withdrawing from His way will stumble. This view is supported here by the quotation דבר פשע (= "matter of embezzlement" or "trespass") which means, according to I.E., an object that has parted with its original owner and is now in the possession of someone else. Similarly, the phrase אז תפשע לבנה (= then did Libnah revolt, II Kings 8:22) should be taken as "then did Libnah withdraw," i.e., Libnah withdrew from under the hand of Judah. It should be noted that this explanation of the term פשע, which I.E. seems to have totally adopted here, is quoted in his commentary on Ex. 22:8 in the name of the 11th-century Qaraite Jeshua b. Judah (or b. 'Ali) as a supplement to a different interpretation of his own. For a discussion of this contradiction, cf. Friedlaender's note (11) to comm. on Is. 1:2.

39 For a similar attempt by I.E. to connect the conclusion of a biblical chapter with its beginning, cf. comm. on Ps. 145:20. Cf. also *Bātēy Midrāshōt*, II, ed. by Abraham Wertheimer (Jerusalem, 1955), p. 382, where the closing passage in Hosea is similarly interpreted as a repetition of the aforementioned phrase, "for thou hast stumbled in thine iniquity" (v. 2).

Bibliography

Abravanel, Don Isaac. *Commentary on the Twelve Minor Prophets and Hagiographa.* Tel-Aviv: Elisha, 1910.

Al-Qumisi, Daniel. *Commentary on the Twelve Minor Prophets.* Jerusalem: Mekizey Nirdamim, 1957.

Bacher, Wilhelm. *Abraham Ibn Esra als Grammatiker.* Strassburg: Karl Trubner, 1882.

Bonfils, Joseph. *Sophnath Paaneah.* Edited by David Herzog. 2 Vols. Heidelberg: Carl Winters, 1911-1930.

Cheyne, T.K. *The Book of Hosea.* Cambridge: University Press, 1905.

Driver, G.R. "Confused Hebrew Roots," *Gaster Anniversary Volume.* Edited by Bruno Schindler. London: Taylors Foreign Press, 1936: 76.

Dunash b. Labrat. *Teshubot Dunash Ben Labrat.* Edited by Hirsch Filipowski. London-Edinburgh: Meorerey Yeshenim, 1855.

Eliezer of Beaugency. *Kommentar zu Ezechiel und den XII kleinen Propheten.* Edited by Samuel Poznanski. Warsaw: H. Eppelberg 1910-1913.

Filwarg, Jonah. *Beney Reshef.* Piotrkow: Solomon Belchatowski, 1900.

Friedlaender, Michael. *Essays on the Writings of Abraham Ibn Ezra.* London: Trubner and Company, 1877.

Gardner, W.R.W. "Notes on Certain Passages in Hosea," *American Journal of Semitic Languages and Literature XVIII* (1901-1902): 177-83.

Gersonides, Levi. *Commentary on the Early Prophets and Hagiographa.* Printed in various editions of the Hebrew Bible.

Gesenius, Wilhelm. *Gesenius' Hebrew Grammar.* Edited by E. Kautzsch and revised by A.E. Cowley. Oxford: The Clarendon Press, 1910.

Harper, William Rainey. *A Critical and Exegetical Commentary on Amos and Hosea.* New York: Charles Scribner's Sons, 1905.

Hayyug, Yehudah. *Grammatische Werke d. R. Jehuda Chajjug.* Edited by Leopold Dukes. Stuttgart: Adolph Kraube, 1844.

Ibn Ezra, Abraham. *Commentary on the Bible*. Printed in various editions of the Hebrew Bible. In addition, the following critical editions were employed: *Abraham Ibn Ezra's Commentary to Exodus*. Edited by Leopold Fleischer. Vienna: Menora, 1926; *The Commentary of Ibn Ezra on Isaiah*. Edited by M. Friedlaender. London: Trubner and Company, 1873; *Ibn Ezra's Short Commentary on Daniel*. Edited by Henry J. Mathews in *Miscellany of Hebrew Literature* II (1877); 1-15; *A Commentary on the Book of Proverbs*. Attributed to Abraham Ibn Ezra. Edited by Samuel R. Driver. Jerusalem: Maqor, 1972; *Abraham Ibn Ezra's Commentary on the Book of Esther*. Edited by Joseph Zedner. London: David Nutt, 1850; *Abraham Ibn Ezra's Commentary on the Canticles*. Edited and translated by Henry J. Mathews. London: Trubner and Company, 1874.

—.*Moznayim*. Edited by Wolf Heidenheim. Offenbach: Hirsh Spitz, 1791.

—.*Sapha Berurah*. Edited by Gabriel Lippman. Furth: D.J. Zurndorffer, 1839.

—.*Sahot Bediqduq*. Edited by Gabriel Lippmann. Furth: D.J. Zurndorffer, 1839.

—.*Sephat Yether*. Edited and published by Gabriel Lippmann. Frankfurt a.M., 1843

—.*Yesod Mora*. Edited by Naphtali Ben-Menachem. Jerusalem: Tishbi, 1970.

Ibn Janah, Jonah. *Sefer Haschoraschim* (= Dictionary). Edited by Wilhelm Bacher. Berlin: H. Itzkowski, 1896.

—.*Hariqmah*. Edited by Michael Wilensky. 2 Vols. Jerusalem: Hebrew Language Academy, 1964.

Ibn Quraish, Yehudah. *Iggeret R. Yehudah b. Quraish*. Edited by Moshe Katz. Tel Aviv: Goldbrener-Lidor, 1950.

Isaiah da Trani. *Commentary on Prophets and Hagiographa*. Edited by Abraham J. Wertheimer. 2 Vols. Jerusalem: Ketab Wasepher, 1959-1965.

Jacob b. Reuben. *Sepher Haosher*. Apperared in print entitled *Mibhar Yesharim* with *Sepher Hamibhar* by Aaron the elder. Eupatoria, 1834.

Kaputa, Chaim Wolf. *Or Linetibah*. Lemberg: Ch. Rohatyn, 1897.

Kil, Yehudah. *Daat Miqra. A commentary on the book of Hosea*. Published by the Society for the Publication of the Bible with a

Traditional Commentary. Jerusalem: Mosad Harav Kook, 1973.

Lipshitz, Abe. *Pirkey Iyyun Bemishnat R. Abraham Ibn Ezra*. Jerusalem: Mosad Harav Kook, 1982.

Maimonides, Abraham. *Commentary on Genesis and Exodus*. Translated by Ephraim Wiesenberg. London: L.Honig and Sons, 1959.

Maimonides, Moses. *Mishneh Torah*. 4 Vols. Warsaw: Joshua Munk, 1880.

—.*The Guide of the Perplexed*. Translated by Shlomo Pines. Chicago and London: The University of Chicago Press, 1969.

Mann, Jacob. "Early Karaite Bible Commentaries." *The Jewish Quarterly Review* (N.S.) XII (1921-1922): 450-501.

Menahem b. Saruq. *Mahberet Menahem*. Edited by Hirsch Filipowski. Edinburgh: Meorerey Yeshenim, 1854.

Nachmanides, Moses. *Commentary on the Torah*. 2 Vols. Edited by Charles B. Chavel. Jerusalem: Mosad Harav Kook, 1959-1960.

Parchon, Solomon. *Mahberet Hearuk*. Edited by Salomo Gottlieb Stern. Pressburg: Anton Schmidt, 1854.

Poznanski, Samuel. "The Arabic Commentary of Abu Zakariya Yahya (Judah ben Samuel) Ibn Balam on the Twelve Minor Prophets." *The Jewish Quarterly Review* (N.S.) XV (1924-1925): 1-53.

—.*Mose B. Samuel Hakkohen Ibn Chiquitilla*. Leipzig: J.C. Heinrichs, 1895.

—."R. Menahem b. Helbo's Interpretations of the Holy Scripture." *Sokolow Jubilee Volume*. Warsaw: Shuldberg, 1904, pp. 389-439.

—."Bibliographie." *Revue des études juives XLI* (1900): 305-7.

Prijs, Leo. *Die Grammatikalische Terminologie Des Abraham Ibn Esra*. Basel: Sepher, 1950.

Qara, Joseph. *Commentary on the Twelve Minor Prophets*. Printed in various editions of the Hebrew Bible.

Qimhi, David. *Commentary on the Bible*. Printed in various editions of the Hebrew Bible. The following critical edition was also employed: *The Commentary of Rabbi David Kimhi on Hosea*. Edited by Harry Cohen. New York: Columbia University Press, 1929.

—.*Sepher Hashorashim* (= Dictionary). Edited by H.R. Biesenthal and F. Lebrecht. Berlin: G. Bethge, 1847.

—.*Miklol*. Edited by Isaac Rittenberg. Lyck: H. Petzoll, 1841.

Qimhi, Joseph. *Sepher Hagaluy*. Edited by Henry J. Mathews. Berlin: Mekitzey Nirdamim, 1887.

—.*Sepher Zikkaron*. Edited by Wilhelm Bacher. Berlin: Mekitzey Nirdamim, 1888.

Rahmer, M. "Die Hebraischen Traditionen in den Werken Hieronymus," *Monatsschrift für Geschichte und Wissenschaft des Judenthums* XIV (1865): 221-24, 460-70.

Roth, Meshullam. *Mebasser Ezra*. Jerusalem. Edited by Joel Zukerow. Jerusalem, 1968.

Saadya Gaon. *Haemunot Wehadeot*. Juzefow: Baruch Zetzer, 1885.

Schroeter, R. "Die in Cod. Hunt 206n aufbewahrte 'arabische Uebersetzung der kleinen Propheten," *Archiv für Wissenschaftliche Erforschung des Alten Testamentes*. Edited by Adalbert Merx. I (1869): 28-48. "Erklärung der kleinen Propheten," *ibid*., 49-52; *ibid*., II: 153-189.

Schröter, Robert. *Kritik des Dunasch ben Labrat über einzelne Stellen aus Saadya's arabischer Uebersetzung des A.T.* Breslau: Schletter, 1866.

Sharim, Isaac. *Hadar Ezer*. Smyrna: Aaron Sigorah, 1865.

Solomon b. Isaac (Rashi). *Commentary on the Bible*. Printed in standard editions of the Hebrew Bible.

Teshubot Talmidey Menahem Wetalmid Dunash. A grammatical discussion between the followers of Menahem b. Saruq and Dunash b. Labrat. Edited and published by Salomo Gottlieb Stern. Vienna, 1870.

The Interpreter's Bible. The Holy Scripture in The King James Version (A.V.) and Revised Standard Versions (R.S.V.). Vol IV. New York-Nashville: Abingdon Press, 1956.

The Septuagint Version of The Old Testament. Translated by Lancelot Charles Lee Brenton. Vol II. London: Samuel Bagster and Sons, 1844.

Wynkoop, J.D. *Commentary on the Book of Hosea*. Printed in Biblia Hebraica, part 1. Edited by Abraham Kahana. Kiew: Levin-Epstein, 1906.

Yefet b. Ali the Qaraite. *The Arabic Commentary on the Book of Hosea*. Edited by Philip Birnbaum. Philadelphia: Dropsie College, 1942.

Zucker, Moshe. *Rav Saadya Gaon's Translation of the Torah*. New York: Feldheim, 1959.

Index

References to the standard commentaries of Rashi, Qara, Ibn Ezra, and Qimhi on Hosea have not been included in this Index due to their abundant occurence. For additional sources cited by Ibn Ezra in this commentary, *see* Introduction, section V.

D

E

F

G

H

I

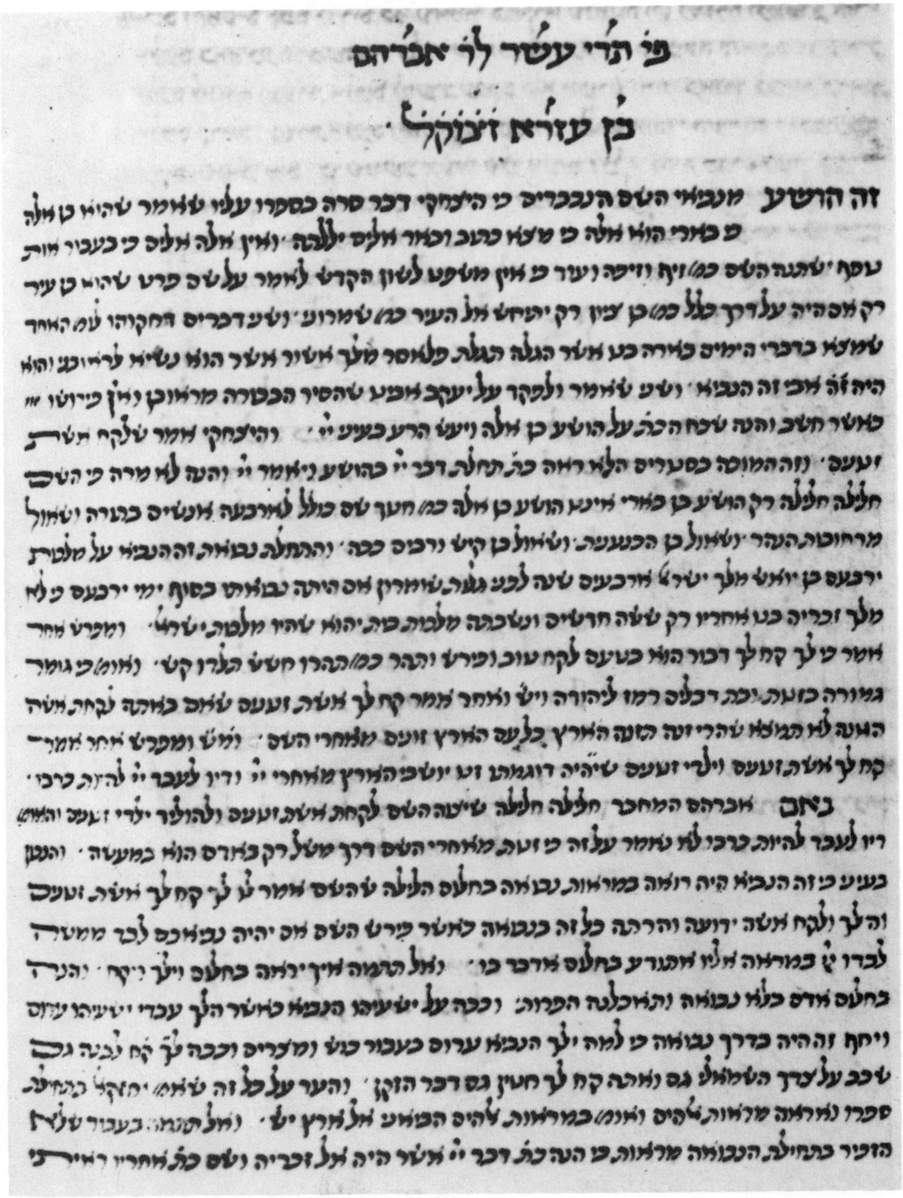

פי' תרי עשר לר' אברהם
בן עזרא זצוק"ל ·

זה הושע מנביאי השם הנכבדים כי היצחקי דבר סרה בספרו עליו שאמר שהיא בן אלה
כי בארי הוא אלה כי שנא כתוב וכאור אלים ילבה · ואין אלה אלים כי כעבור אות
עמף שתנה השם כמ"ו זית וזיתה ועוד כי אין משפט לשון הקדש לאמר על שם פרט שהוא בן עיר
רק אם היה על דרך כלל כמ"ו בן ציון רק יתיחש אל העיר כמו שמרוני · ושני דברים החקיהו עם האחד
שמצא בדברי הימים בארה בנו אשר הגלה הגלה תלגת פלנאסר מלך אשור אשר הוא נשיא לראובני והוא
היה זה אבי זה הנביא · ושני שאמר ולפקד על יעקב אמנע שהסיר הבכורה מראובן ואין פירושו
כאשר חשב והנה שכח הכ' על הושע בן אלה ויעש הרע בעיני יי · והיצחקי אמר שלקח תשרים
ועשם · וזה המוסה בספרים הלא ראה כת' תחלת דבר יי בהושע ויאמר יי והנה לא מרה כי השם
חלילה חלילה רק הושע בן בארי איננו הושע בן אלה כמו חטך שם כולל לארבעה אנשים בגוים ושאול
מרחובות הנהר · ושאול בן הכנענית · ושאול בן קיש ורבים ככה · והתחלת נבואת זה הנביא על מלכות
ירבעם בן יואש מלך ישראל וירבעם שנה לבני גלות שומרון אם היתה נבואתו בסוף ימי ירבעם כי לא
מלך זכריה בנו אחריו רק ששה חדשים ונשכחה מלכות בית יהוא שהיו מלכות ישראל · ומפרש אחר
אמר כי לך קח לך דבור הוא בטעם לקח טוב ופירש יהבו כמו הבו חשש אלרון קשי · ואומר כי גומר
גמורה בזנות · ככה דבלים רמז ליהודה וישראל ואחר אמר קח לך אשה · זנונים שהם באהבה לקחת אשה
הנוה לא תמצא שהרי זנה תזנה הארץ כלומר הארץ זונים מאחרי השם · ויש ומפרש אחר אמר
קח לך אשה זנונים וילדי זנונים שיהיה דוגמתו זנו יושבי הארץ מאחרי יי ודין לעבד יי להיות דרכי ·
באם אברהם המחבר חלילה חלילה שיצוה השם לקחת אשה זנונים ולהוליד ילדי זנונים והאות
ריו לעבד להיות דרכי לא נאמר על זה כי זנות מאחרי השם דרך משל רק באדם הוא במעשה · והנכון
בעיני כי זה הנביא היה רואה במראות נבואה בחלום הלילה שהשם אמר לו לך קח לך אשה זנונים
והלך ולקח אשה ידועה והרתה כל זה בנבואה כאשר פירש השם אם יהיה נביאכם לבד ממעלה
לבדו יי במראה אליו אתודע בחלום אדבר בו · ואל תתמה איך יראה בחלום וילך ויקח · והנה
בחלום אדם בלא נבואה והאכלנה הפרה · וככה על ישעיהו הנביא כאשר הלך עבדי ישעיהו ערום
ויחף וזה היה בדרך נבואה כי למה ילך הנביא ערום בעבור כוש ומצרים וככה לך קח לבנה גם
שכב על צדך השמאלי גם ואתה קח לך חטין גם דבר הזקן · והעד על כל זה שאמר יחזקאל בתחילת
ספרו ואראה מראות אלהים ואומר במראות אלהים הביאני אל ארץ ישראל · ואל תתמה בעבור שלא
הזכיר בתחילת הנבואה מראות כי הנה כת' דבר יי אשר היה אל זכריה ושם כת' אחריו ראיתי

Plate 1: Ms. British Museum Add. 24896

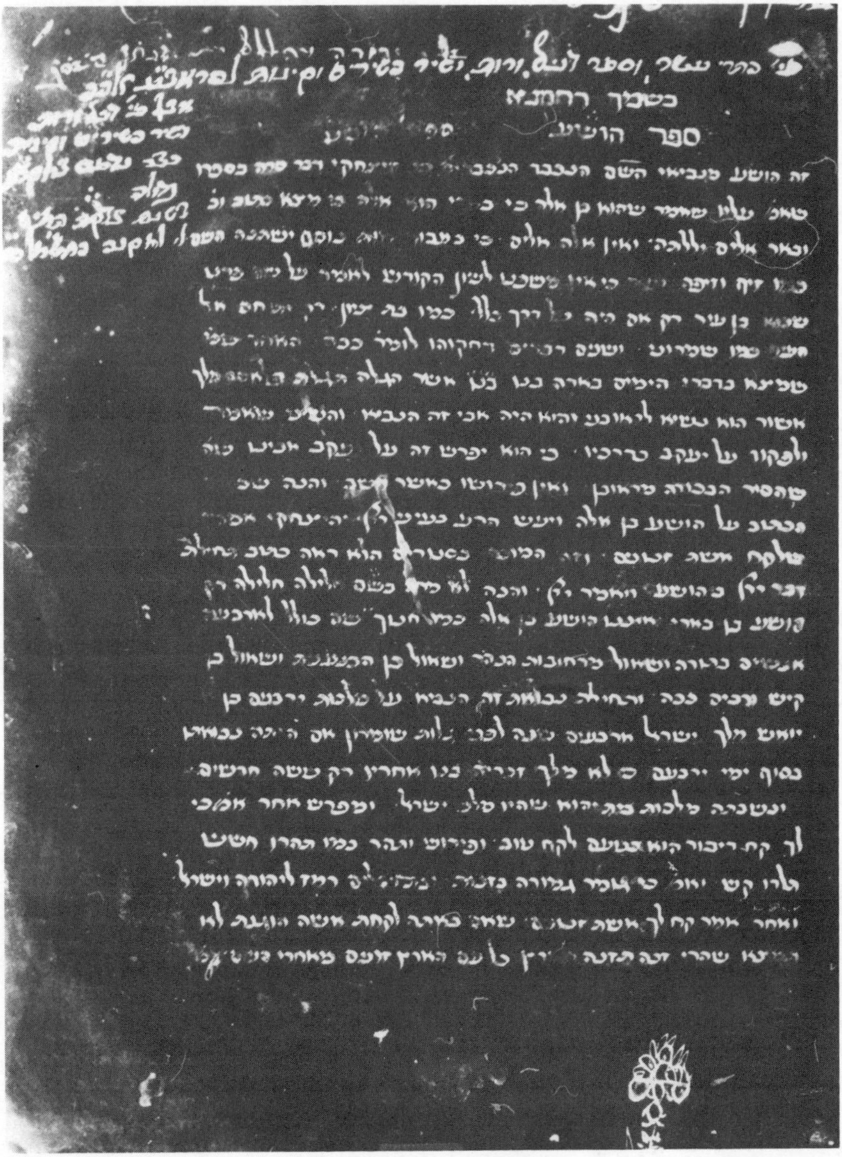
בשמך רחמנא
ספר הושע

Plate 2: Ms. Michael 33 (Bodleian Library, Oxford)

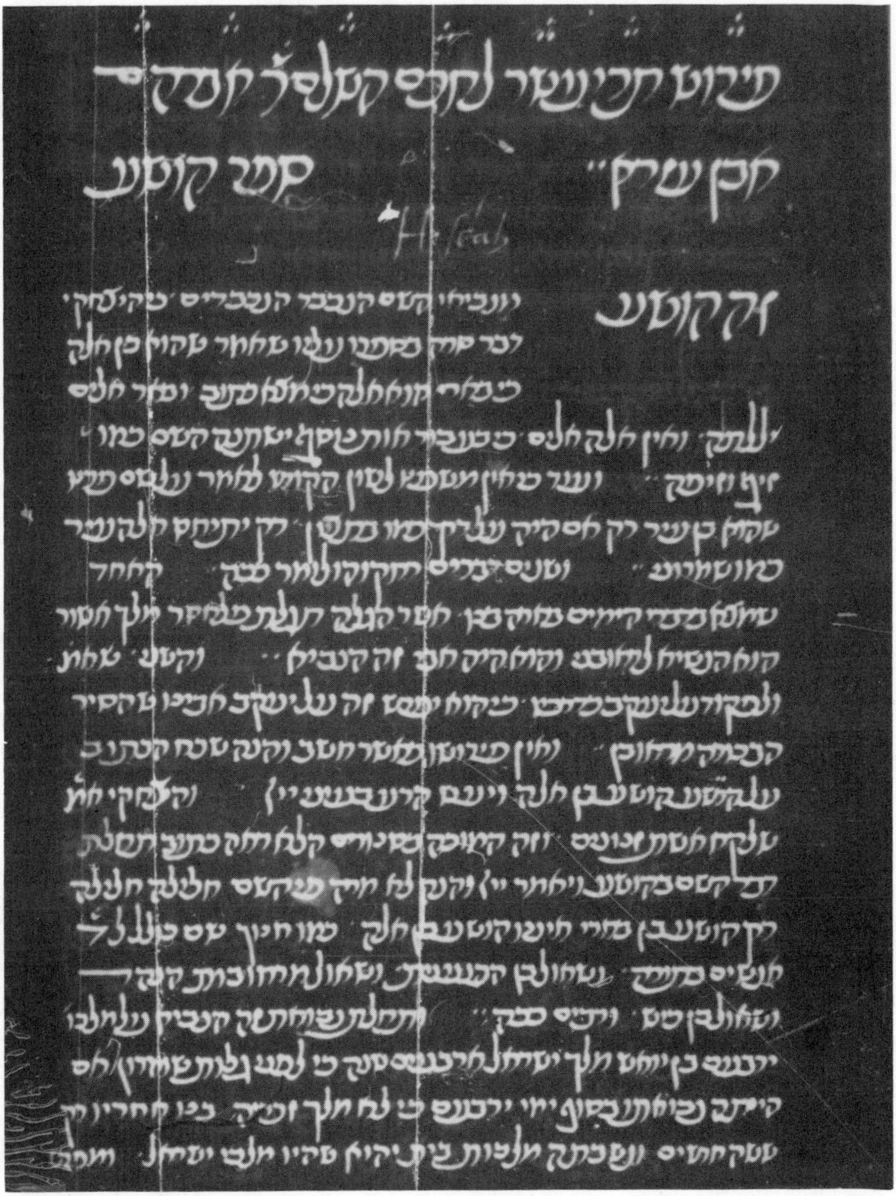

Plate 3: Ms. Vatican 75

HEBREW TEXT

*כשורש[55] *עצי[56] *לבנון:[57] ויך שרשיו. *באורך וברוחב[58] כדרך ׳ומחה *אל[59] *כתף[60] ים כנרת׳ (במדבר לד, יא) *ובמדות שברים ותבריתא:[61]

(8) ישובו. [62]אמר יפת *יושבי[63] בצל *הלבנון.[64] ולפי דעתי יושבי בצל ישראל *והם[65] העבדים *שיהיו[66] *אכריהם וכורמיהם:[67] יחיו דגן. והקמות *יפרחו[68] כגפן: *זכרו. [69]ריחו כדרך ׳אזכרתה׳ (ויקרא ב, ב). ויפת אמר זכר *גפנם[70] למרחק ׳כיין לבנון׳:

(9) אפרים. *באמרו[71] ׳אפרים מה לי עוד׳ *אין לי[72] *צורך אליהם[73] אני אענהו *לתת[74] לו כל *חפצו[75] כדרך ׳והכסף יענה את הכל׳ (קהלת י, יט): ואשורנו. לתת עיני לטוב עליו *עד[76] *שאשורנו[77] נמצא שיהיה ׳כברוש רענן׳, ואל תפחד *בעבור[78] *שאין[79] *לו[80] לברוש פרי כי ממני פריך *נמצא:[81]

(10) *מי חכם. מי ישרת[82] בעבור *אחר.[83] ואלה הם דרכי השם והטעם קשור כי *בשובכם[84] אל השם ירפא אתכם: ופושעים. הם היוצאים *מתחת הרשות[85] כמו ׳על כל דבר פשע׳ (שמות כב, ח), *׳אז תפשע׳[86] (מל"ב ח, כב). *והמעוות[87] *נפשו בדרך הישרה יכשל[88] *והשלים[89] על דרך ׳כי כשלת *בעונך׳[90] (פסוק ב):

רק דק ח׳/ 54 ל: אמר ויך שרשיו כלבנון יהיו, נ: אמרו ושרשיו יהיו/ 55 ל: כשרש/ 56 ו מ ר עצי ח׳/ 57 ר: הלבנון/ 58 ל נ: בארך וברחב/ 59 בבמדבר: על/ 60 ל כתף ח׳/ 61 ב נ: ובמידות שברים ותבריתא, ו מ ובמדות שברים ותבריתא ח׳/ 62 ר: שובו/ 63 ר: ישובו/ 64 ל: העליון/ 65 ל: שהם (עם וא"ו למעלה בין השי"ן וההי"א)/ 66 ו ל מ: שהיו/ 67 ו נ: אכריהם וכרמיהם, ל ר: אכריכם וכרמיכם/ 68 ב נ יפרחו ח׳/ 69 בכ"י: וזכרו/ 70 ב: גפנים/ 71 ל מ נ: כאמרו/ 72 ו מ ר: אין לי ח׳/ 73 ל: צורך עליהם, נ: צורך לי אליהם/ 74 מ ר: ולתת/ 75 מ: צרכו/ 76 מ: עתה/ 77 מ: שאסורנו/ 78 ל בעבור ח׳/ 79 ו מ ר: כי אין/ 80 ו מ ר לו ח׳/ 81 ב נ נמצא ח׳/ 82 נ: מי מי ישרת, ב חכם מי ח׳/ 83 ב נ: אחרת/ 84 ו מ: בשובם/ 85 ע"פ ו ל מ ר, ב נ ובס"ש: מהרשות/ 86 ע"פ ב, נ: אז תפשעי, בשאר כ"י ובס"ש: אז תפשע אדום/ 87 ב ר: והמעות/ 88 ב נ: נפשו בדרך הישר יכשל, ל: נפשו הוא יכשל/ 89 ע"פ כ"י, בס"ש: והשלם/ 90 מ: בעוניך/

לשון נקבה לא חשש *לומר[3] *׳יבוקעו׳[4] כדרך ׳אם תעירו ואם תעוררו׳ (שה״ש ב, ז; ג, ה).

(2) ***שובה.** [5]מעט *מעט[6] *עד[7] השם, וטעם ׳כי כשלת *בעונך׳[8] ואין מי יקימך רק השם *לבדו:[9]

(3) **קחו.** *איננו[10] מבקש מכם כאשר תלכו לבקש רצונו הון או *עולות[11] רק דברים שתודו כדרך *׳ונשא[12] השעיר עליו׳ (ויקרא טז, כב). אמר רבי מרינוס ׳כל תשא עון׳ הפוך *כל עון תשא.[13] והנכון *כל[14] אשר תשא *עונינו[15] **נשוב: וקח טוב.** *מעולה[16] או *הדיבור[17] הטוב שנוכל לומר לפניך[18] והטעם *להתודות.[19] *ורבי יוסף אמר[20] מיעוט מעשים טובים: **ונשלמה.** *שלום[21] פרים כמו ׳כי הכית *את[22] *כל[23] אויבי לחי׳ (תהלים ג, ח) *שפירושו[24] *מכת[25] לחי או *הוא[26] חסר כ״ף. והזכיר *׳פרים׳[27] כי הם גדולים והיקרים *בעולה[28] *וזהו שתאמרו:[29]

(4) ***אשור.** כי[30] *כתוב[31] ׳ואשור הוא מלכו׳ (יא, ה), **לא נשען על אשור ולא על** *סוסינו[32] המובאים ממצרים: **ולא נאמר** *עוד[33] **אלהינו למעשה ידינו.** כנגד מעשה חרשים כי אין מי *שיעזור[34] מי *שאין כח לו כמו[35] **היתום** רק אתה וכתוב ׳אבי יתומים׳ (תהלים סח, ו), וזה כנגד ׳כי כשלת *בעונך׳[36] (פסוק ב) ואין עוזר לך:

(5) **ארפא.** *מלת[37] *משובה[38] לגנאי *בכל המקרא.[39] *ואיננו[40] *כאומר[41] ׳משובתם׳ בכל *מקום[42] *שהכיתים[43] רק *המשובה בנשמה[44] *כחולי[45] בגוף על כן *מלת[46] ׳ארפא׳ כנגד ׳הכה אפרים׳ (ט, טז): **אהבם. אהבת נדבה** הפך ׳ימאסם *אלהי׳[47] (ט, יז): **כי שב** ***אפי.**[48] *הפך[49] ׳חרה אפי בם׳ (ח, ה):

(6) **אהיה** *כטל. [50]*הפך ׳שרשם יבש׳ (ט, טז), ׳ויבוש מקורו׳ (יג, טו).[51] והשושנה תפרח מהרה ובעבור שאין *לה[52] שורש *רק דק[53] *אמר ושרשיו יהיו[54]

שובה ישראל עד ה׳ אלהיך/ 6 מ ר מעט ח׳/ 7 נ ר: עם, ו עד ח׳/ 8 מ ר בעונך ח׳/ 9 ו ל מ ר לבדו ח׳/ 10 ל ר: אינינו/ 11 ל: עגלות/ 12 ו: נשא/ 13 מ: כל תשא עון/ 14 ו מ ר כל ח׳/ 15 מ: עוונינו/ 16 ו: מעולם/ 17 ו: הדבור/ 18 מ וקח טוב מעולה או הדיבור שנוכל לומר לפניך ח׳/ 19 ו: להתוודות/ 20 ו ר: אמר ר׳ יוסף/ 21 ו נ ר: שילום/ 22 מ ר את ח׳/ 23 ע״פ ל ר, בשאר כ״י ובס״ש כל ח׳/ 24 ע״פ ב ו מ נ, ר ל ובס״ש: שפירש/ 25 ו: מבית/ 26 ע״פ ו ל מ נ ר, ב ובס״ש הוא ח׳/ 27 מ פרים ח׳/ 28 מ: בעולא/ 29 ל: וזהו הוידוי שתאמרו/ 30 ל: אשור לא יושיענו כי/ 31 ב: כתב/ 32 ל: סוסיו/ 33 ל עוד ח׳/ 34 נ: שיעור/ 35 ל ר: שאין לו כח כמו, נ: שאין לו כח לו כמו/ 36 ו ל מ ר בעונך ח׳/ 37 מ: מילה, ר: מילת/ 38 מ: תשובה/ 39 מ: בכל מקום המקרא, ל בכל המקרא ח׳/ 40 נ: ואינינו/ 41 ל: כאומרו/ 42 ו ל ח ר: לשון/ 43 ב נ: שהכיתם/ 44 ל: המשובה חלי בנשמה/ 45 ל נ: כחלי, מ ר: כח לו/ 46 מ: מילת/ 47 נ: אלי/ 48 ע״פ ל, בשאר כ״י ובס״ש אפי ח׳/ 49 ב: כנגד, נ הפך ח׳/ 50 ע״פ ל, בשאר כ״י ובס״ש כטל ח׳/ 51 ו מ ר הפך שרשם יבש ויבוש מקורו ח׳/ 52 מ: לו/ 53 ל

(9) *שחתך.[51] כי בי. *ניחום כמו יצר שהוא בעזרך:[52]

(10) *אהי. [53]יש אומרים הפוך כמו איה. והנכון *האומר[54] ׳אהי *מלכך׳[55] *איפוא[56] הוא: *ויושיעך. [57]מידי ומיד החיות: *ושופטיך. [58]*הטעם כפול:[59]

(11) אתן לך *מלך.[60] כשאול שאמר הנביא ׳כי אותי מאסו ממלוך עליהם׳ (שמ"א ח, ז) *עתה[61] אקחנו בעברתי:

(12) צרור. הוא *בלבי[62] לא *אשכחנו[63] כאשר ׳שכחוני׳ הכתוב למעלה (פסוק ו):

(13) חבלי. והבן *שיוליד[64] ידעתי כי *נבל[65] יהיה *כאביו[66] ולא חכם על כן ׳עת לא *יעמוד[67] במשבר בנים׳ כי מיד ימות:

(14) מיד שאול. *הייתי[68] פודה אבותיך עתה *אני[69] אהיה דבר המות *שלך[70] גם ׳אהי קטבך׳ והעד ׳מדבר *באפל[71] *יהלוך[72] *מקטב׳[73] (תהלים צא, ו) כטעם הכרתה. ויש אומרים *כי ׳אהי׳ כמו[74] *איה[75] שאמרו ׳כרתנו ברית את מות׳ (ישעיה כח, טו): *נוחם. שם[76] מגזרת ׳וינחם ה׳ (שמות לב, יד), והטעם שלא אנחם:

(15) *כי הוא בין אחים. [77]מגזרת ׳באחו׳ (בראשית מא, ב): יפריא. כמו *יפרה,[78] *׳החלי׳ (ישעיה נג, י)[79] כמו *החלה.[80] והטעם *דרך משל[81] כאשר הזכיר *׳כמרעיתם׳ (פסוק ו),[82] *סיפר[83] *איך יהרגם השם[84] ויכריתם: *ויבוש.[85] כמו *וייבש[86] או כמשמעו שיכזבו מימיו. *וטעם[87] *זה[88] הרוח משל לאויב *שהוא[89] *ישסה:[90]

יד

(1) תאשם. תהיה שממה: בחרב יפלו. אנשיה: והריותיו. *אחר[1] *שהמלה[2]

אכלה/ 49 ל: וחיית/ 50 ו: תבקש/ 51 ו: שחרך/ 52 ל: ניחום כמו יצר כי בי בעוזרך, ב ניחום כמו יצר שהוא בעזרך ח׳, אבל נשאר רווח לחמש מלים החסרות/ 53 ו: אחי/ 54 ע"פ ב ל נ, מ: כאומר, ו ר ובס"ש: כאומרו/ 55 ו: על כן/ 56 ל: איפה/ 57 ע"פ ל, בשאר כ"י ובס"ש: יושיעך/ 58 ב נ ושופטיך ח׳/ 59 ל: כפול הטעם/ 60 ו מ ר: משל/ 61 ב: ועתה/ 62 מ ר: בליבי/ 63 ב: אשכחוני/ 64 ל: שיולד/ 65 ע"פ ו ל מ נ ר, ב ובס"ש: סכל/ 66 ע"פ ו ל מ נ ר, ב ובס"ש: כאבותיו/ 67 ב ל: יעמד/ 68 ל: היתי/ 69 ל אני ח׳, ר: אני אני/ 70 ע"פ כ"י, בס"ש: שלח/ 71 ו ל ר: באופל/ 72 ב ל נ ר: יהלך/ 73 בכ"י: ומקטב/ 74 ל כי אהי כמו ח׳/ 75 ו ל מ ר: אהיה/ 76 ו מ ר: נוחם יסתר שם/ 77 ב ל נ: כי הוא אחים, ו: כי הוא בן אחים, ר: כי אחים/ 78 ב: יפרד, ו ל מ ר: יפרא/ 79 ע"פ ל, בשאר כ"י ובס"ש: החליא/ 80 ו מ ר: החלא/ 81 ל דרך משל ח׳/ 82 ע"פ ו ל מ נ ר, ב ובס"ש: במרעיתם/ 83 ע"פ ו מ ר, ב נ ו ובס"ש: ספר, ל סיפר ח׳/ 84 מ: אז יהרגם השם, ל איך יהרגם השם ח׳/ 85 מ: ויבש/ 86 ב ו מ נ ר: ייבש, ל: יבש/ 87 נ וטעם ח׳/ 88 נ: וזה/ 89 ב ל נ: הוא/ 90 ו מ ר: משסה/

1 ו ר: אחרי, מ: אחרים/ 2 ו: שהמילה, מ: שהמלה כפולה/ 3 מ ר: לאמר/ 4 ל: תבקעו/ 5 ל:

יואש כאשר אפרש עוד: *ונשא[4] *הוא. שנשאת[5] מלכותו בישראל כי מלך על עשרת השבטים: *ויאשם. וימות. [6]נחשב כמת ועוד כי הרג אביה כל *מחנהו:[7]

(2) ועתה *יוסיפו. הדור[8] הזה *לחטוא:[9] כתבונם. *כתבונתם[10] *כמו[11] 'וצורם לבלות שאול' (תהלים מט, טו) וצורתם: להם הם אומרים. *בני[12] אדם להתל *מהם[13] כי הם מנשקים לבעלים שהם צורות העגלים *כמו[14] *'וכל[15] הפה אשר לא נשק לו' (מל"א יט, יח) והם שופכים דם נקי וזהו 'ודמיו עליו יטוש' (יב, טו). *והנם[16] הפך כל *אדם[17] כי האדם ישק לאדם שהוא *חבירו[18] ויזבח העגלים למאכלו:

(3) לכן. על *כן[19] לא יעמדו: משכים. פירשתיו כי *בחם[20] *השמש[21] לא ימצא: כמוץ. התבן *הדק[22] עם רוח סערה, והיה ראוי *להיות[23] *יסוער[24] בפתח גדול והנה היא *מלה[25] זרה בדקדוק:

(4) ואנכי. *הטעם[26] איך שבת לנשוק *העגל[27] שלא יושיע *ולא ישביע[28] *והנחת[29] אלהיך מימים *הקדמונים[30] שהושיעך:

(5) *אני ידעתיך.[31] וידע כל *צרכיך[32] *כדרך[33] 'יודע צדיק' (משלי יב, י): *תלאובות.[34] 'ארץ ציה וצמא' (יחזקאל יט, יג) וככה בלשון ישמעאל, *ולהיותו[35] כל תלאות בו *הוא[36] דרך דרש *ולא[37] דרך פשט:

(6) *כמרעיתם.[38] *יספר[39] הנביא הטובות *שעשה[40] *השם[41] עם אבותיהם *בבואם[42] מהמדבר אל ארץ כנען:

(7) ואהי. *פועל[43] עבר על הרעות שהביא השם עליהם *אשור. תואר כמו עצום שילכו[44] *אשורי אדם בו[45] ועוד:

(8) אפגשם כדוב שכול. *יש אומרים[46] שנהרגו בניו או הוא תואר יוצא. וטעם *'חית[47] השדה' אני *אוכל[48] קצתם בדבר וברעב *וחית[49] השׂדה *תבקע[50] קצתם:

בישראל שנשאת/ 6 ב: ויאשם וימת, ל: ויאשם בבעל וימות, ר: וישאם וימות/ 7 מ: מנחו/ 8 ל: יוסיפו לחטוא הדור/ 9 ב נ לחטוא ח'/ 10 ל: כתבבניתם/ 11 נ כמו ח'/ 12 ו ל מ נ ר: בשם/ 13 ע"פ כ"י, בס"ש: להם/ 14 ל כמו ח'/ 15 ו מ ר וכל ח'/ 16 ו: והנה/ 17 ו מ ר: האדם/ 18 ל: חברו/ 19 ר כן ח'/ 20 ל: כחם, מ ר: בחום/ 21 ל: השמים/ 22 ו מ ר הדק ח'/ 23 ו מ ר: להיותו/ 24 ל: יוסער/ 25 מ: מילה/ 26 ב הטעם ח'/ 27 ע"פ ו ל, בשאר כ"י ובס"ש: לעגל/ 28 ל ולא ישביע ח'/ 29 מ: הנחת/ 30 ע"פ ו ל, בשאר כ"י ובס"ש: קדמונים/ 31 ע"פ ל, בשאר כ"י ובס"ש אני ידעתיך ח'/ 32 ר: צורכך/ 33 ב: בדרך, ו: כארץ/ 34 ע"פ ל, בשאר כ"י ובס"ש: אני תלאובות/ 35 ו מ ר: להיותו/ 36 ע"פ ל, בשאר כ"י ובס"ש הוא ח'/ 37 ו: לא/ 38 ב: במרעיתם/ 39 ל: ספר/ 40 מ שעשה ח'/ 41 ל השם ח'/ 42 נ: בבאם/ 43 ו: פעל/ 44 ל: אשורנו עצום והוא תואר שילכו/ 45 ע"פ ב נ, ו ל ר: אשור אדם בו, מ: אשור בו, בס"ש: ואשרו בו/ 46 ו ר: ויש אומרים/ 47 ל: חיית/ 48 ע"פ כ"י, בס"ש:

(10) **ואנכי.** הטעם *הלא[87] *תזכור[88] כי אני *העליתיך[89] ממצרים *בעושר[90] רב שלא יגעת בו וכלכלתיך במדבר בהיותך *באהלים[91] כמו כן *אוכל[92] *לעשות[93] לך ׳כימי מועד צאתך ממצרים׳ (דברים טז, ו):

(11) ***ודברתי.**[94] והנה כבר דברתי כזאת וכזאת על הנביאים *שיאמרו[95] *לכם[96] שתניחו *דברי[97] שקר: **וביד הנביאים *אדמה.**[98] *שמתי[99] *דמיונות משלים[100] שתבינו:

(12) *והנה אם היו[101] *אנשי[102] *גלעד[103] לפני הנביאים און: ***אך שוא**[104] **היו.** אחרי כן: **בגלגל** *שורים[105] **זבחו. לבעל: כגלים.** דרך משל *שהיו[106] רבים ונראים:

(13) ***ויברח.** היה[107] לכם לחשוב כי אביכם בברחו *אל ארם[108] *עני היה[109] וכן אמר ׳ונתן לי לחם *לאכול׳[110] (בראשית כח, כ): ***ויעבוד.**[111] **באשה.** זהו ׳הלא ברחל *עבדתי עמך׳[112] (שם כט, כה) ובעבור אשה היה שומר צאן ואני העשרתיו:

(14) ***ובנביא.**[113] גם העליתי בניו על יד נביא הוא *משה ושב[114] ישראל *כמו[115] צאן *ושומרן[116] משה ושכח ישראל כל זה:

(15) **הכעים *אפרים.**[117] השם: ***תמרורים.**[118] בגלוי כמו *׳שמי[119] לך תמרורים׳ (ירמיה לא, כ), ׳ויתמרמר׳ (דניאל ח, ז): **ודמיו.** דמי נקיים *ששפך:[120] **ישוש.** כמו *׳והנה[121] נטושים׳ (שמ״א ל, טז):

יג

(1) **כדבר.** מדיבורו היו *יראים הגוים[1] ואין למלת *׳רתת׳[2] חבר רק בארמית. ורבי משה הכהן *פירש[3] זה על ירבעם שהיה מאפרים כמו זה ירבעם בן

ימצאו לי בני/ 86 ו מ ר: שחטאתם, ל: מחאתי/ 87 ל: לא/ 88 ב ו ל נ ר: תזכר/ 89 ב: העליתוך/ 90 ל: בעשר/ 91 מ: באלהים/ 92 ע״פ ל, ב: ימול, מ ר: יכול, בס״ש:יוכל/ 93 ו מ ר לעשות ח׳/ 94 ר: ודיברתי/ 95 ו מ ר: שאמרו/ 96 מ: להם/ 97 ו ר: דבר/ 98 ב ל נ אדמה ח׳/ 99 ע״פ כ״י, בס״ש: ששמתי/ 100 ל: דמיונות של משלים/ 101 ע״פ ו ל מ ר, בס״ש: אם והנה היו, ב אם ח׳, נ והנה ח׳/ 102 ו מ ר: אנשים/ 103 ע״פ נ, בשאר כ״י ובס״ש: הגלעד/ 104 ו מ ר: עכשיו/ 105 ב ו מ ר: שוורים, ל: ושורים/ 106 ו מ נ: שהם/ 107 ל: ויברח יעקב היה/ 108 ל: אל שדה ארם/ 109 מ ר: היה עני/ 110 ו: לאכל, מ: לאכול ובגד ללבוש/ 111 ל ויעבוד ח׳/ 112 ע״פ ו ל מ ר, ב נ ובס״ש: עבדתיך/ 113 ע״פ מ, בשאר כ״י ובס״ש ובנביא ח׳/ 114 ב ר: משה ואהרן ושב/ 115 ו: כלו/ 116 ב ו ל מ ר: ושומרו/ 117 ע״פ ו מ, בשאר כ״י ובס״ש אפרים ח׳/ 118 ו: ההחריב?/ 119 ו: שומי, בשאר כ״י ובס״ש: שימי/ 120 נ: ששכח/ 121 בכ״י ובס״ש: והנם, בפי׳ א״ע לבמדבר לא, לא: והנה/

1 ל: יראים אנשי הגוים/ 2 ו: חתת/ 3 ל: אמר/ 4 כך בכ״י ובס״ש, בכתוב: נשא/ 5 ל: הוא

ועשיתי לו מעלה על כל הנולדים כי כאשר היה בבטן נתתי לו כח *לאחוז[35] בעקב *עשו[36] *וזהו[37] *כמעשה[38] נס כי אין כח בעומד *בשליה[39] *בעת[40] *ההבקעה[41] *לתפוש[42] *דבר[43] עד שיצא מהרחם לאויר *העולם.[44] והנה *בהיותו[45] בבטן נתתי לו *כח[46] ואחרי כן התאבק עם המלאך ו׳ולא יכול לו׳ (שם לב, כו) והנה *מלאך[47] אחד הרג *כל[48] מחנה אשור (מל״ב יט, לה) ומראותו יפחדו בני *אדם[49] כמו דוד שנבעת (דה״י־ב כא, ל) ואף כי *להתאבק[50] עמו. והנה הטעם שידעו כל *בני[51] העולם כי זרעו *יעמוד[52] לנצח ובסוף *הוא ינצח את אויביו[53] והנה אפרים חושב כי אפרים *הוא[54] מצא האון:

(5) **וישר.** *פירש[55] איך *שר[56] את *אלהים:[57] **ויוכל.** *למלאך[58] וכמעט בכה ויתחנן לו שישלחנו. וטעם ׳עלות השחר׳ (בראשית לב, כה) *לפני[59] שיתחזק האור שלא *יבעת[60] יעקב. וטעם ׳בית אל ימצאנו׳ בשובו *לאביו[61] שם מצא *המלאך,[62] ובעבור שהמלאך נראה בבית אל פעמים הנה המקום שער השמים על כן התנבאתי אני ועמוס על ירבעם בבית אל שהוא מקום מלכותו כאשר אפרש:

(6) **וה׳.** הטעם המלאך *דיבר[63] עם *אביהם[64] והשם *גילה[65] שמו למשה שהוא אלהי המלאכים להיות להם לאלהים על כן ׳ה׳ זכרו׳:

(7) **ואתה.** לו שבת *אל[66] אלהיך היה *עוזרך[67] להשיבך אליו וזהו ׳ואתה באלהיך תשוב׳: *וקוה. אליו ואל[68] *תסמוך[69] אל *עשרך[70] ואל *כוחך[71] כי *הכח מאתו היה[72] לך גם *העושר:[73]

(9) **ויאמר.** טעם *׳אך׳[74] *לא[75] נתן לי *השם[76] *העושר[77] אני מעצמי עשרתי כי *אינני[78] כמו ׳כנען׳ (פסוק ח) הוא הסוחר כמו *׳ולא[79] *יהיה[80] *כנעני עוד׳[81] (זכריה יד, כא). והטעם למה *אמר[82] ׳חסד ומשפט *שמור׳[83] (פסוק ז) ולא יהיה *עושק[84] ככנעני ו׳כל יגיעי לא *ימצאו׳ בני[85] אדם *שחטאתי:[86]

34 ל: אברהם/ 35 ב מ: לאחז/ 36 ע״פ ל, בשאר כ״י ובס״ש עשו ח׳/ 37 ל מ ר: וזה/ 38 ב: מעשה, ל מ: במעשה/ 39 ו מ: בשלייה/ 40 ע״פ ל, בשאר כ״י ובס״ש: ובעת/ 41 ו מ ר: התבקענה/ 42 ב נ: לתפש, מ: לתפוס/ 43 ו דבר ח׳/ 44 ל: שבעולם/ 45 ו מ ר בהיותו ח׳/ 46 ע״פ כ״י, בס״ש: כחו/ 47 נ: המלאך/ 48 ל כל ח׳/ 49 ר: האדם/ 50 ו: להאבק/ 51 ל מ נ ר בני ח׳/ 52 ו ל נ ר: יעמד/ 53 ל: הוא ינצח אויביו, נ: ינצח הוא אויביו/ 54 מ: חושב/ 55 ע״פ כ״י, בס״ש: פירוש/ 56 ב נ: ישר, ל: שרה/ 57 ו: אלהיהם/ 58 ע״פ ו ל מ נ ר, ב ובס״ש: המלאך/ 59 ר: לפי/ 60 ע״פ כ״י, בס״ש: בעת/ 61 ל: אל אביו/ 62 ל: מלאך/ 63 מ ר: דבר/ 64 ע״פ ו מ ר, ב ל נ ובס״ש: אביכם/ 65 ל: גלה/ 66 נ אל ח׳/ 67 ו: עזרך/ 68 ו: וקוה אלהיך אליו ואל, ל: וקוה אל ה׳ כנען ואל/ 69 ו מ נ ר: תסמך/ 70 ל: עושרך/ 71 ב ל: כחך/ 72 מ: הכוח מאתו היה, נ: היה הכח מאתו היה/ 73 נ: העשר/ 74 ו מ: איך/ 75 מ לא ח׳/ 76 מ ר השם ח׳/ 77 ל נ: העשר/ 78 ע״פ ל, ו מ: אינם, נ: איניני, ב ר ובס״ש: אינגו/ 79 ע״פ ב ו ל נ, מ ר ובס״ש: לא/ 80 נ יהיה ח׳/ 81 ע״פ מ נ ר, ב ובס״ש: עוד כנעני, ל: עוד כנעני בבית ה׳/ 82 ע״פ ו ל מ ר, ב ובס״ש: יאמר, נ יאמר ח׳/ 83 ו מ ר: שמר/ 84 ב ו מ נ ר: עשוק/ 85 ו מ ר:

יב

(1) *__סבבוני בכחש.__ אינם הולכים אחרי השם כי אם בכחש ובמרמה[1] לא באמת גם *כן[2] יהודה שהיה אומר כי 'רד עם אל' על משקל 'כי אם תם הכסף' (בראשית מז, יח) שהיה *חושב[3] בעבור *היות[4] *מלכו[5] מבני דוד כי *הוא[6] מלכות השם:

(2) **אפרים.** *איננו[7] הולך אחרי השם כי אם *בדרכיו[8] *כי הוא[9] 'רועה רוח' *כמו[10] 'הקץ לדברי רוח' (איוב טז, ג), והעד 'וברית עם אשור *יכרותו':[11] **ושמן למצרים יובל.** דורון למלך מצרים:

(3) *__וריב.__ [12]*המפרש אמר כי[13] יהודה הוא נאמן והוא יהיה מוכיח *ואמר[14] כי הכתוב לא הזכיר 'וריב לה' על יהודה' רק 'עם' *הטעם[15] כי השם ויהודה יריבו *עם[16] אפרים. והנה *טעה[17] *מדרך[18] *הכתוב[19] והדקדוק כי למעלה *כתוב[20] 'ויהודה את מזורו' (ה, יג) 'ארכיב אפרים *יחרש[21] יהודה' (י, יא) ועל שניהם[22] *אמר[23] 'אכלתם פרי כחש' (י, יג), גם *שכח[24] *'ויריבו רועי גרר עם רועי יצחק' (בראשית כו, כ),[25] 'וירב העם עם משה' (שמות יז, ב) ורבים *אחרים[26] על כן *חבר[27] אפרים עם יהודה ואמר 'ולפקוד על יעקב כדרכיו' שזה השם כולל שניהם:

(4) **בבטן.** *המפרש[28] בבטן גזר השם דבר הבכורה והברכה לא ידעתי *מה[29] טעם *'בבטן'[30] *והכתוב אמר 'בטרם[31] אצרך בבטן ידעתיך' (ירמיה א, ה). ולפי דעתי כי הוא כמשמעו כי בבטן עקב את אחיו וזהו מפורש 'וידו אוחזת בעקב עשו' (בראשית כה, כו). והטעם למה *לא[32] *זכרו בני יעקב[33] שאני בחרתי *אביהם[34]

אשיב שבותם (מ: 'שביתם' במקום 'שבותם') רק אינם הולכים אחרי השם כי אם (בס"ש: "הם" במקום "אם") סבבוני בכחש ומרמה (ר: "ובמרמה" במקום "ומרמה"), ופרק יא מסתיים עם המלים "כי הוא מלכות השם" (יב, א)/

1 ע"פ ל, ראה ההערה בסוף פרק יא/ 2 ו כן ח'/ 3 ל: חשוב/ 4 מ: היותו/ 5 ע"פ ב ל מ נ ר, ו ובס"ש: מלכי/ 6 ו ל מ: היא/ 7 נ: אינינו/ 8 ע"פ ו מ ר, ב ל נ ובס"ש: בדבריו/ 9 ע"פ כ"י, בס"ש: כי אם הוא/ 10 ל כמו ח'/ 11 ו ר: יכרתו/ 12 ל: וריב לה' עם יהודה/ 13 ע"פ ו מ ר, ל: המפרשים כי, בס"ש: המפרש כי/ 14 ל ואמר ח'/ 15 ראה למטה הערה 22/ 16 ע"פ ו מ ר, בשאר כ"י ובס"ש: על/ 17 מ נ: טעם/ 18 ר מדרך ח'/ 19 ע"פ ו מ, ב: הכת', נ ר ובס"ש: הכתב/ 20 ע"פ ו מ נ ר, ב ובס"ש: כתב/ 21 ר: יחרוש/ 22 ראה למעלה הערה 15, ל: הטעם וריב לה' על אפרים עם יהודה כי עם יהודה ישוב על אפרים כמ' ארכיב אפרים יחרוש יהודה כי שם יהודה ישוב על אפרים יחרש יהודה ועל שניהם/ 23 מ: אומר/ 24 ר: שכחו/ 25 ו: ויריבו רועה גרר עם רועה יצחק, ל: ויריבו רועי יצחק/ 26 ל: ככה/ 27 מ ר: חיבר/ 28 ל: המפרשים/ 29 ל מה ח'/ 30 ל בבטן ח'/ 31 ב ל נ: וכתוב בטרם, ר: וכתוב אומר בטרם/ 32 ל לא ח'/ 33 ע"פ ו מ ר, ב ל נ: יזכרו בני יעקב, בס"ש: יזכרו את בני יעקב/

(6) *וחלה. כמו[43] 'יחולו על ראש יואב' (שמ"ב ג, כט) 'ולא חלו *בה[44] *ידים'[45] (איכה ד, ו) ידי *האויבים:[46] וכלתה בדיו. סעיפיו *כמו[47] 'ותעש בדים' (יחזקאל יז, ו) וזאת הרעה באה *להם[48] *ממועצותיהם:[49]

(7) *ועמי[50] *תלואים. [51]באל"ף כמו 'אשר תלאום' (שמ"ב כא, יב) ויו"ד 'למשובתי' *אינו[52] סימן *הפועל[53] כמו *'ושמחתים[54] בבית *תפלתי'[55] (ישעיה נו, ז), 'אשתחוה אל היכל קדשך ביראתך' (תהלים ה, ח) *כי[56] משובה לעולם לגנאי. והנה הטעם *שהם עושים[57] דרך משובה עמי כאדם תלוי באויר *אינו עולה למעלה ואינו יורד[58] למטה: ואל על. כמו *'נאם[59] הגבר הוקם על' (שמ"א כג, א) שהוא תואר כמו עליון. והנה פירושו ואל עליון *יקראוהו[60] הקוראים *והם[61] נביאי השם *וכולם[62] על דרך *אחד[63] לא *ירימו[64] ראש:

(8) איך. *אמגנך. כמו[65] 'אתנך' *כמו[66] 'אשר מגן צריך' (בראשית יד, כ), 'עטרת תפארת *תמגנך' (משלי ד, ט) תתן לך[67] כמו *'כי[68] ארץ *הנגב[69] נתתני' (יהושע טו, יט): נכמרו. יקדו ונצרבו *כמו[70] *'עורנו[71] כתנור נכמרו' (איכה ה, י): *נחומי. [72]מגזרת 'וינחם ה' ' (שמות לב, יד), ודברה תורה *כלשון[73] בני אדם:

(9) לא. *אל.[74] שאוכל לסבול *הכעס[75] ועוד כי בקרבך לבדך הייתי *קדוש:[76] כי אל *אנכי. ולא[77] *אבוא[78] בעיר. על דרך 'ישב אלהים את האדם' (דה"י־ב ו, יח). והגאון אמר לא *אבוא[79] בעיר אחרת רק בירושלים לבדה:

(10) אחרי. אם *ישובו[80] ללכת אחרי השם כמו 'אחרי ה' *אלהיכם[81] תלכו' (דברים יג, ה) עתה ישאג כאריה 'ויחרדו בנים' הם ישראל *שהלכו[82] אל *מערב[83] שהיא מצרים כי כן *הוא[84] מערבית דרומית וככה אשור:

(11) וטעם 'יחרדו *כצפור'[85] *שהצפור[86] תחרד מקול האריה ואני *אעיפם[87] כעוף וכיונה הפך שאמר 'כיונה פותה אין לב' (ז, יא): והושבתים על בתיהם. הטעם אשיב שבותם:[88]

אחד ח'/ 41 ו ההולכים ח'/ 42 ע"פ ב ו מ נ ר, ל ובס"ש: ארצו/ 43 ל: וחלה חרב כמו/ 44 ע"פ ו ל נ ר, ב מ ובס"ש: בהם/ 45 ל: יד, ר: ידיים/ 46 ב: האוהבים/ 47 ב נ כמו ח'/ 48 ל: אליהם/ 49 ו: ממעצותיהם/ 50 ל ועמי ח'/ 51 נ: תלאים/ 52 ו ל מ ר: אינגו/ 53 ל: הפעל/ 54 ל ר ובס"ש: ושימחתים/ 55 מ ר: תפילתי/ 56 ב: לכי/ 57 ב: שהן עושין/ 58 ב מ: איננו עולה למעלה ואיננו יורד, ל: לא עולה ולא יורד, ר: עולה למעלה ואיננו יורד/ 59 ל מ: נאום, בשמואל: 'ונאם'/ 60 ל: יקראו/ 61 ב: והשם/ 62 ל: וכלם/ 63 ו מ ר: אחת/ 64 ע"פ כ"י, בס"ש: ירומו/ 65 נ: אמגנך ישראל כמו/ 66 ב ל נ כמו ח'/ 67 ו מ ר: תמגנך אתנך אתן לך, ל: תמגנך תתן להם/ 68 ל כי ח'/ 69 נ הנגב ח'/ 70 בכ"י כמו ח'/ 71 ב מ: עורינו/ 72 ל: נחמי/ 73 ע"פ ו מ ר, בשאר כ"י ובס"ש: כנגד/ 74 מ אל ח'/ 75 מ: הרעה/ 76 ר: קודש/ 77 ע"פ ו ל מ ר, ב נ ובס"ש: אנכי ולא איש ולא/ 78 נ: אבא/ 79 נ: אבא/ 80 ל: ישוב/ 81 ב נ אלהיכם ח'/ 82 נ: שהלי/ 83 מ: מארב/ 84 ו נ ר: היא/ 85 מ: כציפור, נ כצפור ח'/ 86 מ: שהציפור/ 87 ע"פ מ נ, ו ר: אעופם, ב ל ובס"ש: אעופה/ 88 ע"פ ל, בשאר כ"י ובס"ש:

מלכי ישראל לא סרו *מחטאות[104] *ירבעם. וטעם[105] 'בשחר' כי *יושדו בלילה ובשחר[106] *יכרת[107] מלכם:

יא

(1) **כי נער.** *זהו[1] 'מלומדה' (י, יא) *ממני[2] כי *מהיותו[3] נער, והטעם בצאתו ממצרים, אז *החילותי[4] *ליסרו[5] בעבור שאהבתיו:

(2) **קראו.** הטעם 'ממצרים קראתי לבני' (פסוק א) לעבדני והם עתה 'קראו להם' לבעלים וכאשר *קראו לבעלים כן הלכו[6] ונדדו מארצם מפניהם. ויש אומרים 'קראו' *להם' נביאי[8] והם הלכו אחורנית:[9]

(3—4) **ואנכי *תרגלתי.** תי"ו[10] *תרגלתי[11] תחת ה"א ואין *כמוהו[12] במקרא. והטעם *הרגלתיו[13] ללכת על רגליו כאשר יורגל הנער שיוקח על זרועותיו וזהו כדרך רפואה לחזק הנער עד שיוכל ללכת. ובעבור *שדמה[14] ישראל ל'עגלה *מלומדה'[15] (י, יא) אמר *'בחבלי אדם אמשכם בעבתות אהבה'[16] לא כמו העבותות *המושכות[17] *בצואר[18] *העגלה[19] החורשת:

(4) **ואהיה להם.** כאנשים *המרחמים[20] *על[21] העגלה *להרים[22] העול *שהוא[23] על *לחיה[24] רגע *אחר[25] רגע: **ואט.** כמו[26] *ואטה,[27] *ומלת[28] *'אוכיל'[29] שם דבר כמו *'אכל[30] בכסף' (דברים ב, כח) והייתי מטה אליו אוכל. ורבי מרינוס אמר כי *'אוכיל'[31] ראוי להיותו *אאכיל[32] כמו 'ויוסף עוד דוד את כל בחור *בישראל'[33] (שמ"ב ג, כט). *ופירש[34] 'ואט' כמשמעו *שהיית[35] *מאכילו[36] *אט.[37]

(5) **לא ישוב.** *ואשור[38] *שם[39] מלכו. כאשר הזכרתי 'ושמו להם ראש *אחד'[40] (ב, ב): **כי מאנו לשוב.** אלי *ההולכים[41] למצרים לשוב אל *ארצי.[42]

בשאר כ"י ובס"ש: ככה/ 104 ע"פ ב ו מ ר, ל נ ובס"ש: מחטאת/ 105 ל: ירבעם בן נבט וטעם/ 106 ל: ישד בן בלמה ובשר/ 107 ל מ ר: ירידת/

1 ו מ ר: זה הוא, ל זהו ח'/ 2 ע"פ ב נ, בשאר כ"י ובס"ש: ממנו/ 3 ל: מהיותי/ 4 ב ו ל: החלותי/ 5 ב ל: לייסרו/ 6 ע"פ נ, מ ר: קראו להם נביאי והם הלכו, בס"ש: קראו להם לבעלים כן הלכו/ 7 ו "לבעלים כן הלכו ונדדו מארצם מפניהם ויש אומרים קראו" ח'/ 8 ל: להם לבעלים נביאי/ 9 ל: אחרנית/ 10 ל: תרגלתי לאפרים תיו/ 11 ל תרגלתי ח'/ 12 נ: כמהו/ 13 ל: תרגלתיו/ 14 מ ר: שדימה/ 15 ל: מלמדה/ 16 ע"פ ו ל מ ר, ב נ ובס"ש: בחבלי אדם בעבותות אמשכם אהבה/ 17 ל נ: המושמות/ 18 ב נ בצואר ח'/ 19 ע"פ כ"י, בס"ש: העגל/ 20 ע"פ ל, בשאר כ"י ובס"ש: המרימים/ 21 ע"פ ב ל נ, ו מ ר ובס"ש: עול/ 22 ו מ ר: להשים/ 23 מ שהוא ח'/ 24 ו מ ר: לחייה/ 25 ר: אחרי/ 26 ל: ואט אליו כמו/ 27 ע"פ ל, ב ו מ נ ר ובס"ש: אטה/ 28 מ: ומילת/ 29 ו: אוביל/ 30 ו מ נ ר: אוכל/ 31 ו: אוביל/ 32 נ: מאכיל/ 33 ב ו ר: ישראל, ל בישראל ח'/ 34 נ ר: ופרש/ 35 ל: שהיתי/ 36 ע"פ ב נ, בשאר כ"י ובס"ש: מאכיל/ 37 מ: אני/ 38 ו: ואשר/ 39 מ: הוא/ 40 ר

רק *זועה׳[51] (ישעיה כח, יט) והיום לא יפחדו שתשיגם *מלחמה[52] כאשר *השיגה[53] *את[54] *בני[55] *בנימין[56] מהשבטים. וזה *הכתוב[57] *כמו[58] ׳כריח שדה׳ (בראשית כז, כז) שטעמו *ראה ריח בני אשר ברכו ה׳ כריח שדה:[59]

(10) **באותי ואסרם.** מגזרת מוסר והיו״ד מובלע בדגשת *עי״ן הפועל[60] כדרך ׳בטרם אצרך *בבטן׳[61] (ירמיה א, ה), ׳כי אצק מים׳ (ישעיה מד, ג). *ופירוש[62] *׳ואספו[63] עליהם׳ *איך[64] איסרם על *ידי[65] עמים *רבים[66] *שיתאספו[67] עליהם *ואסרם[68] כמו יאסרו *השורים:[69] **לשתי עונותם.** כמו ׳כבחצי מענה׳ (שמ״א יד, יד), ׳האריכו למעניתם׳ (תהלים קכט, ג). וטעם *׳שתי׳[70] בעבור יהודה ואפרים:

(11—12) ***ואפרים.**[71] אני למדתיו *מתחילה[72] *לסבול עול[73] *מצותי:[74] **ואני עברתי.** *החוק[75] על כל חורש שהטיבותי לצוארה והרכבתי אפרים עם יהודה: ***יחרש. יעקב.** כולו[76] השדה *שלי[77] דרך משל על *התורה[78] *וצויתים[79] *זרעו[80] וקצרו הוא התגמול, נירו להסיר הקוצים לסקל הנתיב ועת תדרשו השם *לרוות[81] הזרע אז *יבא[82] מלקוש ׳ויורה צדק *לכם׳[83] כמו ׳יורה ומלקוש׳ (דברים יא, יד). וכל המפרשים אומרים בקשו אתם *תורתו[84] והוא *יבא[85] *ויורה אתכם:[86]

(13) ***חרשתם.**[87] *וכל[88] זה עשיתם שלא סבלתם *עולי[89] *כי[90] *בטחתם[91] *בגבוריכם[92] *ובעבור זה:[93]

(14) **וקאם. *כשוד[94] *שלמן.**[95] אולי הוא *שלמנאסר:[96] ***בית[97] ארבאל.** שם מקום: ***רטשה.**[98] שם דבר ׳אם על *בנים׳.[99] ולהיותו מגזרת *אורב[100] *אין טעם לו:[101]

(15) ***ככה.**[102] **בית אל.** ששם העגל שהוא *סבת[103] הרע מכל רעתם כי רוב

דורו כאילו עמדו עם בני בנימין/ 49 ו: הם עולה, ר: הם עלוה/ 50 ו מ ר והיה ח׳/ 51 מ נ: זעוה/ 52 ל מלחמה ח׳/ 53 ל: השיג/ 54 ל את ח׳/ 55 ו מ בני ח׳/ 56 נ: בנימן/ 57 ע״פ כ״י, בס״ש: הכתב/ 58 ו ר כמו ח׳/ 59 ל: ראה ריח בני כריח השדה אשר ברכו ה׳/ 60 מ: העי״ן הפועל, נ: עי״ן הפעל/ 61 ו ל מ ר בבטן ח׳/ 62 ע״פ כ״י, בס״ש: ופירש/ 63 ל: ואוספו/ 64 ל: אך/ 65 כ״י: יד/ 66 ע״פ ו ל מ ר, ב נ ובס״ש רבים ח׳/ 67 ו: יתאספו/ 68 ב ל נ ויאסרום/ 69 ע״פ ל מ נ, ב: השוורים, ו ר ובס״ש: קשורים/ 70 ע״פ ו מ ר, בשאר כ״י ובס״ש: שתים/ 71 ל: מלמדה/ 72 ל: בתחילה, נ: מתחלה/ 73 נ: לסבל על/ 74 ו מ ר: המצות/ 75 ב נ: החק/ 76 ע״פ מ, ל: חרש יעקב כל, נ: יחרש יעקב כלו, בס״ש: יחרש יעקב יעקב כלו (ועם התיבה ״יחרש״ מסתיים דיבור המתחיל הקודם)/ 77 ע״פ ו ל מ נ ר, ב ובס״ש: שלו/ 78 ב נ התורה ח׳/ 79 ו: וצויתם, מ נ: וציויתים, ר: וציויתם/ 80 מ ר זרעו ח׳/ 81 ו מ ר: לצאת, ל: לזרות/ 82 מ ר: יבוא/ 83 ל לכם ח׳/ 84 ע״פ ל נ, בשאר כ״י ובס״ש: תורתי/ 85 ב מ ר: יבוא/ 86 ל: ויורה צדק אתכם, נ: וירויה אתכם/ 87 ב נ חרשתם ח׳/ 88 ל: כל/ 89 ב: עוד, נ: עוזי, ר: עלי/ 90 ו מ כי ח׳/ 91 מ: ובטחתם/ 92 ב מ: בגיבוריכם, ר: בגבוריכם, ל: בגבורכם, נ: בגבוריהם, נ: בגיבורכים/ 93 ל ובעבור זה ח׳/ 94 ב: כשד, ו: כשור/ 95 ר: שלשמן/ 96 ע״פ ו ל מ ר, ב נ ובס״ש שלמנאצר/ 97 כ״י: בבית/ 98 מ: נטשה/ 99 ל: הבנים/ 100 ל: אומ׳/ 101 ו מ ר: אין לו טעם/ 102 ל ככה ח׳/ 103 ע״פ ל,

׳הוא *יערף[8] מזבחותם׳ שהרבו כדרך *׳וערפתו׳[9] (שמות יג, יג) הריסות:

(3) **כי.** כאשר חלק *לבם[10] לא *רצו[11] *להיות[12] עליהם מלך ולא יראו *מהשם[13] על כן אין להם *מורא[14] והכל יעשה *כרצונו:[15]

(4) ***דברו.**[16] **אלות *שוא.**[17] דרך *זרה כאילו[18] *המלה[19] *מורכבת[20] משם *הפועל[21] הסמוך *ושאינו[22] סמוך או היה כן בעבור אות הגרון. ומשל ׳משפט׳ שהוא מתוק *והפך[23] למר כמו *׳ההופכים ללענה[24] משפט׳ (עמוס ה, ז) והוא *יפרח[25] *׳כראש משפט׳[26] *שאינו[27] ישר: על ***תלמי.** כמו[28] ׳תלמיה רוה׳ (תהלים סה, יא). *׳ו׳שדי׳[29] כמו שדה *והעד[30] ׳יעלוז שדי׳ (שם צו, יב):

(5) ***לעגלות.** הם[31] עגלי הזהב בבית אל: ***יגורו.** יפחדו[32] **השוכנים בשומרון: כי אבל עליו.** *הטעם על כל עגל בבית אל כאשר תחרב: **וכמריו.** אשר עליו[33] יגילו היום יתאבלו: **כי.** הטעם כפול:

(6) ***גם.** עגל[34] שומרון: **לאשור *יובל.**[35] כי הוא זהב: ***בשנה.**[36] *בתוספת[37] הנו"ן כמו ׳שבענה בנים׳ (איוב מב, יג):

(7) **נדמה.** ישרת בעבור אחר וכן הוא נדמה שומרון נדמה מלכה: **כקצף.** כמו *׳ותאנתי[38] *לקצפה׳[39] (יואל א, ז):

(8) **ונשמדו.** במות הבעלים בסור *העגלים:[40] ***ואמרו.**[41] *אמר[42] רבי משה *הכהן[43] *כי אמרו[44] דרך משל בעבור המזבחות כדרך ׳כי היא שמעה׳ (יהושע כד, כז), והטעם שלא יראו *עוד.[45] ויפת אמר ויאמרו עובדיהם מרוב צרתם:

(9) ***מימי.** יותר[46] כמו ׳מזקנים אתבונן׳ (תהלים קיט, ק), ׳מאויבי *תחכמני׳ (שם שם, צח). ופירוש[47] ׳שם עמדו׳ על *חטאי דורו כאילו בגבעה עמדו עם בני בנימין[48] *הם ׳בני עלוה׳[49] כמו עולה ׳והי[י]ת(ה) לזעוה׳ (דברים כח, כה) *׳והיה[50]

ובס"ש: **חלק אחד**/ 6 ל **שהוא ח׳**/ 7 ל: **וכמו**/ 8 ו ל: **יערוף**/ 9 ב נ: **וערפתי**/ 10 ב: **ליבם**/ 11 ו ל מ נ ר: **ירצו**/ 12 ר: **להיותם**/ 13 ל: **מאת השם**/ 14 ו מ: **מורה**, ל: **מוראה**/ 15 ב ל נ: **רצונו**/ 16 ל: **דברו ח׳**/ 1 ב ו ר **שוא ח׳**/ 18 ל נ: **זרה כאלו**, ו ר **זרה כאילו ח׳**/ 19 מ: **המילה**/ 20 ו: **המורכבת**/ 21 מ: **פועל**/ 22 ו מ ר: **ושאיננו**/ 23 בכ"י: **וההפך**/ 24 נ: **וההופכים לענה**/ 25 ו: **יכריח**/ 26 ע"פ ל, ו: **כראש משפטים**, נ ר: **בראש משפט**, ב מ ובס"ש: **בראש משפטם**/ 27 ו ל מ: **שאיננו**/ 28 מ: **תלמי שדי כמו**/ 29 ל: **שדי**/ 30 ו: **זה עד**/ 31 ל: **לעגלות בית און הם**/ 32 ל: **יגורו שכן יפחדו**/ 33 ו מ ר **הטעם על כל עגל בבית אל כאשר תחרב וכמריו אשר עליו ח׳**/ 34 ל: **גם אותו עגל**/ 35 ב ו: **וכל**/ 36 ו ל מ: **בושנה**/ 37 ע"פ כ"י, בס"ש: **בתוספות**/ 38 ל נ **ותאנתי ח׳**/ 39 ו: **לגפנה**/ 40 ל: **הבעלים**/ 41 ל **ואמרו ח׳**/ 42 ל: **ויאמר**/ 43 ע"פ ו מ ר, ב ל נ ובס"ש **הכהן ח׳**/ 44 ר **כי אמרו ח׳**/ 45 מ **עוד ח׳**/ 46 ל: **מימי הגבעה יותר**/ 47 ב: **תחכמני ופי׳**, ו ר: **תחכמני מצותיך ופירוש**, מ נ: **תחכמני מצוותיך ופירוש**, בס"ש: **תחכמני ופירש**/ 48 ע"פ נ, ב: **על חטאי דורו כאילו עמדו עם בני בנימין**, ו: **על חטא דורו בגבעה עמדו עם בנימין**, ל: **על חטאי דורו כאילו בגבעה עמדו על חטאי דורו כאילו בגבעה עמדו עם בני בנימין**, מ: **על חטאי דור בגבעה עמדו עם בנימין**, ר: **על חטא דור בגבעה עמדו שם עם בני בנימין**, בס"ש: **על חטאי**

ואם יגיע ימות[62] *הוולד[63] לפני הלידה. והוא *שם[64] *דבר[65] כמו *דיעה[66] על כן *אחריו אם[67] ילדו ויגדלו את בניהם אשכלם שלא יגיעו *להיותם[68] *אדם:[69]

(12) **בשורי מהם.** שי״ן תחת סמ״ך:

(13) **אפרים.** יהיה כצור שהיתה *שתולה[70] בנוה *וכסוה[71] המים כך ראיתי בנבואה שיוציא האב אל הורג בניו:

(14) **תן.** יתפלל הנביא *אחר[72] *שגזרת[73] *עליהם[74] שיוציא כל אחד בניו אל ההורג אולי ימותו קטנים ולא יהיה צערם גדול. *וזהו[75] *׳תן להם רחם[76] משכיל׳ שימותו בבטן *והילדים[77] ימותו באפס חלב: ***צומקים.**[78] *כמו ׳צמוקים׳[79] (שמ״א טז, א) יבשים:

(15) **כל.** טעם ׳בגלגל׳ הוא *המקום[80] שהיו שם בעברם את הירדן *היה[81] ראוי שיזכירו את *טובתי[82] בהיות *אבותיהם[83] שם שהבאתים אל ארצי ועתה אגרשם מביתי:

(16) ***הוכה.**[84] הטעם *הוכה[84] העץ משל לאבות *ובנים:[85]

(17) ***ימאסם.** אמר הנביא אמר השם אלי כי איננו אלהיהם:[86]

ט

(1) **גפן בוקק.** רק אין בו כח לפרות ואין פרי: **ישוה לו.** *יחשוב[1] כי יפרה *או פריו יהיה[2] שוה *כגפן[3] שהוא בוקק כי כאשר הרביתי פריו *׳הרבה[4] למזבחות׳:

(2) **חלק.** כי אין להם *אלוה אחד:[5] **עתה יאשמו.** מגזרת שממה כמו ׳תאשם שומרון׳ (יד, א) *שהוא[6] *כמו[7] ׳והאדמה לא תשם׳ (בראשית מז, יט), ולבם שנחלק

62 ע״פ ו מ ר, ב ל נ ובס״ש: ההריון ואם היה לא יגיע להראות ואם הגיע ימות/ 63 ע״פ ב מ נ ר, ו ל ובס״ש: הולד/ 64 ר שם ח׳/ 65 ע״פ כ״י, בס״ש דבר ח׳/ 66 ל: דעה/ 67 ל מ: אחריו כי אם/ 68 ע״פ ו ל מ נ ר, ב ובס״ש: להיות/ 69 ב: האדם/ 70 ו מ ר: שתולה ח׳/ 71 מ ר: וכיסוה/ 72 ו: אחרי/ 73 ו: שגזרה/ 74 ל המאמר מן ״שיוציא האב אל הורג״ עד ״שגזרת עליהם״ ח׳/ 75 ע״פ ב ל מ נ ר, ו ובס״ש: וזה/ 76 ע״פ ל מ, בשאר כ״י ובס״ש להם ח׳/ 77 ע״פ ל, מ: והלדים, בשאר כ״י ובס״ש: והילודים/ 78 ל: צמקים, ר: צמוקים/ 79 ו מ ר כמו צמוקים ח׳/ 80 ו מ ר המקום ח׳, ל: מקום/ 81 ו: יהיה/ 82 ו טובת, מ: טובתו/ 83 ל מ: אבותיכם/ 84 ו ל מ ר: הכה/ 85 ל: ולבנים, מ: אבנים/ 86 ל: ימאסם אמר הנביא אלהי כי איננו אלהים רק לו, מ ר: ימאסם אמר הנביא אלהי כי אינימו אלהיהם, נ: ימאסם אמר הנביא אלי כי אינינו אלהיהם, ו הפירוש על פסוק יז ח׳/

1 ל: יחשב/ 2 ע״פ ב ל נ, ו: את פריו יהיה, מ ר: את פריו יהי, בס״ש: את פריו והיה/ 3 ל: לגפן/ 4 ע״פ ו, בשאר כ״י ובס״ש: הרבו/ 5 ע״פ ל, ב: חלק אלוה אחד, ו: חלק אחר, נ: חלק אלוה אחר, מ ר

(4) לא. הנשארים *ואילו[14] היה להם 'לא יערבו לו': כלחם אונים. כמו 'לא אכלתי באוני' (דברים כו, יד) והוא שם דבר ולשון רבים אונים:

(5) מה. חג ה'. כנגד זבחיכם:

(6) כי הנה *הלכו.[15] מפחד *שוד שיבואם[16] יש *מהם[17] שימותו במצרים גם בדרכים, על כן אמר 'מחמד לכספם' והנה לשוד ילכו:

(7) באו ימי *השלם.[18] *שישלם לכם השם[19] שהייתם אומרים על נביא *השם[20] *שהוא[21] אויל ואיש *אשר[22] רוח השם בו הוא משוגע: על *רב[23] *עונך. משטמה. שיש[24] בלב *כל אחד:[25]

(8) *צופה. הטעם[26] שאמר כי נביא השם הוא אויל והוא *עושה[27] מעצמו *צופה[28] והוא כמו[29] *נביא[30] שהוא צופה *מה להיות[31] וזה נביא השקר הוא *'פח[32] יקוש' וטעם 'משטמה בבית *אלהיו'[33] כדרך שהזכיר *בתחילה[34] *'וכשלת[35] היום וכשל גם נביא' (ד, ה):

(9) העמיקו. להרע: כימי הגבעה. שמרד בנימין:

(10) כענבים. כדרך *'ימצאהו[36] בארץ מדבר' (דברים לב, י), *וטעם 'כענבים במדבר'[37] שאין שם *ישוב[38] כל מוצאם ישמח *בהם[39] וככה *'כבכורה[40] בתאנה' ולא היתה *שמחתי רק[41] מעט *כי[42] *לא[43] עמדה *כי[44] *השתחוו[45] לבעל פעור וינזרו מאחרי: *לבשת.[46] כמו *'והבשת[47] *אכלה יגיע'[48] שם לאליל: ויהיו *שקוצים.[49] שנטמאו[50] בעבור אהבת *נשי[51] *מדין:[52]

(11) *אפרים.[53] טעם 'כעוף' על *המהירות[54] שלא ישמחו ולא יהיה להם כבוד מהלידה גם מבטן כאשר תראה *בטן[55] ההרה *שהתנפחה[56] *מהריון[57] כאשר *יפסק[58] דם *האשה. והנה[59] הטעם *כי[60] *ימעט[61] *ההריון ולא יהיה מגיע להראות

אוכלין/ 13 ל: ויתנו מגז' אתנן/ 14 ע"פ ו מ נ ר, ב ל ובס"ש: ואלו/ 15 ל: ילכו/ 16 ו ר מ: שוד מצרים שיבואם/ 17 ל: מהם ח'/ 18 ב ל נ: השלום, ו מ ר: השילום/ 19 ב נ: שישלם להם השם, ו ל מ: שישלם השם לכם/ 20 ל השם ח'/ 21 ו מ ר: הוא/ 22 ו אשר ח'/ 23 ל מ ר: רוב/ 24 ב: עונך ורבה המשטמה שיש, ו מ ר: עונך ורוב המשטמה שיש, ל: עונך ורוב שיש, נ: עונך ורב המשטמה שיש/ 25 ל: כל אחד מהם/ 26 ב ו מ נ ר: צפה הטעם, ל: צפה אפרים הטעם/ 27 נ: עשה/ 28 ל נ: צפה/ 29 ו מ נ המאמר "נביא השם הוא אויל והוא עושה עצמו צופה והוא כמו" ח'/ 30 ו מ ר: הנביא/ 31 מ ר: מה לו להיות/ 32 ר פח ח'/ 33 מ: אלהיי/ 34 ו ל מ ר: בתחלה/ 35 ע"פ ל, בשאר כ"י ובס"ש: וכשל/ 36 ע"פ כ"י, בס"ש: ימצאוהו/ 37 ל וטעם כענבים במדבר ח'/ 38 ו נ ר ובס"ש: יישוב/ 39 ע"פ ו ל מ ר, ב נ ובס"ש: בהן/ 40 ל: כבורה/ 41 ל: שמחתי בך רק/ 42 ל כי ח'/ 43 ל: ולא/ 44 מ כי ח'/ 45 ל: השחיתו/ 46 ר: לבושת/ 47 ע"פ ב נ, מ: והובשת, בשאר כ"י ובס"ש: והבושת/ 48 ו ר אכלה יגיע ח', בירמיה ג, כד: 'והבשת אכלה את יגיע'/ 49 ב: שקיצים, מ ר: שיקוצים/ 50 ל המאמר "לבעל פעור... שקוצים שנטמאו ח'/ 51 מ: אנשי/ 52 ל: מדיין/ 53 ל אפרים ח'/ 54 ו ל מ ר: מהירות/ 55 ע"פ ו ל מ ר, ב נ ובס"ש: הבטן/ 56 ע"פ כ"י, בס"ש: שתתנפחה/ 57 ע"פ ו מ ר, ב ל נ ובס"ש: מההריון/ 58 ל: יפסוק/ 59 ע"פ ל מ נ ר, ב: האשה הנידה והנה, בס"ש: האשה הנדה והנה/ 60 ו מ ר כי ח'/ 61 ר ימעט ח'/

(9) *כי.[41] **פרא.** כמו 'פרא אדם' (בראשית טז, יב). וטעם 'בודד' כי לא היתה עצתם אחת *ומלת[42] 'התנו' מגזרת 'אתנן' (ט, א) *שהיה[43] *כל אחד נותן[44] מנחות של אהבים לשרי האומות:

(10) *גם. טעם[45] 'אקבצם' *במצרים[46] אז *יחלו[47] להתאונן ולהתרעם *מעט מרוב משא מלך מצרים[48] ואשור ושריהם. ולא יתכן מדרך *הדקדוק[49] לפרש 'ויחלו' רק *כמו[50] 'וממקדשי תחלו' (יחזקאל ט, ו):

(11) *כי הרבה. וטעם[51] 'היו לו מזבחות לחטוא' כבר *היו[52] לו *שירש[53] מאבותיו ולמה הרבה עוד:

(12) *אכתוב. ואני[54] *הוכחתיו[55] *וחוקי[56] כתובים היו לו:

(13) *זבחי. אמר[57] ר' משה *הכהן[58] *'הבהבי'[59] *כדברי[60] *רז"ל[61] 'ולא *הבהבה'[62] (שבת פרק ב, משנה ג). ויפת אמר מגזרת *הב הב[63] *והיו"ד נוסף[64] כמו שַׁדַי והוא הנכון: *יזכור[65] עונם. שישובו *אל מצרים[66] *למרות[67] פיו *'לא[68] *תוסיפו[69] לשוב בדרך הזה עוד' (דברים יז, טז):

(14) *וישכח.[70] היכלות. *לבצר[71] *בהם:[72] ואכלה. *ארמנות[73] כל עיר ועיר:

ט

(1) **אל.** הטעם כל *גוי אם ישמח[1] *בבא[1a] להם *גילה[2] דין הוא כי אין אחד מהם *שיזנה[3] *תחת[4] אלהיו כאשר עשית אתה אהבת לתת *אתנן לבעלים[5] תחת *מעשר[6] אלהיך וזאת הזנות על כן *'גרן[7] ויקב' כי זרים יקחום:[8]

(2) **יכחש בם.** *כאילו[9] לא יכירם:

(3) *לא ישבו.[10] **ובאשור טמא יאכלו.** כי כן *היו[11] *אוכלים[12] בארץ ה' אחר שלא יתנו קודש השם *ויתנו אתנן:[13]

איני/ 41 ל כי ח'/ 42 ר: ומילת/ 43 ב: שיהיה, ל: שיהא/ 44 ו מ: כל אחת נותן, ר: נותן כל אחד/ 45 ל גם טעם ח'/ 46 ל במצרים ח'/ 47 ל: יחל/ 48 ל: מעט ממשא מלך ושרים מרוב משא המלך מצרים/ 49 ב מ: הדיקדוק/ 50 ל כמו ח'/ 51 ל כי הרבה וטעם ח'/ 52 מ נ: והיו/ 53 מ ר: שורש/ 54 ל: אכתב לו רובי תורתי ואני/ 55 ו: הזנחתים, מ ר: הוכחתים/ 56 ו: וחוקים, ל: וחקי/ 57 ל: זבחי הבהבי אמר/ 58 ב ל מ הכהן ח'/ 59 מ: הבבי/ 60 ל: כדרך/ 61 ו ל מ ר: חכמינו, נ: רבותינו/ 62 ו: אבהבה/ 63 ע"פ מ ר, ל: בב הב, ב ו ובס"ש: הבהב/ 64 ל והיו"ד נוסף ח'/ 65 ב ו ל מ נ: יפקד, ר: יפקוד/ 66 ל: אל ארץ מצרים/ 67 נ: לפרות/ 68 ר: ולא/ 69 כ"י: תוסיפון/ 70 ל וישכח ח'/ 71 ל: להבצר/ 72 ב נ: אותם, ל: מהם/ 73 ע"פ כ"י, בס"ש: ארמנותיה/

1 ל: גוים ישמחו/ a 1 ל מ ר: בבוא/ 2 ו ל מ נ ר: גדולה/ 3 ו ל מ ר: שזנה/ 4 ל מ נ ר: מתחת/ 5 ו: אתנן זונה לבעלים/ 6 ל: המעשר/ 7 מ ר: גורן/ 8 ע"פ ב מ נ, בשאר כ"י ובס"ש אין סימני הפסק אחר "יקחום"/ 9 ו: כאלו/ 10 ל לא ישבו ח'/ 11 ר היו ח'/ 12 ע"פ ב ל מ נ ר, ו: יאכלום, בס"ש:

ח

(1) **אל.** *דברי השם אל הנביא שים[1] 'אל *חכך[2] שופר' ודאה כנשר *אל[3] בית ה'. ויפת אמר שים *חכך[4] שופר כי *אויב[5] *ידאה כנשר[6] *על[7] בית ה', ויפה *פירש[8] בעבור מלת 'יען':

(2) **לי.** ככה הוא לי יזעקו בני ישראל או יחסר בית ישראל:

(3) **זנח.** ***טוב.** [9]הוא השם הנכבד שהיה טוב לו: ***ירדפו.**[10] כמו *'אשר יקראו[11] *ה' צדקנו'[12] (ירמיה כג, ו):

(4) **הם.** כי לא שאלו *השם[13] להמליך ירבעם וכתוב 'אשר יבחר ה' אלהיך בו' (דברים יז, יב) גם *כן[14] *מלכי[15] ישראל: **השירו.** מעלומי העי"ן קם שב *שר[16] והטעם כפול. ויפת אמר כמו *סמ"ך[17] כמו *'בשורי[18] מהם' (ט, יב), והטעם הפוך אם המליכו או אם *הסירו.[19] וטעם 'למען יכרת' בעבור יכרת מהם הכסף והזהב:

(5) ***זנח. שומרון.**[20] כפול *כאילו[21] *כתוב[22] אותך זנח עגלך אותך שומרון כאילו מאס בך כי העיר תחרב *ואנשיה[23] *ילכו[24] בשבי: **חרה אפי בם. בעגל ובשומרון: עד מתי.** יהיה *חרון[25] *אפי[26] *בם[27] עד *שיהיו[28] נקיים ולא *יוכלו[29] נקיון שיהיה להם *ממנו:[30]

(6) ***כי.**[31] *מעצת ישראל הוא[32] *ומעצת[33] המלך שהמליכוהו נעשה עגל שומרון: **כי *שבבים.** [34]כמו שביבים. ויפת אמר כי עגל שומרון *יעשה ישראל להיות שובב, וזה[35] איננו נכון:

(7) ***כי.**[36] תי"ו סופתה נוסף *כמו 'אימתה'[37] (שמות טו, טו): **אולי.** ואם תאמרו 'אולי יעשה' *דעו[38] כי 'זרים *יבלעוהו':[39]

(8) **נבלע.** הטעם יבלעו קצירכם גם יבלעו הזורעים: **ככלי *אין[40] חפץ בו.** שאדם ישליכנו מביתו:

ח'/ 125 ע"פ ו, בשאר כ"י ובס"ש: ואני/ 126 ל: על צריהם/ 127 ב נ: זו זה לעגם, ר: זה לעגם/ 128 ו: אלי/

1 ל: דברי הנביא השם אמר שים/ 2 ב: חיכך/ 3 ל אל ח'/ 4 מ ר: חיכך/ 5 ל: האויב/ 6 נ: כנשר ידא, ר: ידאה מנשר/ 7 נ: אל, ל על ח'/ 8 ע"פ כ"י, בס"ש: פירוש/ 9 ב ל נ טוב ח'/ 10 ל: אויב ירדפו/ 11 ב: כאשר יקרחו/ 12 בכ"י ה'צדקנו ח'/ 13 ע"פ ו ל מ ר, נ: לשם, בס"ש: להשם/ 14 ל: כל, ר: כי/ 15 ע"פ ו ל מ נ ר, ב ובס"ש: מלך/ 16 נ: סר/ 17 ל: בסמך/ 18 ל: בסורי/ 19 ע"פ ו מ ר, ב ל נ ובס"ש: השירו/ 20 ל: זנח עגלך שומרון/ 21 ע"פ ב מ, בשאר כ"י ובס"ש: כאלו/ 22 ל: אמר/ 23 ע"פ ב ל מ נ ר, ו ובס"ש: ואנשים/ 24 ו מ ר: הלכו/ 25 ב נ: הרה/ 26 מ: אפו/ 27 מ בם ח'/ 28 ל: שיהו/ 29 ל: יוכלון/ 30 מ: ממון/ 31 מ כי ח'/ 32 נ: מעצת מעצת ישראל הוא, ל מעצת ישראל הוא ח'/ 33 ל: מעצת/ 34 ל: לשבבים, ר: שובבים/ 35 ו: יעשה ישראל שובב ישראל יעשה שובב וזה, מ ר: יעשה ישראל שובב וזה/ 36 ל כי ח'/ 37 ל: כמו תי"ו אימתה/ 38 ו ר: דע/ 39 מ: יבעלוהו/ 40 ר:

(11) **ויהי אפרים.** *בקלותו[85] וחוסר דעתו שהיו *הולכים[86] אל מצרים ואשור לבקש עזרה והם *לא ידעו כי כאשר[87] *׳ילכו אפרוש[88] *עליהם רשתי׳[89] *והנה אתפשם כי לא יוכלו לברוח על כן אמר[90] *׳עליהם׳[91] ולא להם, ובעבור שהזכיר *׳כיונה׳[92] (פסוק יא) אמר *׳כעוף[93] השמים אורידם׳:

(12) ***איסירם.**[94] כמו *איסרם[95] רק הוא *מהבנין[96] הנוסף ולא החליפו היו״ד *בוי״ו[97] כמו ׳ועפעפיך *יישרו[98] נגדך׳ (משלי ד, כה) ולא *אמר[99] אוסירם כמו אושיבם אורידם והעמידו המלה על *בנינה[100] *ששרשה[101] יסר או העתיד ייסר. *והטעם[102] אני *איסר[103] אלה ההולכים למצרים אז *יהיו[104] *׳כשמע[105] לעדתם׳ היושבים *בארצם:[106]

(13) ***אוי.**[107] טעם נדדו בעבור שהיו בורחים *שוד[108] *יבא עליהם:[109] **ואנכי.** *בלבי[110] *ומחשבתי לפדותם[111] והם היו אומרים כי כל לבי להרע להם:

(14) **ולא.** הטעם *כאשר הלילו[112] על משכבותם *ואמרו[113] אוי *להם על הרעה הבאה עליהם לא יזעקו אלי[114] כאשר *יזעק[115] החולה אל הרופא. וטעם ׳על דגן ותירוש *יתגוררו׳[116] שיתחברו ביום *לאכול ולשתות כמו ׳נהרגו ממגורות׳ (יואל א, יז): **יסורו בי.** ידברו סרה בי, והנה[117] *בלילה[118] לא *יזעקו[119] אלי וביום *מורדים[120] לדבר כזבים:

(15) ***ואני יסרתי.** הטעם[121] אני *יסרתים[122] לא לרעתם רק לחזק *זרועותם[123] *כדרך[124] *׳ואנכי[125] תרגלתי לאפרים׳ (יא, ג):

(16) **ישובו לא על.** הטעם ישובו אל מצרים לא על צורך רק להלשין *על שריהם[126] וזה טעם ׳היו כקשת רמיה׳, והעד ׳מזעם לשונם׳: ***זו לעגם.**[127] הקרוב *בעיני[128] כי המ״ם סימן אנשי הלשון:

ר: לגויים/ 84 ל: לעוזרם/ 85 מ: בלקותו/ 86 ו מ ר: הולכין/ 87 ע״פ ל, מ: לא ידעו באשור, בשאר כ״י ובס״ש: לא ידעו כאשר/ 88 ע״פ ל, ב: ילכו כי אני אפרש, בשאר כ״י ובס״ש: ילכו כי אני אפרוש/ 89 ע״פ ו מ, בשאר כ״י ובס״ש: רשתי עליהם/ 90 ל: והנה אחפשם כי לא יוכל על כן אמר, ו מ ר והנה אחפשם כי לא יוכלו לברוח על כן אמר ח׳/ 91 ר עליהם ח׳/ 92 ו: ביונה/ 93 ו: בעוף/ 94 ו מ: אייסרם, נ: איסרם, ר: אייסירם/ 95 מ: אסדם/ 96 מ מהבינייו, ר: מהבניין/ 97 ו ל מ: בר״ו, נ: בוא״ו/ 98 בכ״י ובס״ש: יישירו/ 99 ב נ אמר ח׳/ 100 ב נ ר: בניינה, מ: ביניינה/ 101 מ: ששרשיה/ 102 ו מ: וטעם/ 103 ו מ: אייסר/ 104 ל: יהיה/ 105 ע״פ ל מ נ ר, ב ובס״ש: כשמועה/ 106 מ: לארצם/ 107 ל אוי ח׳/ 108 ל שוד ח׳/ 109 ו ר: יבא להם, ל: יבא אוי להם/ 110 נ: בליבי/ 111 ו ר: ומחשבותי לפדותם, מ: ומחשבותם לפדותם, נ: ומחשבתי כלבם לפדותם/ 112 ע״פ ב ל נ ר, ו ובס״ש: כאשר אפדם הלילו, מ: כאשר אפדים הלילו/ 113 ו ל מ נ: ואומרים/ 114 מ להם על הרעה הבאה עליהם לא יזעקו אלי ח׳/ 115 ל יזעק ח׳/ 116 נ: יתגודדו/ 117 ו מ ר לאכול ולשתות כמו נהרסו ממגורות יסורו בי ידברו סרה בי והנה ח׳/ 118 ו מ ר: והלילה/ 119 ו מ ר: יצעקו/ 120 מ מורדים ח׳/ 121 ב ו מ נ ר: ואני הטעם, ל ואני מוסר הטעם/ 122 ב נ: ייסרתים/ 123 ל: זרועותיהם/ 124 ר כדרך

*ששרשו[33] ליץ על כן *הוא[34] *מכפולי הלמ"ד,[35] על *כן[36] *'תופפות'[37] (תהלים סח, כו) ו'מתופפות' (נחום ב, ח) שנים שרשים. ומלת 'החלו' *מחלי כמו הראו ו'מלכנו'[38] הוא הפעול והשרים *הם הפועלים: **החלו שרים.**[39] את המלך מן *השכרות[40] *וכמוהו[41] 'מחלה לב' (משלי יג, יב) *פועלת מחלה את הלב[42] *מהבנין[43] הנוסף שהוא החלה. וטעם *'חמת[44] מיין' בחסרון בי"ת בחמת מלא *יין[45] ופירושו כמו 'מן החמת' (בראשית כא, טו), *ונסמך[46] ככה כמו *דלת[47] 'וסגור *דלתך[48] *בעדך'[49] (ישעיה כו, כ), והעד 'מספח חמתך ואף שכר' (חבקוק ב, טו) *שהוא[50] כטעם הזה:

(6) ***כי.**[51] מלת 'בארבם' על מחשבות רעות שיחשבו כל הלילה, והנה לבם קרוב כתנור רק כל אופה ישן בלילה רק *בבקר[52] *יבעיר[53] התנור *ואלה[54] *אין[55] לבם ישן רק חושב כל הלילה:

(7) ***כלם.**[56] הטעם *אוכלים[57] *אלה[58] את אלה אפילו *שופטיהם[59] גם קושרים על מלכיהם על כן כתוב:

(8) ***אפרים.**[60] *הוא[61] **יתבולל.** כמו *'בלול'[62] (שמות כט, מ) *מעורב.[63] והטעם שהם מבקשים *עזר[64] *מן האומות[65] לזה מפני זה וזהו 'מצרים קראו אשור הלכו' (פסוק יא) על כן יתבולל *בעמים ומצרים[66] הם *הקרואים.[67] וטעם 'עוגה בלי הפוכה' אז תהי נשרפת *כשאינה הפוכה[68] והטעם על עצתם, ובעבור כי דמה *יצרם ולבם[69] *לתנור[70] *דמה העצה לעוגה:[71]

(9) **אכלו.** הטעם על *השחד[72] *שהיו[73] *נותנים לאשור[74] *ולמצרים[75] כאשר כתוב על המלכים. וטעם 'גם שיבה' שנחלש *כחם[76] ואבד *הונם:[77] **זרקה בו.** *התולדה[78] זרקה בו שיבה שהשיבה *תבוא[79] מתולדת האדם:

(10) **וענה.** פירשתיו: **ולא שבו *אל ה'.**[80] *בענים[81] שאין להם מה *שיתנו[82] עוד *לגוים[83] *שיעזרום:[84]

ששורשו/ 34 ל: היא/ 35 ו מ ר: מעלומי העי"ן ומכפולי הלמ"ד, ל: מעלומי העי"ן וכפולי הלמ"ד/ 36 מ כן ח'/ 37 ו: תופפותו/ 38 ב: מחלי הלמ"ד (ועל הגליון נוסף: מנחי) כמו הראו ומלכנו, ו מ ר: מחלי כמו הראו ומלכינו, ל: ממחלה ומלכינו, נ: מחלי הלמ"ד כמו הראו ומלכנו/ 39 ו מ ר הם הפועלים החלו שרים ח'/ 40 ו מ ר: מן השררות/ 41 ב ו: וכמהו/ 42 ל פועלת מחלה את הלב ח'/ 43 מ: מהבינייו, נ: מהבניין, ר: ומהבניין/ 44 ל חמת ח'/ 45 נ: מיין/ 46 מ: ונמסך/ 47 ל דלת ח'/ 48 ר: דלתיך/ 49 ו מ ר בעדך ח'/ 50 ו ר: הוא/ 51 ל כי ח', נ: בי/ 52 ר ובס"ש: בבוקר/ 53 מ: בעיר/ 54 ו מ ר ואלה ח'/ 55 ו מ ר: ואין/ 56 מ כלם ח', ב ו ר: כולם/ 57 ב: אוכלין/ 58 נ אלה ח'/ 59 ל: השופטים/ 60 ל: אפריים/ 61 ל הוא ח'/ 62 ב נ: בליל/ 63 ו מ ר: ומעורב/ 64 מ נ: עוד/ 65 ל: מהאומות/ 66 ע"פ ל, בשאר כ"י ובס"ש: בעמים כמו בלול ומצרים/ 67 ע"פ ב נ, בשאר כ"י ובס"ש: הקוראים/ 68 ל כשאינה הפוכה ח'/ 69 ל: לבם ויצרם/ 70 ל: לתנות, ר: כתנור/ 71 ל: דמם לעוגה/ 72 מ: השוחד/ 73 ל שהיו ח'/ 74 ל: נתנים לאשור, ר: נותנים על אשור/ 75 ב ולמצרים ח'/ 76 מ: כוחם/ 77 ל: ממונם/ 78 ו ל מ: התולדת, ר: התולדות/ 79 ב נ ובס"ש: תבא/ 80 ב ל נ: אלי/ 81 ע"פ נ, ו: בערים, ר: כערים, בס"ש: כעניים/ 82 ע"פ מ, ו: שיתכן, בשאר כ"י ובס"ש: יתנו/ 83 ל: בגוים,

(ירמיה כט, יז): *שם[78] *זנות[79] לאפרים. רמז *לעגלים[80] בבית אל *שהוא[81] לאפרים:

(11) גם יהודה. אחר שהזכיר אפרים. *ו'שת[82] קציר' כמו 'ועשה קציר כמו נטע' (איוב יד, ט). והטעם ששת קציר לך ועזרך *לעבוד[83] הבעל בבית אל כאשר היה בלבי להשיב שבות עמי שיאמרו 'לכו ונשובה *אל ה'[84] (פסוק א), ובעבור יהודה *שהניח[85] *ביתי[86] ועזרך *לא אשיב[87] שבותך:

ז

(1) כרפאי. בעבור שאמרו 'כי הוא טרף וירפאנו' (ו, א) אמר כאשר ארצה לרפאם *עמד[1] *לפני[2] *רשעם בלבם[3] שלא עזבוהו עד עתה 'כי פעלו שקר' *ובלילה[4] *יגנבו[5] וביום פושטים *גדודים חוץ מן הערים:[6]

(2) *ובל.[7] והם חושבים *כי[8] *אינני[9] *רואם[10] ולא ידעו כי מעלליהם סובבים אותם והם נגד פני:

(3) ברעתם ישמחו מלך. ושרים שימליכוהו:

(4) *כלם. גם מלכם עמהם.[11] *'ותנור'[12] לשון זכר על כן מלת *'בוערה' מלעיל[13] כמו לילה, 'נחלה עבר על *נפשנו'[14] (תהלים קכד, ד). וזה הפסוק הפוך *הוא[15] וככה טעמו כמו תנור אופה *בוערה[16] 'מלוש *בצק[17] עד *חומצתו'[18] עד ישבות אופה מעיר *כי צריך[19] להבעירו *ולהסיקו[20] הרבה:

(5) יום. שימליכו מלכם שיקרא אותו היום יום *מלכנו[21] *ישכירוהו[22] ביין אז *ימשך[23] ידו עם *הלוצצים.[24] וזאת המלה *מפועלי[25] הכפל *שהוא לץ[26] *ואילו[27] *היתה[28] *מלוצצים[29] *היתה[30] *מהפעלים[31] שהם *עלומי[32] העי"ן מגזרת לץ

ח'/ 76 ל הטעם ח'/ 77 ר: התאנים/ 78 ו: שהם, מ: שהים, ל שם ח'/ 79 ו: זכות/ 80 מ לעגלים ח'/ 81 ר: שהיא/ 82 ל: שת/ 83 ל: לעבד/ 84 ל אל ה' ח'/ 85 ל: שהסיח/ 86 מ: ביתו/ 87 ל: לא ארצה להשיב, מ: לא אשוב/

1 ל: עומד/ 2 ל: לפניי/ 3 ע"פ כ"י (מלבד מ שהמעתיק הוסיף על הגליון את המלה "שיש": רשעם שיש בלבם), בס"ש: רשעים בלבם/ 4 ע"פ כ"י, בס"ש: בלילה/ 5 ל מ ר: יגנובו/ 6 ל: גדודים על הערים בחוץ/ 7 ל: ולא/ 8 נ כי ח'/ 9 ע"פ ב ו ל, מ ר: איני, נ: שאינני/ 10 ל: רואה/ 11 ע"פ ב נ, ו מ ר: כולם גם מלכם עמהם, ל: כלם עמהם, בס"ש: כלם גם כלכם עמהם/ 12 ל: תנור/ 13 ל: בוערה היא מלעיל/ 14 מ: נפשינו/ 15 ע"פ ו ל מ ר, ב נ ובס"ש הוא ח'/ 16 ו: בערה/ 17 ו: צבצק/ 18 ל: חמצתו/ 19 ל: כי אז צריך/ 20 בכ"י: ולהשיקו/ 21 ע"פ ל, בשאר כ"י ובס"ש: מלכינו/ 22 ב ו: ישכירהו/ 23 ו ל: ימשוך, ר: ימשיך/ 24 ו מ ר: הליצנים/ 25 ל מ ר: מפעלי/ 26 נ: שהוא לץ/ 27 ו ר: ולו, מ: ולא/ 28 ר: הייתה/ 29 ל: מלצים/ 30 מ: הויתה/ 31 ל: מפעלים/ 32 ל: מעלומי/ 33 ל:

אנוש' (דה"י־א א, א) גם[35] יחסר *אות[36] בי"ת כדרך *'כי ששת ימים'[37] (שמות כ, יא) וככה הוא כמלקוש *ויורה בארץ:[38]

(4) **מה.** הטעם *שהחסד הזה[39] שאמרתם שתשובו *לדעת[40] השם: **כענן *בקר.**[41] שלא *יעמוד.[42] ומלת 'משכים' *איננו פועל כמו 'משכים היו'[43] (ירמיה ה, ח) כאילו *הוא[44] שם *לשחר, ולפי[45] דעתי *שמשכים היו כל אחד אם כן[46] יהיה גם זה *כן:[47]

(5) ***על.**[48] **חצבתי.** כמו 'חוצב בהר' (מל"א ה, כט) והטעם *שהרגתי[49] קצת הנביאים שלהם שהיו מתעים אותם שלא ישובו: **הרגתים.** בעבור שהם אמרו שקר לאמר אמרי פיהם על *כן[50] *הרגתים[51] גם אני באמרי פי אולי *תשוב[52] ישראל: **ומשפטיך אור *יצא.**[53] כמו 'והוציא כאור צדקך' (תהלים לז, ו) ועוד בעבור *שאמר[54] 'כשחר נכון מוצאו' (פסוק ג):

(6) ***כי חסד חפצתי.** חסד נכון[55] לא חסד כענן:

(7) ***והמה.**[56] על נביאי *שקר:[57]

(8) ***גלעד.**[58] *עקובה. כמו 'עקוב הלב' (ירמיה יז, ט), 'עשה בעקבה'[59] (מל"ב י, יט) *עקובה[60] מדם שנשפך:

(9) **וכחכי.** היו"ד תחת ה"א על דרך 'לכלא הפשע' (דניאל ט, כד) גם הוא באל"ף תחת ה"א, ואלה *השתים[61] מלות זרות *הן[62] כי משפט בעלי הה"א בסמוך *לכלות[63] לחכות. והטעם כאשר יחכו *גדודים[64] איש *שיבא[65] *ויפשיטוהו[66] ככה הם *חבר[67] *כהנים[68] והנה הזכיר נביאי השקר גם הכהנים: **שכמה.** כמו *'לעבדו[69] שכם *אחד[70] (צפניה ג, ט). והנה 'גדודים' ישרת בעבור *אחרת[71] *כגדודים בדרך ירצחו[72] *כולם,[73] הטעם שהכהנים יקחו מתנות כהונה בחזקה:

(10) ***בבית.**[74] ***שערוריה.**[75] *הטעם[76] דבר מגועל *'כתאנים[77] השוערים'

ארץ וככה חסר/ 34 ב מ נ ר: וא"ו, ו ל: ו"ו/ 35 ע"פ ו ל מ ר, ב נ ובס"ש: אדם שת גם/ 36 ל: מלת/ 37 ל: כי ששת ימים עשה ה' וככה/ 38 ע"פ כ"י, בס"ש: ויורה ארץ/ 39 ע"פ ל, בשאר כ"י ובס"ש: הזה שהחסד/ 40 ר: מלדעת/ 41 ב מ ר ובס"ש: בוקר/ 42 ו נ: יעמד/ 43 ל איננו פועל כמו משכים היו ח'/ 44 ו: היה, ר: היו/ 45 נ: לשחר ומלת ולפי/ 46 ל: שמשכים היה כל אחד מהם על כן חצבתי בנביאים הרגתים באמרי פי אם כן/ 47 ו כן ח'/ 48 ו ל מ על ח'/ 49 ע"פ ו, ב ל מ נ ר ובס"ש: שהרג/ 50 ל כן ח'/ 51 ע"פ ו ל מ נ ר, ב ובס"ש: הרגתי/ 52 ע"פ ל מ נ ר, ב ובס"ש: תשובו/ 53 ו: יוצא/ 54 ב: שאמרו/ 55 ל: כי חפצתי חסד נכון/ 56 ל: והמשל/ 57 ל: השקר, ו מ ר הפירוש על פסוקים 6־7 ח'/ 58 ו מ ר גלעד ח'/ 59 ו המאמר "עקובה כמו עקוב הלב עשה בעקבה" נשנה פעמיים/ 60 ב ל מ עקובה ח'/ 61 ל: השתיים/ 62 ו ל מ הן ח'/ 63 מ נ ר: לחלות/ 64 ו: הגדודים/ 65 מ: שיבוא/ 66 ע"פ מ ר, ו: ויפשיטהו, ב ל נ ובס"ש: ויפשטוהו/ 67 מ חבר ח'/ 68 ו: הכהנים/ 69 ו: לעובדו, ל: ולעבדו, מ ר: לעוברו/ 70 ע"פ ו, בשאר כ"י ובס"ש אחד ח'/ 71 ע"פ ו מ ר, בשאר כ"י ובס"ש: אחר/ 72 ו: גדודים כדרך ירצחו, מ ר: גדודים בדרך ירצחו/ 73 ל: כלם/ 74 ל בבית ח'/ 75 ב נ שערוריה

*׳תאשם[89] שומרון׳ (הושע יד, א), ׳והאדמה לא *תשם׳[90] (בראשית מז, יט) חסר אל״ף: ישחרונני. *יבקשוני[91] *כשחר[92] *ויאמרו[93] *אלה לאלה:[94]

ו

(1) לכו. *אמר[1] ׳טרף׳ בעבור ככפיר: יך. [2]מכה: ויחבשנו. כמו *׳ולא חבשו׳[3] (ישעיה א, ו) כי המכה צריכה לזור *ולחבש ולרכך באחרונה[4] בשמן. *ובאה[5] מלת ׳טרף׳ *פועל עבר[6] *עם ׳יך׳ שהוא[7] עתיד על דרך *הזמן העומד[8] כאשר פירשתי *בספרי:[9]

(2) *יחיינו.[10] ירפאנו כמו ׳וימרחו על השחין ויחי׳ (ישעיה לח, כא), ׳עד חיותם׳ (יהושע ה, ח), וטעם *יומים[11] *זמן קרוב: שלישי. הפך כל נשבר[12] כי אז *יכאב:[13]

(3) *ונדעה. שנרדפה[14] לדעת את ה׳ כי זה סוד כל *החכמות[15] ובעבור זה לבדו *נברא האדם[16] רק לא יוכל לדעת *את[17] השם עד *שילמד[18] *חכמות[19] *הרבה[20] שהם כמו סולם לעלות אל זאת המעלה העליונה. וטעם ׳כשחר׳ *כי[21] *בתחילה[22] *ידע המשכיל השם יתברך במעשיו[23] כמו השחר בצאתו ורגע *אחר[24] רגע יגדל האור עד שיראה האמת: *ויבוא[25] כגשם.[26] הטעם שהשם *יעזרנו[27] ויורנו האמת על דרך *׳יערף[28] כמטר לקחי׳ (דברים לב, ב). *ואחרים[29] אמרו כי *יבוא[30] לנו מרפא מהשם *כגשם[31] ׳אשר לא יקוה לאיש׳ (מיכה ה, ו), והטעם כי אין מרפא *כי אם מאתו:[32] כמלקוש יורה *ארץ. חסר[33] *וי״ו[34] כדרך *׳אדם שת

89 ע״פ כ״י, בס״ש: תשם/ 90 ר: תאשם/ 91 ר: ובקשוני/ 92 נ: בשחר/ 93 ו ר: ויאמר/ 94 ל: אילו לאילו, בס״ש: אלה לאלה לכו אמר טרף בעבור ככפיר, ראה הערה 2 לפרק ו/

1 ב נ אמר ח׳/ 2 בס״ש מתחיל פרק ו עם ׳יך׳/ 3 ו ל מ ר: לא חובשו/ 4 ו: ולחבוש וליבך, ר: ולחבש באחרונה/ 5 ע״פ ו ל מ ר, ב נ ובס״ש: ובאת/ 6 ו: פעל עבר, ל פועל עבר ח׳/ 7 ל: עם יך ויחבשנו שהוא/ 8 נ: הזמן העתיד העומד/ 9 ל: בספר ישעיה/ 10 ב נ: יחינו/ 11 ב נ ר: יומיים/ 12 ו ל ר: עד שלישי זמן קרוב כל נשבר, מ: עד שלישי זמן קרובים כל נשבר/ 13 ו: נכאב. ב־ו מ ר יש כאן הוספה: עד אשר יאשמו (ה, טו) עד אשר יהיו שוממים ויבקשו פני וכאשר צר להם אז ישחרונני ויאמרו כך כל הארץ לכו ונשובה אל ה׳ כי הוא יחיינו מיומיים כעין משל כלו׳ כי הוא רופא נאמן שיתן להם רפואה לשני ימים כלו׳ לזמן מועט וביום השלישי יקימנו (ו: יקיימנו, מ: יקימינו)/ 14 ל: ונדעה נרדפה שנרדפה/ 15 מ: החוכמות/ 16 ב מ: נברא כל האדם, ל: נברא אדם, ר: נברא כל העולם/ 17 ו מ ר את ח׳/ 18 ל: שילמדו, ו מ ר: שילמוד/ 19 ב ל נ: חכמת/ 20 ו מ נ ר הרבה ח׳, ל: הדבור/ 21 ו כי ח׳/ 22 ו ל נ ר: בתחלה/ 23 ב נ: יגע המשכיל במעשיו, ו ל מ ר: ידע המשכיל השם במעשיו/ 24 מ נ ר: אחרי/ 25 ב ו ל מ נ ובס״ש: ויבא/ 26 ב ל כגשם ח׳/ 27 ע״פ ו ל מ ר, ב נ ובס״ש: יעירנו/ 28 ב ל נ ר: יערוף/ 29 ב: והאחרים/ 30 ב נ ובס״ש: יבא/ 31 ו: בגשם, ר: כשגם/ 32 ו ל מ ר: רק מאתו/ 33 ל:

(6) **בצאנם.** שב אל יהודה לבדו שבית המקדש בנחלתם: *חלץ. כבודו מהם[44] כאשר *יאמר[45] *'אלך אשובה[46] אל מקומי' (פסוק טו) ולמה חלץ מהם כי 'בה' בגדו' (פסוק ז):

(7) **עתה.** *יאכל[47] *אלה[48] הבנים עם חלקיהם חדש רע כמו *'כי[49] קרוב יום אידם' (דברים לב, לה). ור' ישועה *אמר[50] חדש אב. ויפת אמר כי *'חדש'[51] *הוא חרב[52] כמו *'והוא[53] חגור חדשה' (שמ"ב כא, טז)[54]:

(8) **תקעו.** *הטעם[55] השמיעו זאת וידעו *הכל[56] *כי[57] 'אפרים' (פסוק ט):

(9) **הודעתי נאמנה.** משפט נאמן כמו *גזרה[58] והדומה לה:

(10) ***היו.**[59] *עושים[60] רע לאשר הם ברשותם: ***כמסיגי**[61] **גבול.** בסתר על כן אענישם:

(11) **עשוק** ***אפרים.**[62] עשקוהו *מלכיו[63] *ורימוהו:[64] ***כי הואיל**[65] **הלך.** שנים *פועלים[66] עוברים כמו *'הגשם[67] *חלף[68] הלך *לו'[69] (שה"ש ב, א) כי *הואיל[70] שהלך אחרי מצות אנשים *והוא[71] *צו[72] כמו 'צו לצו' (ישעיה כח, י). ויפת אמר כי אפרים יהיה עשוק *מהגוים:[73]

(12) **ואני.** *הטעם[74] שאכלם:

(13) ***וירא.**[75] **את מזורו.** מכה שהיא צריכה שיזורו *אותה:[76] **וישלח.** יהודה כי *כן[77] אחריו: **ירב.** שם מקום באשור: ***יגהה.**[78] כמו 'ייטיב *גהה'[79] (משלי יז, כב) *מראה[80] העין:

(14) **כי.** בתחילה אמר 'ואני כעש' (פסוק יב) בפנים מהגוף ועתה 'כשחל' בחוץ *ומי[81] יוכל *לרפא[82] לכם: ***ואלך.** לי ואין[83] רודף אחרי או אלך עם הטרפה. והנכון שאטרפם ואלך לי *כאשר[84] *כתוב אחריו:[85]

(15) ***אלך.**[86] ***עד**[87] **אשר יאשמו.** שיודו *שאשמו[88] או כטעם שממה

יענה/ 42 ו ל נ ר: **ואין טעם לו**, מ: **ואין טעם לא**/ 43 ל: **עוני**/ 44 ל: **חלץ מהם חלץ כבודו מהם**/ 45 ל: **אמר**/ 46 ע"פ ב נ, ו ל מ ר ובס"ש: **אלכה ואשובה**/ 47 ע"פ כ"י, בס"ש: **יאכלם**/ 48 מ: **אל**/ 49 ו מ ר כי ח'/ 50 ע"פ ב ו נ, ל מ ר ובס"ש: **אומר**/ 51 מ: **חודש**/ 52 ע"פ כ"י, בס"ש: **חדש הוא חגור חרב**/ 53 ב נ **והוא ח'**/ 54 ל: **עתה יאכל אלה הבנים חדש רע כמו והוא חגור חדש, והשאר ח'**/ 55 ר: **כטעם**/ 56 ל: **כל**/ 57 ו מ ר **כי ח'**/ 58 ו מ **גזרה ח'**/ 59 ר: **יהיו**/ 60 ב ו מ נ ר: **עושין**/ 61 ב ו מ נ ר: **כמשיגי**/ 62 ב **אפרים ח'**/ 63 ו נ: **מלאכיו**/ 64 ב נ: **וכמהו**, ו: **וכמוהו**, מ: **מרימיה**, ל **ורימוהו ח'**/ 65 ו: **כי אולי הואיל**/ 66 ב נ: **פעולים**, ו מ ר: **פעלים**/ 67 ר: **השגם**/ 68 מ **חלף ח'**/ 69 מ ל **לו ח'**/ 70 ל: **הוא**/ 71 ו: **והם**/ 72 ל **צו ח'**/ 73 ל: **מן הגוים**/ 74 ב ר ובס"ש: **טעם**/ 75 ל **וירא ח'**/ 76 ב מ נ: **אותו**/ 77 ב נ: **אין**/ 78 ל **יגהה ח'**, מ: **יהגה**/ 79 מ ר: **גאה**/ 80 ע"פ ב ל נ, ו מ ר ובס"ש: **מראית**/ 81 ע"פ ב מ נ ר, ו ל ובס"ש: **מי**/ 82 ו: **לרפוא**/ 83 ו ר: **ואלך ואלך לי ואין**, ל: **ואלך לי כאשר נכתב אחריו ואין**/ 84 מ **כאשר ח'**/ 85 ל: **נכתב אחריו**, מ: **כתוב אחריו אחריו**/ 86 מ: **הלך**/ 87 ב נ **עד ח'**/ 88 מ: **שאשמיו**/

ה

(1) **שמעו זאת הכהנים.** *גם[1] *הקשיבו[2] בית ישראל *שהוכחתים או בית ישראל[3] הם *הסנהדרין,[4] ׳ובית המלך *האזינו׳ כי[5] *כולם[6] *שופטים:[7] **כי פח הייתם למצפה.** שלא *תניחו[8] לעלות *החוגגים אל בית השם:[9]

(2) **ושחטה.** *ולשחוט[10] *בדרך:[11] ***שטים.** הם[12] עובדי הבעל: **העמיקו.** הפח *אלו[13] הנזכרים אולי לא יראוהו העוברים ואני *איסרם כולם[14] על זאת הרעה שעשו כי לא נעלם *ממני[15] אשר העמיקו *על כן ׳אני ידעתי׳:[16]

(3) ***אני.**[17] דע כי אשת יעקב אבינו *היא[18] רחל *והנה[19] לאה נכנסה במקומה גם רחל נתנה שפחתה *לו[20] *ובעבור קנאת לאה נתנה לו גם השפחה האחרת[21] על כן כאשר ילדה רחל *את[22] יוסף אמר *׳שלחני׳[23] (בראשית כט, כג־כה; ל, ד־ט; כה) ויעקב אמר *על[24] אפרים ומנשה *׳ויקרא בהם שמי׳[25] (שם מח, טז) על כן יקראו כל ישראל אפרים. ויפת אמר *אולי[26] *ממלכת[27] יהוא *היתה[28] מאפרים ובעבור שמצא ׳ואת *ראמת[29] בגלעד לגדי׳ (דברים ד, מג) הוצרך לומר איננה *הכתובה בדברי יהוא (מל״ב ט, א־ב), ובספר[30] עמוס אפרש *שהוא[31] מאפרים. והנכון בעיני כי כאשר *באו[32] אבותינו ארץ כנען והנה עמד יהודה על גבולו מנגב ובית יוסף שהוא כל שבט אפרים וחצי שבט *מנשה[33] מצפון *על כן יזכור[34] יהודה *ואפרים,[35] וככה *בירמיהו[36] ׳הבן יקיר לי *אפרים׳ (ירמיה לא, יט) ואין[37] מלך בימים ההם מאפרים: **הזנית. נפשך גם אחרים:**

(4) **לא יתנו.** לא יעשו *מעשים[38] שישובו או לא *׳יניחו[39] על דרך ׳על כן לא נתתיך׳ (בראשית כ, ו):[40]

(5) **וענה.** אמר יפת *כמו ׳בפני יענה׳[41] (איוב טז, ח) *ואין לו טעם[42] רק הוא מגזרת *עני:[43]

1 ל: גם ח׳/ 2 ל: והקשיבו/ 3 ל שהוכחתים או בית ישראל ח׳/ 4 מ: הסנהדרים/ 5 ב: האזינו לי כי/ 6 ו: מלם שופד/ 7 נ: שפטים/ 8 מ: תנוחו/ 9 ו מ ר: אל בית השם החוגגים/ 10 ל: לשחוט/ 11 ו בדרך ח׳/ 12 ל: שטים העמיקו הם, מ: שטים הם, בשאר כ״י ובס״ש: סטים הם/ 13 ב ו ר: אילו/ 14 ל: איסר לכולם/ 15 ו מ: ממנו/ 16 ע״פ ל, בשאר כ״י ובס״ש אני ידעתי ח׳/ 17 ל אני ח׳/ 18 ל: היה/ 19 ל: והיא/ 20 ב נ: לה/ 21 נ: ובעבור הנאת לאה נתנה לו גם השפחה האחרת, ל: בעבור קנאת לאה ובעבור קנאת רחל נתנה לו גם היא השפחה האחרת/ 22 ו את ח׳/ 23 נ: שלחיני/ 24 ו ובס״ש: אל/ 25 ל: ויקרא שמי בהם/ 26 ל אולי ח׳/ 27 ל: שמלכות, מ: ממלכות/ 28 ר: הייתה/ 29 ל ר: ראמות, ב ו מ נ ובס״ש: רמות/ 30 ל: כתובה בדבר יהוא היתה מאפרים ובספר/ 31 ל: שהיא/ 32 ר: ראו/ 33 ל: המנשה/ 34 ל: על כן לא יזכר, נ: על כן יזכר/ 35 ב ו מ נ ר: מאפרים/ 36 ו ר: בירמיה/ 37 ל: אפרים אם ילד שעשועים ואין/ 38 ל: מעשיהם/ 39 ע״פ כ״י, בס״ש: ינוחו/ 40 ל: כמו על כן לא נתתיך לנגוע אליך, מ: על דרך לא נתתיך/ 41 ע״פ ב ו נ ר, ל: כמו כחשי בפני יענה, מ: כבני יענה, בס״ש: כמו בני

והנה הטעם למה *תראו[91] כי אתם בני השם *ואתם באים[92] בית און, יותר טוב שלא תעשו *זה וזה[93] או *פירושו[94] כנגד 'אלה וכחש' הכתוב בתחלת הפרשה (פסוק ב):

(16) *כי.[95] סורר הוא שיסור מן הדרך *שצוה[96] שלא ילך בה, והנה *דמה[97] ישראל *לפרה[98] סוררה שלא יוכל אדם לחרוש בה. וטעם 'עתה' *השם היה רועה[99] *אותם[100] 'ככבש במרחב', *לולי[101] *היותם[102] סוררים או הטעם עתה ירעם השם ככבש לבדו במקום מרחב והוא טועה:

(17) *חבור.[103] יש אומרים כי עצבים כמו *'וכל עצביכם'[104] (ישעיה נח, ג). והנכון כמו 'העצב נבזה' (ירמיה כב, כח), 'לעצבי כנען' (תהלים קו, לח) והכל מגזרת 'עצבון' (בראשית ג, יז) כי אין תועלת *בפסיליהם[105] רק עצבים, והטעם *מחוברים[106] הם *לפסילים[107] *והם[108] *חברתם:[109] הנח לו. *עד[110] *שיסיר[111] *אותם[112] אולי יפקחו עיניהם:

(18) *סר. באה[113] עליהם רעה שסר סבאם מחסרון התירוש ולא *שבו[114] מדרכם הרעה, *רק[115] מלכיה הזנו אחרים בעבור מתנות שהם אומרים הבו. ובאה *מלת[116] 'הבו' *כמו[117] *'את אשר[118] תאפו אפו' (שמות טז, כג) *ועקרו[119] *אפו כי גם הוא גם 'אהבו[120] *הבו'[121] גם 'הבו לכם' (דברים א, יג) *הכל[122] כמו רדו, צאו והשנוי *היה בעבור[123] אות הגרון: *מגניה.[124] הם המלכים כמו *'כי לה' מגיננו'[125] (תהלים פט, יט), וסוף הפסוק מוכיח כי הטעם כפול *ו'מגניה' שב[126] אל בית און:

(19) צרר. כאדם *שיצרור[127] רוח *בכנפיו[128] שלא ימצא *מאומה[129] או 'בכנפיה' בכנפי בית און: ויבשו. *המגינים:[130] מזבחותם. בבית און:[131]

תשבע/ 91 נ: תיראו/ 92 ו: ואינם באין/ 93 ב נ: זה בזה/ 94 ר: פירוש/ 95 ל כי ח'/ 96 ו מ ר: שיצוה, ל: שיצווה/ 97 ו מ ר: דימה/ 98 ע"פ מ, בשאר כ"י ובס"ש: כפרה/ 99 ו ל נ ר: היה השם רועה, מ: היה שם רועה/ 100 מ ר: אותן/ 101 ע"פ ל מ ר, ו נ: לולא, ב ובס"ש: אילולי/ 102 ע"פ ל, ו מ ר: שאתם ובס"ש: הייתם/ 103 ל חבור ח'/ 104 ב נ: לכל עצביהם, ל וכל ח'; מ: וכל עצביכם תנגשו/ 105 ל: בפסילים/ 106 ל: מחברים/ 107 ר: לפסיליהם/ 108 ע"פ ו מ ר, ב ל נ ובס"ש: הם/ 109 ו: מחברתם/ 110 ל עד ח'/ 111 ו מ נ ר: שיסור/ 112 ע"פ ל נ, ב: אינם, ו מ ר ובס"ש: אותו/ 113 ל: סר סבאם באה/ 114 ר: שב/ 115 ו ר: כי/ 116 מ ו: מילת/ 117 ר כמו ח'/ 118 ל את אשר ח'/ 119 ע"פ ל מ ר, ב ו נ ובס"ש: ועיקר/ 120 ע"פ מ, ו: אפו גם הוא אהבו, ר: אפו גם היא אהבו, בס"ש: אפו גם אהבו/ 121 ל הבו ח'/ 122 ו: והכל/ 123 ע"פ ו מ ר, ל היה ח', ב נ ובס"ש: היה בו בעבור/ 124 ב ו מ נ: ומגניה, ל: ומגיניה/ 125 ע"פ ל נ, ב: כי לה' מגינינו, ו מ ר ובס"ש: כי לה' מגיני ארץ/ 126 ל נ ר: ומגיניה שב, ב: ומגניה הם שב/ 127 ו מ ר: שיצור, ל: שיצרר/ 128 ל: בכפיו/ 129 ל מאומה ח'/ 130 ב ו ובס"ש: המגנים/ 131 מ מן 'ויבשו' עד 'בבית און' ח'/

(13) **על ראשי.** טעם 'ראשי' בגלוי וככה 'על הגבעות'.[54] **יזבחו.** יאמרו לכהני הבעל שיזבחו, ובעבור *שהולכים[55] האנשים להקטיר חוץ *מהערים תשארנה[56] הבנות והכלות בבתים, 'על כן *תזנינה'.[57]

(14) ***לא.** הטעם[58] אין לתמוה אם הבנות תזנינה כי הם בעלותם לראשי ההרים *להקטיר[59] הם אוכלים ושותים עם הזונות *וזונים כולם.[60] ומלת 'יפרדו' אנשים *ידועים[61] עם זונה אחת. ומלת 'ילבט' בלשון ישמעאל כמשתבש שלא ידע מה לעשות *וכמוהו[62] 'ואויל שפתים ילבט' (משלי י, ח). והנה אין טעם 'לא *אפקוד'[63] שלא *יפקוד[64] *עליהם,[65] רק *דבר[66] כנגד האבות כי הם מלמדים אותם לזנות *ולעשות[67] כמעשיהם אולי הבנות *קטנות[68] *הן[69] על כן לא אפקוד:

(15) ***אם.** ישראל[70] חטאו *עם[71] ירבעם שפחד *שתבוא[72] המלוכה לבית דוד *על[73] כן עשה שני עגלים *בשני קצות ארץ ישראל למה[74] יאשם יהודה שהניח בית המקדש שהוא *בחלקו[75] *וילך[76] למקום רחוק לעכו"ם, והנביא מוכיחם 'אל יאשם יהודה ואל תבואו הגלגל ואל תעלו בית און' *הוא[77] בית אל בעבור *העגל[78] ששם שם ירבעם.

כתוב בתורה 'ובשמו תשבע' (דברים י, כ) והטעם 'את ה' אלהיך תירא' שלא תעבור *על מצות לא תעשה לא בעבור[79] יראת מלך או *דבה או נזק[80] בגוף רק בעבור יראת השם, ו'אותו תעבוד' מצות עשה מהם בפה ומהם במחשבה, 'ובו תדבק' *במחשבת הלב שלא יעבור רגע בכל יכולתו שלא יחשוב בלבו[81] מעשה השם ונפלאותיו בעליונים *ובשפלים ובאותות[82] הנביאים. ואחר שיהיה דבק בשם חייב הוא להזכיר השם בכל *דרכיו[83] *ולהשבע[84] בשמו בעבור שיבינו ממנו *כל הברואים[85] שהוא *דבק בשם ובאהבתו ותמיד[86] שמו וזכרו שגור בפיו ובאהבתו אותו *כל[87] העם ישמעו וילמדו ממנו האהבה והיראה. וככה מנהג הנביאים *שישבעו[88] כדוד ואליהו ואלישע *וכמוהו[89] *'תשבע כל לשון'[90] (ישעיה מה, כג).

אלהים/ 54 בכ"י ובס"ש אין סימני הפסק/ 55 ו מ ר: שהלכו/ 56 מ: מהערים שיזבחו תשארנה/ 57 ו מ ר: תזנינה בנותיכם/ 58 ל: לא אפקוד הטעם/ 59 ב נ להקטיר ח'/ 60 ו: וזונים כלם; ל: וכלם זונים/ 61 ע"פ כ"י; בס"ש: יודעים/ 62 נ: וכמהו/ 63 ב נ: אפקד/ 64 ב נ: יפקד/ 65 ב ל עליהם ח'/ 66 מ ר: דיבר/ 67 ע"פ ל, בשאר כ"י ובס"ש: לעשות/ 68 ר: הקטנות/ 69 ו מ הן ח'. ל: הם/ 70 ל: אם זונה אם ישראל/ 71 ב נ: עד/ 72 נ: שתבא/ 73 ר על ח'/ 74 ר: בשני קצות הארץ ישראל למה/ 75 ו מ ר: חלקו/ 76 ל: והלך/ 77 ל: היא/ 78 ל העגל ח'/ 79 ר: על מצות על תעשה אלא בעבור/ 80 ל: דבר נזק/ 81 ע"פ ו מ ר, ב נ ובס"ש: במחשבת הלב שלא יעבור רגע בכל יכולתו שיחשוב בלבו, ל: במחשבת הלב שיחשוב בלבו, והמאמר "שלא יעבור רגע בכל יכולתו" ח'/ 82 ע"פ ו ל מ נ ר, ב ובס"ש: ובשפלים ובתחתונים ובאותות/ 83 ע"פ ו ל מ ר, ב נ ובס"ש: דבריו/ 84 ב: להשבע/ 85 ע"פ ב ל נ ר, ו מ ובס"ש: כל השומעים הברואים/ 86 ע"פ ו מ ר, ב ל נ ובס"ש: דבק באהבת השם ותמיד/ 87 ע"פ ל, בשאר כ"י ובס"ש: וכל/ 88 ל שישבעו ח'/ 89 ו נ: וכמהו/ 90 ע"פ ו ל מ נ ר, ב ובס"ש: כל לשון לך

(6) ***נדמו[18] עמי מבלי *הדעת.** זאת[19] *המלה[20] *אם היתה[21] מגזרת *דמות[22] יהיה אחריה אל *בשלש[23] נקודות *כמו[24] 'אל מי דמית' (יחזקאל לא, ב), ובאפס מלת אל מטעם כריתה כמו 'ודמיתי אמך' (פסוק ה), והטעם שלא תלד עוד אחר שיהיה *במקומך[25] *כהן[26] *ואתה[27] תכשל במהרה גם ימותו בניך: [28]**נדמו.** אומר לכהן בחסרון דעתך נכרתו *עמי:[29] **כי *אתה[30] הדעת *מאסת[31] ואמאסך מכהן לי ותשכח תורת אלהיך.** הטעם כפול 'כי אתה הדעת *מאסת'[32] כי לכהן *ניתנה[33] התורה. *ועוד[34] כי הם השופטים 'כי שפתי כהן ישמרו דעת' (מלאכי ב, ז): **אשכח בניך.** חלילה שהשם ישכח, רק הטעם שיכשלו בני הכהן וילכו לאבדון:

(7) ***כרבם.**[35] אני הרביתי בניך: **כן חטאו לי.** חטאים רבים, על כן 'כבודם בקלון אמיר', אחליף:

(8) **חטאת עמי יאכלו.** בני הכהן ונפש עמי ישאו על עונם, *כאומר[36] סמוך עלי לכפר העון כדרך 'ואליו הוא נושא את נפשו' (דברים כד, טו), *וזה[37] עון גדול, על כן יבא רע *על[38] *הכהן[39] ועל העם ולא תהיה מעלה לכהן על ישראל:

(9) **והיה.** כבר אמרתי כי דרך *הכפי"ן[40] דרך קצרה, והיה *העם[41] ככהן והכהן כעם *וכמוהו[42] 'כעמי כעמך' (מל"א כב, ד): **ופקדתי עליו.** על כל אחד מהם:

(10) **ואכלו.** זאת היא הפקידה: **הזנו.** נפשם גם אחרים ולא ירבו כמו 'ויפרץ האיש' (בראשית ל, מג): **כי את ה' עזבו לשמור.** דרכו או תורתו:

(11) **זנות.** *בחסרון וי"ן[43] כמו 'שמש ירח עמד *זבלה'[44] (חבקוק ג, יא), *והטעם[45] כי הזנות *גם[46] היין *כל[47] אחד *מהם יקח לב ולקיחת הלב כאילו נשארו[48] בלא לב להבין:

(12) ***עמי.** והאות[49] כי *הם[50] בלא לב ששב עמי לשאול בעצו *הוא[51] הפסל: **כי רוח זנונים התעה.** אותו: *ויזנו, [52]כולם 'מתחת *אלהיהם'[53] כאשר הזכיר 'עמי':

ודמיתי אמך והכרתי אמך, מ ר: ודמיתי והכרתי אמך/ 18 ב ל מ: נדמה/ 19 ב: הדעת ודמה שהוא פעל זאת, נ: הדעת נדמה שהוא פעל זאת/ 20 מ: המילה/ 21 נ אם היתה ח'/ 22 ו: למות, מ: תמות/ 23 ל מ: בשלוש/ 24 ב ל נ כמו ח'/ 25 בכ"י: מקומך/ 26 ו: בהן/ 27 ו מ נ ר: ואת/ 28 ע"פ ב ל מ, בס"ש אין סימני הפסק/ 29 ו: עמיך/ 30 ל אתה ח'/ 31 ב: מאסתה/ 32 ב ל מ ר ובס"ש: מאסתה/ 33 ו נ: נתנה/ 34 ב נ: עוד/ 35 ל: כרובם/ 36 ע"פ ו ל מ, ב נ: כלומר, ר ובס"ש: כאמור/ 37 ל: וזהו/ 38 מ ר על ח'/ 39 מ ר: לכהן/ 40 ו: כפי"ן/ 41 ו ל: כעם/ 42 ו: וכמהו/ 43 ב נ: בחסרון וי"ו ויין, ל: בחסרון ו"ו, מ: בחסרון ואויין, ר: בחסרון וא"ו יין/ 44 ב: זבולה, ל זבלה ח'/ 45 ל: הטעם/ 46 ל: עם/ 47 ו כל ח'/ 48 ב ו: מהם יקח לב כדרך עמד זבולה כאילו נשארו, מ: מהם יסיר כדרך עמד זבולה כאילו נשארו, נ: מהם יקח לב כדרך עמד זבולה ולקחת הלב כאילו נשארו, ר: מהם יקח לב כדרך עמד זבולה נשארו/ 49 ל: עמי בעצו ישאל והאות/ 50 ו: מם/ 51 ו מ ר: והוא/ 52 ב: ויתעו/ 53 ע"פ כ"י; בס"ש:

לעולם' (יחזקאל לז, כה): ופחדו אל ה'. שישובו *במהרה[59] *בבא[60] הקץ אל ארצם במרוצה פתע פתאום, כדרך *'יחרדו כצפור[61] ממצרים' (יא, יא) *ושם[62] כתוב 'והושבתים על בתיהם *נאם ה'.[63] והעד הנאמן על זה הפירוש *שאמר 'באחרית הימים'[64] והם סוף *נבואת[65] הנביאים כמו 'והיה באחרית הימים נכון יהיה הר *בית[66] ה' (ישעיה ב, ב) ושם כתוב 'וכתתו חרבותם *לאתים'[67] (שם ב, ד) וכל אלה לעתיד:

ד

(1) **שמעו. עם יושבי הארץ.** *היא[1] ארץ ישראל *שהשם בחרה,[2] והנכון יושבי הארץ שלו, כמו 'ומארצו יצאו' (יחזקאל לו, כ):

(2) **אלה. שבועה,** *'ואת אלית'[3] (שופטים יז, ב) *מגזרת[4] שבועה: **פרצו.** מגזרת *'פריצים'[5] (ירמיה ז, יא): **ודמים.** *דמי[6] הרוג אחד *נוגעים בדמי הרוג אחר:[7]

(3) **על כן.** למ"ד 'אומלל' כפול, וטעם 'בחית השדה ובעוף השמים' שלא ימצאו מה יצודו, והעד *'וגם[8] דגי הים יאספו'. ויפת אמר כי אלה רעים מדור המבול כי דגי הים *לא מתו, וזה[9] דרך דרש:

(4) **אך.** אין איש *שיריב[10] אחר או יוכיחנו, ומשפט הכהנים היה להוכיח *את ישראל[11] ועתה שבו *הם להוכיח הכהן[12] כי גם הוא רע מעללים כאשר יפרש וזהו 'ועמך כמריבי כהן':

(5) **וכשלת.** *עם הכהן הגדול שהיה בימי זה הנביא מדבר ומתנבא[13] עליו 'וכשלת היום', *והטעם ביום שהוא[14] אור כאילו *היית[15] בלילה אתה ונביא שקר המפתה אותך, וזהו 'וכשל גם *נביא[16] עמך לילה': *ודמיתי. והכרתי:[17]

להשם ואין תרפים לעכו"ם שקראם/ 56 ו מ: שהמה/ 57 ל כללם ח'/ 58 ו מ ר: את/ 59 ל: מהרה/ 60 מ: בבוא/ 61 ר: יחרדו כדרך כצפור/ 62 ע"פ ו ל מ ר, ב נ ובס"ש: ששם/ 63 ב ל נ נאם ה' ח'/ 64 מ: שאמר באחרית הימים נכון יהיה, ומן "והם סוף" עד 'והיה באחרית הימים' ח'/ 65 נ: נבואות/ 66 ר: הבית/ 67 ו: לאיטים, ל: לאיתים/

1 ב: הוא/ 2 ע"פ ב ו מ נ ר, ל: שבחרה השם, בס"ש: שהשם בחר/ 3 ל: וגם אלית/ 4 ב: מגזיר'/ 5 ל: פרצים/ 6 ו: ומי/ 7 ו מ ר: נוגעים בדמי אחר, ל: פוגעים דמי הרוג אחר, נ: נוגעים דמי הרוג אחר/ 8 ו: עם/ 9 מ: לא מתו במבול וזה/ 10 ו ר: שירב/ 11 ע"פ ל מ ר, ב ו נ ובס"ש: להוכיח לישראל/ 12 ו: הם להזכירו להוכיח הכהן, ל: להוכיח אתם הכהן/ 13 ל: עם הכהן הגדול ידבר שהיה בימי זה הנביא ומתנבא/ 14 ל: טעם היום שהוא, מ ר: והטעם כיום שהוא, נ: והטעם ביום הוא/ 15 ע"פ ו, ל מ ר: הייתה, נ ובס"ש: היתה/ 16 ב ו מ: נביאך, נ ר: נביאיך/ 17 ו: ודמיתי והפרתי אמך, ל:

ראוי להיות ואכירה או יהיה *מבניין[16] הקל ואם לא *נמצא,[17] *אף על פי שלא נמצא[18] *לשון הכר משקל קל[19] *הנה[20] יהיה על משקל *׳ואתנה׳[21] (מל״א יד, ח) או הפתח הקטן *תחת הגדול[22] כמו ׳ואעדך עדי׳ (יחזקאל טז, יא) שהוא מן עדה, ׳פן אכלך בדרך׳ (שמות לג, ג) מן כלה *ובאה,[23] *זאת[23a] המלה על דרך ׳וידבקו׳ (דה״י־א י, ב) ורבים ככה. וטעם ׳בחמשה עשר כסף׳ כמשמעו לכתובתה: **וחומר. ולתך.** מאכלה. ולפי דעתי שהוא משל ליהודה. ואלה חמשה עשר *הם[24] מלכי יהודה *שתחלתם[25] *רחבעם[26] *מלך[27] ולא תחשוב מלכות בני יאשיהו רק *מלכות אחת[28] כי אחים היו וחומר ולתך הם הכהנים הגדולים שהיו במלכות יהודה:[29]

(3) **ואומר. ימים רבים.** *והטעם[30] אם *תרצי[31] שתהיי לי תשבי ימים רבים שלא תזני ולא תהיי לאיש אחר. והטעם לא *תעבדי[32] אלהים אחרים בסתר: **ולא *תהיי[33] לאיש *וגם אני.** ומלת[34] לא תשרת בעבור אחרת, והטעם וגם אני לא *אבוא[35] *אליך.[36] ויש אומרים אם *תשובי אלי[37] גם אני אשוב *אליך,[38] *ופירש[39] זה הדבר הנביא:

(4) **כי ימים רבים. אין מלך.** ואין טענה *מן החשמונאים[40] כי אינם מבני יהודה: **ואין זבח.** אמר יפת *בן עלי[41] זהו ׳תשבי *לי׳[42] (פסוק ג) כי לא *תעשי *לי[43][44] זבח *ומצבה.[45] *לפי דעתי[46] *אין[47] המצבה אסורה רק כאשר *דברה[48] תורה, והנה מה יעשה במלת תרפים. *ואחרים[49] *אמרו[50] *הכל לעכו״ם[51] *ולא מצאנו אפוד לגנאי.[52] והנכון *בעיני[53] אין זבח *לשם[54] ולא מצבה לבעל, *אין אפוד השם ואין תרפים לעכו״ם שקראם[55] לבן אלהיו (בראשית לא, ל):

(5) **אחר ישובו בני ישראל.** *שהם[56] בני יהודה וישראל שגלו בתחלה, על כן *כללם.[57] וטעם *׳ואת[58] דוד מלכם׳ זהו המשיח כמו ׳ודוד עבדי נשיא להם

כמו תכרו מאיתם ואיננו, ר: כמו תכרו מאתכם ואיננו/ 14 מ: ובדיקדוק/ 15 ר: והיא/ 16 מ: מהביניין, ר: מהבנין/ 17 ו: ימצאו/ 18 נ: אעפ הגהה שלא נמצא/ 19 ו מ: לשון הזכר משקל קל, ר: לשון משקל קל לה/ 20 נ הנה ח׳/ 21 ע״פ ב, ו מ ר: אתנח, נ: ואתנה, בס״ש: אתנה/ 22 ע״פ ו מ ר, ב נ: תחת גדול, בס״ש: תחת הפתח גדול/ 23 ר: ובאת/ 23 a ע״פ ו מ ר, ב נ ובס״ש: זו/ 24 ו מ ר: גם/ 25 מ: שתחילתם/ 26 ו מ ר: ירבעם/ 27 ו ר מלך ח׳/ 28 ו: מלכות אחד, מ: מלכות אחאב/ 29 ר המשך ״ואומר ימים רבים והטעם אם״ ח׳, ראה בסמוך הערה 31/ 30 ו מ: הטעם/ 31 ו: תרצה, ראה למעלה הערה 29/ 32 ע״פ כ״י, בס״ש: תעבדו/ 33 ו: תהיה/ 34 ו: וגם אני אליך ומלת, מ ר: וגם אני אלייך ומלת/ 35 נ: אבא/ 36 מ נ ר: אלייך/ 37 ע״פ ב מ נ ר, ו: תשובו לי; בס״ש: תשובו אלי/ 38 מ ר: אלייך/ 39 ו: ופירשו, מ: ופירשו, בס״ש: ופירוש/ 40 ו ר: מהחשמונאים, מ: בהחשמונאים/ 41 נ בן עלי ח׳/ 42 ו מ לי ח׳/ 43 ע״פ ב ו מ נ ר; ל: תעשה; בס״ש: תעשו/ 44 נ לי ח׳/ 45 מ: ומנחה/ 46 ו מ: ולפי דעתי/ 47 נ אין ח׳/ 48 ב: דיברה/ 49 נ ואחרים ח׳/ 50 ב נ אמרו ח׳/ 51 ב נ: הכל לפי ע״ז/ 52 ו: ולא מצאנו אשר לגנאי, ל: ולא מצאנו לגנאי, ר: ולא מצאנו מצבה לבעל, ומן ׳אפוד לגנאי׳ עד ׳לשם ולא׳ ח׳/ 53 נ: בעיניי/ 54 נ לשם ח׳/ 55 ע״פ מ, ב ל נ: אין אפוד השם ואין תרפים שקראם, ו: אין אפוד ואין תרפים לע״ז שקראם, ר: אין אפוד השם ואין תרפים לע״ז שקראם, בס״ש: אין אפוד

(23) **והיה. אענה.** כמו ׳והכסף יענה את הכל׳ (קהלת י, יט) *ימציא.[106] וטעם ׳אענה׳ פעמים תמיד כדרך ׳נשאו נהרות ה׳ (תהלים צג, ג) כמו שפירשתי: **אענה את השמים.** הפך ׳ונתתי את שמיכם כברזל׳ (ויקרא כו, יט): **והם יענו את הארץ.** שיתנו טלם *וגשמיהם[107] *בעתם:[108]

(24) **והם יענו את יזרעאל.** שם מקום הנזכר[109] שישוב כאשר היה *ברוב אדם:[110]

(25) **וזרעתיה.** שירבו ויפרו כזרע הארץ: *ורחמתי[111] **את לא רוחמה.** הם האבות: **ואמרתי *ללא עמי.** הם[112] שנולדו בגלותם וזאת הנבואה לעתיד או היא *קשורה. פירוש אילו[113] שבו הגולים מדרכם הרעה *היו שבים[114] אל ארצם. ואל תתמה *לומר[115] אחר שהשם גזר עליהם *שיעמדו בגולה שנים רבות[116] איך ישובו כי הנה אמר ירמיהו על ירושלים *׳ביד[117] מלך בבל *תנתן׳[118] (ירמיה לז, יז) *והוא[119] מצוה *׳עשו[120] משפט׳ (שם כב, ג) ואם תעשו כן לא יחרב הבית ואם לא *תעשו[121] *כן[122] יהיה לחרבה:

ג

(1) ***ויאמר.**[1] בדרך נבואה: **לך אהב אשה.** וקחנה לאשה כי זה *משמע[2] לשון אשה כי לא הזכיר זונה, והעד ׳ואכרה לי׳ (פסוק ב). **ואחרי כן תהיה** *׳אהובת רע׳,[3] והטעם אדם אחר ותנאף עמו. והמשל *׳כאהבת ה׳[4] את בני ישראל׳ שאהב אותם ׳והם פונים אל אלהים אחרים׳, *זה הוא[5] ׳אהובת *רע׳[6] ואינם *אוהבים[7] השם רק אוהבים היין *שיתעם.[8] *מלת[9] ׳אשישי׳ כמו ׳סמכוני באשישות׳ (שה״ש ב, ה), והטעם באשישות היין, וככה אשישי *יין[10] ענבים, *וכמוהו[11] ׳ואשישה אחת׳ (שמ״ב ו, יט), ואין *צורך[12] להזכיר יין:

(2) **ואכרה.** יש אומרים ואקנה אותה *כמו ׳תכרו מאתם׳ (דברים ב, ו), ואינו[13] נכון בטעם *ובדקדוק,[14] *והוא[15] מגזרת ׳הכר נא׳ (בראשית לז, לב) רק היה

לבדי תהיי, ח: תהיו לי לבדי/ 105 למעלה פסוק י: והיא לא ידעה/ 106 ב נ ימציא ח׳/ 107 ר: וגשמיכם/ 108 מ: בעיתם/ 109 למעלה א, ד, ב, ב/ 110 ב: ברוב מקום/ 111 ר: וריחמתי/ 112 ר: ללא עמי עמי הם/ 113 ב נ: קשורה אילו, ו מ ר: קשורה לו פירוש אילו/ 114 נ: היושבים/ 115 ר: לאמר/ 116 ע״פ ב, ו מ ר: שיעמדו בגולה ימים רבים שנים רבות, נ: שיעמדו עליהם בגולה שנים רבות, בס״ש: שיעמדו בגולה שלש שנים רבות/ 117 ב: מיד/ 118 ב נ: תתנך/ 119 ע״פ כ״י, בס״ש: והיא/ 120 מ: שעשו/ 121 מ נ ר: תעשה/ 122 ו מ ר כן ח׳/

1 נ: ואמר/ 2 ב נ: משפט/ 3 ר: אהובת ריע, בס״ש: אוהבת רע/ 4 ו: לאהבת ה׳, בס״ש: כאוהב׳ ה׳/ 5 מ ר: זהו/ 6 ר: ריע/ 7 ב: אהובים/ 8 ו מ ר: שתתעם/ 9 ו מ: ומלת/ 10 ר: היין/ 11 ו: וכמהו, נ: מלת אשישי יין וכמוהו, ומן ׳כמו׳ עד ׳וככה׳ ח׳/ 12 ר: צריך/ 13 ב: כמו עב תכרו מאותם ואיננו, מ:

*החדש[75] שתתחדש הלבנה גם תי"ו *שבתה[76] חסרה או מובלעת בדגשות תי"ו שבתה:

(14) **והשימותי. אתנה.** האל"ף נוסף *כמו מתנה.[77] ורבי מרינוס אמר *שהוא[78] *כמו[79] 'אתנן זונה' (דברים כג, יט):

(15) **ופקדתי.** וטעם 'ותעד' משל לאשה זונה שתשים הנזם על אפה והחלי בצוארה *ליפות עצמה[80] *למצא חן[81] בעיני הנואף:

(16) **לכן.** אחר שתדע כי *כל[82] זאת הרעה *באה עליה[83] *בעבור[84] ששכחה *אותי[85] ולא ידעה *בתחילתה[86] כי אני הטיבותי עמה ובאמרה 'אלכה *ואשובה[87] אל אישי הראשון' (פסוק ט) *אז[88] אפתיה בדברים: **והולכתיה. אל ארצה** *ששב כמדבר:[89]

(17) **ונתתי** *לה[90] **את כרמיה.** הפך 'והשימותי גפנה' (פסוק יד) ותחת עמק עכור שעכרתיה שהוא עמק יזרעאל ישוב לפתח תקוה: **וענתה.** תנגן ותשיר כמו 'ותען להם מרים' (שמות טו, כא). ויש אומרים ותדור שמה מגזרת 'מעון' (תהלים כו, ח) ויפרש ככה 'וענה איים באלמנותיו' (ישעיה יג, כב), והוא רחוק *בעיני:[91]

(18) **והיה.** *תקראי אישי ולא[92] **תקראי לי עוד בעלי.** כי כן כתוב 'את ימי *הבעלים' (פסוק טו). ור'[93] מרינוס אמר אפי' שם *שהוא[94] ספק כמו בעל *שהוא שם ע"ז[95] או *כמו[96] 'כי יבעל בחור' (ישעיה סב, ה) לא *תזכרי[97] עוד:

(19) **והסירותי.** על דרך 'ומל ה' אלהיך' (דברים ל, ו) כי כאשר ישוב השובב מחטאו השם יעזרהו וישיבהו בכל לבו:

(20) **וכרתי.** הפך *'ואכלתם חית[98] השדה' (פסוק יד). 'וקשת וחרב' וכלי מלחמה כמו 'באוכלי שולחניך' (שמ"ב יט, כו), 'חמור לחם' (שמ"א טז, כ) בעבור שהזכיר *תחלה[99] 'ושברתי את קשת ישראל' (א, ה), והנה *הטעם[100] שישבו לבטח:

(21) ***וארשתיך.*** כמו 'מאורשה לאיש' (דברים כב, כג) יש אומרים שתעשי צדק ומשפט גם אני אעשה חסד ורחמים ואין צורך:[101]

(22) ***וארשתיך[102] *לי באמונה.[103] *תהיי לי לבדי[104] באמונה: וידעת את ה'.*** הפך *ולא ידעה:[105]

תוי"ן/ 74 נ כן ח'/ 75 ו נ: **החודש**/ 76 ו מ נ ר: **שבת**/ 77 ע"פ כ"י, בס"ש **כמו מתנה** ח'/ 78 ב נ **שהוא** ח'/ 79 ו **כמו** ח'/ 80 מ ר: **ליפות את עצמה**/ 81 ו מ ר **למצא חן** ח'/ 82 ו **כל** ח'/ 83 מ ר: **הבאה עליה**, ו: **הבאה עליו**/ 84 ו **בעבור** ח'/ 85 מ: **אותו**/ 86 נ ר: **בתחלה**/ 87 ב: **אשובה**/ 88 ב נ: **או**/ 89 ו ר: **שב כמדבר**, מ: **שב במדבר**/ 90 ב ו מ נ ר **לה** ח'/ 91 נ **בעיני** ח'/ 92 ב נ: **תקראי לי אישי ולא**, ו מ ר: **תקראי לי אישי הראשון ולא**, ל: **תקראי אישי הראשון ולא**/ 93 ל: **הבעלים מפיה ור'**/ 94 ר: **הוא**/ 95 ב: **שהוא ע"ז**, ל: **שהוא שם של ע"ז**/ 96 ר **כמו** ח'/ 97 ע"פ ב נ, ו מ: **תזכר**, ר: **תזכור**, בס"ש: **תזכרו**/ 98 ר: **ואכלתם את חית**/ 99 ב נ: **תחילה**, ו ר ל: **בתחלה**, מ: **בתחילה**/ 100 ל: **בטעם**/ 101 ב ל ו הפירוש על פסוק 21 ח'/ 102 מ: **ואירשתיך**/ 103 ב נ **לי באמונה** ח'/ 104 ב נ: **לי תהיי לבדי**, ל: **לי**

*להכירם:[39] **וגדרתי את גדרה.** שאשים גדר *בדרכיה[40] *כדרך[41] *׳גדר[42] דרכי בגזית׳ (איכה ג, ט):

(9) **ורדפה.** האומר כי דגשות הדל״ת כי כן *הוא[43] כל דבר תמיד *שאדם[44] מתעסק בו ואין לו *סוף[45] אולי יפרש לנו *זה המדקדק[46] מה הפרש *בין ׳הדובר[47] בי׳ (זכריה א, ט) ובין ׳רוח ה׳ *דבר[48] בי׳ (שמ״ב כג, ב), ׳הנני גורש מפניך׳ (שמות לד, יא), ׳לא אגרשנו׳ (שם כג, כט), ׳ויגרש את האדם׳ (בראשית ג, כד), אלה הגזרות *נמצאות[49] *בבנין הקל ובבנין[50] הכבד ורבים ככה. והנכון כי רדף הקל לעולם הוא *אחר[51] הבורח ומלת ׳ירדף חשך׳ (נחום א, ח) *יוצאה[52] *לשנים פעולים[53] וככה ׳ורדפה *את מאהביה׳[54] שתרדף *אחריהם[55] בברחה להם: *ובקשתם.[56] חסר דגש בקו״ף כי הוא *מבנין[57] הכבד וככה ׳שלחו באש מקדשך׳ (תהלים עד, ז) להקל על הלשון על כן אלה *חסרים[58] דגש:

(10) **והיא.** עד עתה כי *היתה אומרת[59] *כי הבעלים[60] שתקטיר להם הם הטיבו לה כדרך *׳ומן אז[61] חדלנו לקטר למלאכת השמים׳ (ירמיה מד, יח): **עשו לבעל.** הצורפים עשו *צורות[62] *מזהב[63] *וכסף[64] ליפות הבעל. ובספרד היה חכם מפרש הבעל *בעל הבית[65] הצומח בחכמת המזלות כי כן יקראו בתים למזלות ולהם הם עובדים כי הם צבא השמים:

(11) **לכן.** טעם ׳בעתו׳ *בעת[66] שאביא אויביה *לקחתו:[67] **והצלתי.** *והפרשתי, וכן[68] כל לשון הצלה ׳והצלתי צמרי ופשתי׳ שנתתי *לה[69] לכסות את *ערותה:[70]

(12) **ועתה אגלה את נבלותה.** מגזרת נבלה על משקל ׳כי הילדות והשחרות הבל׳ (קהלת יא, י) כי גלוי הערוה נבלה היא:

(13) **והשבתי.** שלא להתחבר שנים תוי״ן חסרו האחד *וככה שבתו[71] כי שבת שרשו וככה ׳וכרתי להם ברית׳ (פסוק כ) כי כרת שרשו ואין *נאה[72] להתחבר *שנים תוי״ן[73] לומר והשבתתי וכרתתי כי *כן[74] היה ראוי: **חדשה.** הוא ראש

38 ר המקומות ח׳/ 39 ע״פ כ״י, בס״ש: להכירה/ 40 ו מ ר: בדרך/ 41 מ כדרך ח׳/ 42 ו: גזר/ 43 ב הוא ח׳/ 44 ל: אדם/ 45 ו: ספק/ 46 ו מ: זה המפרש המדקדק/ 47 מ: בין בין הדובר/ 48 מ: דיבר/ 49 ע״פ ב, ו מ נ ר: הנמצאות, בס״ש: נמצאו/ 50 מ: בבינייין הקל ובביניין/ 51 נ: אחרי/ 52 ר: יוציאה/ 53 ו מ ר: לשני פעולים/ 54 ב נ את מאהביה ח׳/ 55 ע״פ ב נ, ו מ ר ובס״ש:אחריה/ 56 ו ובקשת/ 57 נ: מהביניין/ 58 ו מ: החסרים/ 59 נ: היא אומרת, ר: הייתה אומרת/ 60 ל: שהבעלים/ 61 ע״פ מ ר, בשאר כ״י ובס״ש: ומאז/ 62 ר צורת/ 63 מ: בזהב/ 64 ל: ומכסף, ו למלאכת השמים עשו לבעל הצורפים עשו צורות מזהב וכסף ח׳/ 65 מ ר בעל הבית ח׳/ 66 ע״פ ל, בשאר כ״י ובס״ש בעת ח׳/ 67 ל לקחתו ח׳/ 68 ו ר: והצלתי לשון הפרשה וכן/ 69 מ: להם/ 70 ו ר: ערוותה/ 71 ב ל וככה שבתו ח׳, נ: הגהה (במקום ״וככה שבתו״)/ 72 ע״פ כ״י, בס״ש: נראה/ 73 ע״פ כ״י, בס״ש: שני

*זהו[10] סנחריב: **ועלו מן הארץ כי גדול יום יזרעאל.** שנפקד *עון בית ישראל[11] והנה הכל לגנאי *ולא[12] לשבח או הטעם כי גדול *יהיה[13] יום *אידם כיום[14] יזרעאל. *והמפרש[15] יותר מיום *יזרעאל[16] אין משפט *הלשון[17] לחסר מ״ם כי הדבר יבא להפך, ועוד *מה טעם[18] ׳כי גדול׳ ואין שם *זכר מה:[19]

(3) **אמרו.**[20] כדרך ׳ויהתל בהם אליהו *ויאמר[21] קראו בקול׳ (מל״א יח, כז), ׳שמח בחור בילדותך׳ (קהלת יא, ט), ׳באו בית אל׳ (עמוס ד, ד), ורבים ככה על כן *אחריו ׳ריבו באמכם ריבו׳ איך[22] אתם ׳בני אל חי׳ (פסוק א) והאם זנתה[23] הם האבות:

(4) **ריבו.** הנביא מוכיח הגולים אולי ישובו וישיב *השם[24] שבותם או *יוכיח אלו[25] הדורות לפני גלותם: **זנוניה.** כפול העי״ן כמו ׳בינה הגיגי׳ (תהלים ה, ב): **ונאפופיה.** *כפול[26] הלמ״ד כמו ׳סגריר׳ (משלי כז, טו):

(5) **פן. כיום** *הולדה. בהיותה במצרים[27] כאשר הזכיר יחזקאל ׳ואת ערום ועריה׳ (יחזקאל לז, ז): **והצגתיה.** כמו ׳ויצג את המקלות׳ (בראשית ל, לח): **ושמתיה כמדבר.** *אין אדם[28] בו. וטעם ׳בצמא׳ שהיא אומרת ׳נתני לחמי ומימי ושקויי׳:[29]

(6) **ואת בניה לא ארחם.** הם שילכו בגולה:

(7) *כי **הובישה.** נפשה.[30] וטעם ׳מאהבי׳ פועל יוצא *לשנים פעולים[31] כי בקשו שהייתי אוהבת אותם בעבור מתנותם. *והאומר[32] כי ׳מימי׳ הוא התירוש והביא ראיה *׳ותירושי[33] במועדו׳ (פסוק יא) לא *דבר[34] נכונה כי התירוש ׳ותירושי׳ כנגד ׳ושקויי׳. וטעם ׳מימי׳ כמו ׳ואכלכלם לחם ומים׳ (מל״א יח, יג), והנביא אמר ׳לחם לא אכלתי ומים לא שתיתי׳ (דברים ט, ט), ׳ומים בכסף תתן לי׳ (שם ב, כח):

(8) **לכן.** *שך. מגזרת ׳לשכים׳ (במדבר לג, נה) וכמוהו[35] ׳הלא אתה *שכת[36] בעדו׳ (איוב א, י): **בסירים.** קוצים ׳כי כקול הסירים׳ (קהלת ז, ו), ׳כי עד סירים סבכים׳ (נחום א, י): *ונתיבותיה.[37] *המקומות[38] הידועים שיש בהם סימנים

ובס״ש אין סימני הפסק/ 10 ל: זה, נ: זה הוא/ 11 ו ל מ ר: **עון ישראל**/ 12 מ ר: **לא**/ 13 ב **יהיה ח׳**/ 14 ר: **אידם שלהם כיום**/ 15 ו: **והפרוש**/ 16 ר **יזרעאל ח׳** ועל הגליון נוסף ׳יזרעל׳/ 17 ר **הלשון ח׳**/ 18 ע״פ כ״י, בס״ש: מם טעם/ 19 ע״פ ב ל נ, בשאר כ״י ובס״ש: זכר מם/ 20 ראה למעלה פסוק א הערה 5/ 21 נ: **ויאמרו**/ 22 ב ל נ: **אחריו ריבו איך**, ו: **אחריו ריבו באמכם איך**/ 23 **פסוק ז**/ 24 נ: **העם**/ 25 מ נ: **יוכיח אלה**, ר: **מוכיח אלה**/ 26 מ **כפול ח׳**/ 27 נ: **היולדה בהיותה מצרים**/ 28 מ: **לאדם**/ 29 **פסוק ז**: ׳נתני לחמי ומימי צמרי ופשתי שמני ושקויי׳/ 30 ע״פ כ״י, בס״ש: כי הובישה הורתם/ 31 ו מ ר: **לשני פעולים**/ 32 ע״פ כ״י, בס״ש: ושאומר/ 33 נ: **ותירוש**/ 34 מ ר: **דיבר**/ 35 ב: **שך מגז׳ שכים וכמוהו**, נ: **שן מגזרת שנים וכמהו**/ 36 ו מ ר: **שכתה**/ 37 ע״פ ו נ ר, ב מ ובס״ש: **נתיבותיה**/

(5) *והיה. [72]קשת ישראל. מלכות זכריה כי *בו[73] *נפסקה[74] מלכות יהוא:

(6) *ותהר. [75]ותלד בת. *זה[76] הדור הבא אחריו וקראו בת *כי כתוב[77] *אחרי[78] ירבעם 'הוא השיב את גבול ישראל' (מל"ב יד, כה) *ואחרי[79] מות זכריה בנו מלך מנחם ובימיו בא מלך אשור. ואין *צורך[80] להזכיר *מלכות[81] *שלום[82] *כי לא מלך אלא[83] ירח ימים, ובימי פקח בן רמליה הגלה *תגלת[84] פלאסר רבים מערי *ישראל,[85] ובימי הושע בן אלה נלכדה שומרון על כן קרא זה הדור בת. ופירש 'לא רוחמה כי לא אוסיף עוד ארחם', תחסר *אות[86] שי"ן, 'לא אוסיף עוד' שארחם *וכמוהו 'ונדעה ונרדפה'[87] (ו, ג), 'אל תרבו תדברו' (שמ"א ב, ג). יש אומר 'כי נשוא' שהייתי עד עתה נושא להם עונם ואין זכר לעון. והנכון *בעיני[88] כי זאת המלה באה כדרך *'הרגו[89] לאבנר' (שמ"א ב, ג), והטעם *כדרך[90] *'ישאני עושני' (איוב לב, כב).[91] והנה *ספר גלות[92] השבטים:

(7) ואת בית *יהודה.[93] שנמלטו אנשי ירושלים מיד סנחריב: והושעתים בה'. שיצא *מלאך[94] השם והכה כל מחנה אשור:

(8-9) ותגמל. הולידו בנים השבטים שגלו בגלותם ושם עמדו *ולא[95] שבו לארצם על כן קראם 'לא עמי': *ואנכי[96] לא אהיה. להם לאלהים ומרוב הכעס לא הזכירו:

ב

(1) והיה. זאת הפרשה דבקה היא כי במקום שגלו *שם[1] יולידו בנים רבים רק אינם יראים את השם. ופירוש *'והיה'[2] במקום כמו 'תחת אשר לא עבדת' (דברים כח, מז).[3] והטעם שהם קוראים עצמם *'בני אל חי' והם[4] באמת 'לא עמי' בעבור מעשיהם הרעים:[5]

(2) *ונקבצו.[6] *וטעם[7] 'ונקבצו' *שרבים מבני יהודה תפש[8] סנחריב וכן כתוב כי תפש כל ערי יהודה הבצורות (מל"ב יח, יג): [9]ושמו להם ראש אחד.

זה ירבעם/ 71 ל: בעיני השם הרע/ 72 ל והיה ח'/ 73 ע"פ ו ל מ נ ר, ב ובס"ש בו ח'/ 74 נ: נפסק/ 75 ל ותהר ח'/ 76 ל זה ח'/ 77 ל כי כן כתוב/ 78 ע"פ כ"י, בס"ש: אחר/ 79 ב: ואחר/ 80 ל: צרך/ 81 ב נ מלכות ח'/ 82 ל שלום ח'/ 83 ל: שמלך, ו מ נ ר כי לא מלך אלא ח'/ 84 ל: תלגת/ 85 נ: יהודה/ 86 ב נ אות ח'/ 87 מ: וכמוהו ורדפה ונדעה נרדפה, נ: וכמהו נרדפה, ר: וכמוהו נרדפה/ 88 ו מ ר בעיני ח'/ 89 מ: הורגו/ 90 נ כדרך ח'/ 91 מ ר: ישאיני עושיני/ 92 ב נ: גלות ספר/ 93 בכ"י יהודה ח'/ 94 ר: מלך/ 95 ו ר: לא/ 96 ל ואנכי ח'/

1 ר שם ח'/ 2 ר והיה ח'/ 3 ר: תחת אשר לא עבדת את ה'/ 4 ו מ ר: בני אל והם, ל: בני אלהים והם/ 5 ו מ ר מכאן והלאה מפורש פסוק 3 ('אמרו') ואחריו פסוק 2 ('ונקבצו')/ 6 ל ר ונקבצו ח'/ 7 ע"פ כ"י, בס"ש: טעם/ 8 ו מ ר: שרבים מהם תפש, ל: שרבים מערי יהודה תפש/ 9 ע"פ ב, בשאר כ"י

עם הארץ זונים מאחרי השם. ומפרש אחר אמר קח לך אשת זנונים וילדי זנונים שהרי דוגמתו זנו יושבי הארץ מאחרי השם ודיו *לעֲבֵד להיות[37] כרבו (מדרש תהלים כז, ה).

נאם אברהם המחבר: חלילה חלילה *שיצוה[38] השם לקחת אשת זנונים *ולהוליד[39] ילדי זנונים והאומר דיו לעבד להיות כרבו לא נאמר על זה כי זנות מאחרי השם דרך משל רק באדם הוא *במעשה.[40] והנכון בעיני כי זה הנביא היה רואה במראות נבואה בחלום הלילה שהשם אמר לו ׳קח לך *אשת[41] *זנונים׳[42] והלך ולקח אשה ידועה והרתה *וילדה[43] כל זה *במראות הנבואה[44] כאשר פירש *השם[45] ׳אם יהיה נביאכם׳ לבד ממשה *רבינו[46] לבדו ׳ה׳ במראה אליו *אתודע[47] בחלום אדבר בו׳ (במדבר יב, ו). ואל תתמה איך יראה בחלום ׳וילך ויקח׳ (פסוק ג) והנה בחלום *אדם[48] בלא נבואה ׳ותאכלנה הפרות׳ (בראשית מא, ד) וככה על ישעיהו הנביא ׳כאשר הלך עבדי *ישעיהו[49] ערום ויחף׳ (ישעיה כ, ג), זה היה *בדרך נבואה[50] כי למה ילך הנביא ערום בעבור כוש ומצרים וככה *׳קח לך[51] *לבנה׳[52] (יחזקאל ד, א) גם *׳שכב[53] על צדך *השמאלי׳[54] (שם ד, ד) גם ׳ואתה קח לך *חטין׳[55] (שם ד, ט) *גם[56] דבר הזקן (שם ה, א). והעד *על כל זה[57] שאמר יחזקאל בתחלת ספרו ׳ואראה מראות אלהים׳ (שם א, א) *ואומר[58] ׳במראות אלהים הביאני אל ארץ ישראל׳ (שם מ, ב). ואל תתמה בעבור שלא הזכיר בתחילת הנבואה מראות כי *הנה דבר[59] ה׳ אשר היה אל זכריה ושם *כתוב[60] אחריו ׳ראיתי הלילה (זכריה א, ח), ׳ואשא עיני ואראה׳ (שם ה, א), והנה *כתוב[61] באברהם ׳במחזה׳ (בראשית טו, א) וכן *היתה[62] כל נבואתו. *והנה[63] אמר לו בדרך *הנבואה[64] למה ׳אשת זנונים׳ ׳כי זנה תזנה הארץ׳:

(3) וילך ויקח. *האשה[65] *הנזכרת[66] *כך[67] היה רואה במראה. וטעם ׳ותלד בן׳ הדור הבא אחרי ירבעם בן יואש:

(4) דמי יזרעאל. הם בית אחאב על בית יהוא שלא *מלא[68] אחרי השם גם יהואחז בנו ויהואש *בן[69] בנו *גם זה ירבעם[70] גם זכריה בנו כולם עשו *הרע בעיני ה׳[71] כי כן כתוב:

כי/ 37 ב נ: לעבד ה׳ להיות/ 38 ר: יצוה/ 39 ר: ולהוליד ח׳/ 40 ל: מעשה/ 41 ל: אשה/ 42 ב ל: זנונים ח׳/ 43 נ: וילדה ח׳/ 44 ב ל נ: בנבואה/ 45 ע״פ ל נ, בשאר כ״י ובס״ש השם ח׳/ 46 ע״פ ו נ, בשאר כ״י ובס״ש רבינו ח׳/ 47 ו: יתודע/ 48 ר: אדם ח׳/ 49 מ: ישעיה/ 50 ע״פ כ״י, בס״ש: במראה הנבואה/ 51 ב: לך קח/ 52 ו: לבינה/ 53 ל: ושכב/ 54 ל: השמאלית, נ: השמל/ 55 ל מ נ ר: חטים/ 56 ל: גם ח׳/ 57 ו: על כל שזה, ל: על כל אלה, ר: על כל זה ח׳/ 58 ו: ואמ׳/ 59 ע״פ ו מ ר, ל נ: הנה כתוב דבר, ב ובס״ש: הנה כתב דבר/ 60 ע״פ ו ל נ, בשאר כ״י ובס״ש: כתב/ 61 ע״פ ל נ, ב ובס״ש: כתב, ו מ ר: כתב ח׳/ 62 מ ר: היה/ 63 ל: וכן/ 64 ב נ: הנבואה ח׳/ 65 ו ר: אשה/ 66 ב ו מ נ: הנזכרה/ 67 ו: וככה/ 68 ו מ: מילא/ 69 ל ר: בן ח׳/ 70 ב: גם ירבעם, ו: גם הוא ירבעם, מ: גם זה גם

פירוש הראב״ע על הושע

א

(1—2) זה הושע מנביאי *השם הנכבדים[1] כי היצחקי דבר סרה בספרו עליו שאמר שהוא בן אלה *כי[2] בארי הוא אלה כי *מצא[3] כתוב ׳ובאר אלים יללתה׳ (ישעיה טו, ח). ואין אלה *אלים כי[4] בעבור אות נוסף ישתנה השם כמו ׳זיף וזיפה׳ (דה״י־א ד, טז) ועוד כי אין משפט לשון הקדש לאמר על שם פרט שהוא בן עיר רק אם היה על דרך *כלל[5] כמו *׳בת[6] ציון׳ (מל״ב יט, כו) רק *יתיחס[7] על העיר כמו שמרוני. *ושני[8] דברים דחקוהו *לומר[9] *ככה[10] האחד שמצא בדברי הימים ׳בארה בנו אשר הגלה *תגלת פלאסר[11] מלך *אשור הוא[12] נשיא לראובני׳ (דה״י־א ה, ו) והוא היה *אבי זה[13] הנביא; *והשני[14] שאמר ׳ולפקד על יעקב *כדרכיו׳ (יב, ג) כי הוא יפרש זה על יעקב[15] אבינו שהסיר הבכורה מראובן. ואין פירושו כאשר חשב והנה שכח *הכתוב על[16] הושע בן *אלה[17] ׳ויעש הרע בעיני ה׳ (מל״א יז, ב). *והיצחקי[18] אמר שלקח אשת זנונים וזה המוכה בסנורים הלא ראה כתוב ׳תחלת דבר *ה׳[19] בהושע ויאמר ה׳׳ והנה לא מרה *פי השם[20] חלילה *חלילה,[21] רק הושע בן בארי איננו הושע בן אלה כמו חנוך שם כולל לארבעה אנשים בתורה (בראשית ד, יז; ה, יח; כה, ד; במדבר כו, ה) *ו׳שאול מרחובות הנהר׳ (בראשית לו, לז) ׳ושאול בן הכנענית׳ (שמות ו, י),[22] *ו׳שאול בן קיש׳ (שמ״א י, כא), ורבים ככה.[23] *ותחלת[24] נבואת זה הנביא על מלכות ירבעם בן יואש *מלך ישראל[25] ארבעים שנה *לפני[26] גלות שומרון אם היתה נבואתו בסוף ימי ירבעם כי לא מלך זכריה בנו אחריו רק ששה חדשים ונשבתה מלכות בית יהוא שהיו *מלכי[27] ישראל. ומפרש אחר אמר כי *׳לך[28] קח *לך׳[29] *דבור[30] הוא כטעם ׳לקח טוב׳ (משלי יד, ב) *ופירש[31] ׳ותהר׳ (פסוק ג) כמו ׳תהרו חשש תלדו קש׳ (ישעיה לג, יא) *ואמר[32] כי ׳גומר׳ גמורה בזנות ו׳בת דבלים׳ רמז ליהודה *וישראל.[33] ואחר אמר ׳קח לך אשת זנונים׳ שאם *באת[34] לקחת אשה *הוגנת[35] לא תמצא *שהרי[36] ׳זנה תזנה הארץ׳ כל

1 ו מ נ ר: השם הנכבד הנכבדים, ל: השם הנכבד מן הנכבדים/ 2 ל: בן/ 3 ע״פ כ״י, בס״ש: ימצא/ 4 ל: ואלים שוה כי/ 5 ו: כלל ח׳/ 6 ב: בן/ 7 ע״פ ל מ נ ר, ב ו ובס״ש: יתיחש/ 8 ו ל מ ר: ושנים/ 9 מ: לומר ח׳/ 10 ב מ: ככה ח׳/ 11 בדה״י־א ה, ו: תלגת פלנאסר/ 12 ב נ: אשור אשר הוא/ 13 ב: זה אבי/ 14 ב: ושני, ל נ: והשיני/ 15 ב נ: כדרכיו כי הוא יפרש זה על יעקב ח׳/ 16 ל: הכתוב בו על/ 17 נ: אלה ח׳/ 18 ר: זה יצחקי/ 19 ר: ה׳ ח׳/ 20 מ: בשם/ 21 ל: חלילה ח׳/ 22 ו: ושאול בן הכנענית ושאול מרחובות הנהר/ 23 ל: ושאול בן קיש ורבים ככה ח׳/ 24 נ: והתחלת/ 25 ר: מלך על ישראל/ 26 ר: כי/ 27 ב נ: מלכות/ 28 ל נ: לך ח׳/ 29 ו מ ר: לך ח׳/ 30 מ: דיבור/ 31 מ: ופירוש, נ: ופרש/ 32 ב נ: ואומר/ 33 ל: ולישראל/ 34 ע״פ ר, בשאר כ״י ובס״ש: באתה/ 35 ב נ: הגונה/ 36 ל:

קיצורים

1. סימני כתבי־יד

ב	=	כתב־יד המוזיאום הבריטי 24896
ו	=	כתב־יד ואטיקאן 75
ל	=	כתב־יד ליוורדן 2, 4
מ	=	כתב־יד מיכאל 33 (אוקספורד)
נ	=	כתב־יד מונטיפיורי 2, 34
ר	=	כתב־יד רומא־אנגליקה 2, 80

2. ראשי תיבות

בס״ש	=	בספרים שלנו
ח׳	=	חסר
כת״י	=	כתב־יד
ע״פ	=	על פי
דה״י־א, דה״י־ב	=	דברי הימים־א, דברי הימים־ב
מל״א, מל״ב	=	מלכים־א, מלכים־ב
שה״ש	=	שיר השירים
שמ״א, שמ״ב	=	שמואל־א, שמואל־ב

במבוא למהדורתי של "פירוש רבי אברהם אבן־עזרא על יואל", שיצאה לאור על פי ששה כתבי־יד ב"ספר יובל" לכבוד רבי יוסף דוב סולובייציק (ירושלים תשמ"ד), דברתי באריכות על העזובה הרבה השוררת בפירושי אבן־עזרא על תרי עשר ועל הצורך לנקותם מן הטעויות.

הפעם נטלתי על עצמי את המשימה להוציא מהדורה חדשה של פירוש אבן־עזרא על הושע על פי ששת כתבי־היד הנזכרים ולנכש ממנו את העשבים השוטים שצמחו בו. למלאכת ההדרה של הטקסט צירפתי תרגום אנגלי המלווה בהערות והארות, בהן השתדלתי להצביע על המקבילות שבכתבי הראב"ע ולהתחקות אחרי המקורות ששימשו יסוד מוסד לפירושיו.

אמנם בקיץ תשמ"ג (=1983) הרשה לי פרופ' אוריאל סימון מאוניברסיטת בר־אילן ברמת־גן להעיף עין על העתק של פירוש מקוטע על הושע, שנרשם לדעתו מפי הראב"ע על ידי תלמידו, ותודתי נתונה לו על כך. אלא שמבחינת התוכן לא עוררו אצלי הקטעים האלה עניין מיוחד. נוסף לכך עמדה לפניי שאלת אותנטיותם המחכה לליבון ולבירור. בשל הנימוקים האלה אין דעתנו נתונה עליהם במהדורה זו.

פירוש רבי אברהם אבן־עזרא

על הושע

הוגה ונערך על־פי ששה כתבי יד
בצירוף חילופי נוסח ותרגום אנגלי

על ידי
אברהם ליפשיץ